About Time –

Delay Analysis in Construction

Stephen Lowsley

and

Christopher Linnett

RICS BOOKS

DISCLAIMER: The authors are not lawyers and so any commentary on case law, contracts or any other legal issue referred to in this book should not be relied upon as legal opinion. If the reader wishes to study the general workings of the British legal system, the common law, the hierarchy of the courts or the specific legal principles arising out of the cases and contracts referred to, they should refer to appropriate legal textbooks or consult a specialist construction lawyer.

Published by RICS Business Services Limited
a wholly owned subsidiary of
The Royal Institution of Chartered Surveyors
under the RICS Books imprint
Surveyor Court
Westwood Business Park
Coventry CV4 8JE
UK
www.ricsbooks.com

ISBN 978 1 84219 247 7
ISBN 1 84219 247 7 (prior to 1 January 2007)

Reprinted 2006

Typeset by Columns Design Ltd, Reading
Printed and bound in Europe by the Alden Group, Oxford

Contents

Illustrations

Preface

Over the years the problem of delays on construction projects has prompted a steady flow of reports, academic analyses and court cases, but these have provided very little straightforward practical advice to construction professionals on how to evaluate delays.

Some very useful guidance was provided by The Society of Construction Law in October 2002 with their *Delay and Disruption Protocol*, and, without doubt, this publication dramatically elevated the level of understanding and level of debate about the problems of construction delay analysis. However, the Protocol has been met with a certain amount of criticism (which is perhaps inevitable given the difficulties with the subject), but it is highly questionable whether the Protocol fulfils its aim of providing 'the best way to deal with delay and disruption issues' or of being 'applicable to any contract that provides for the management of delay and disruption'.

For example, the guidance in the Protocol requires that:

> 'As early as possible in the project, the Contractor should submit … a programme (using commercially available critical path method project planning software) showing the manner and sequence in which the Contractor plans to carry out the works.'

While the Protocol recognises that this 'may be thought to be onerous for smaller projects', others find it too prescriptive and wholly unrealistic, particularly for the huge number of small subcontract firms upon which the UK construction industry depends so heavily.

Everyone connected to the construction industry, from architects, engineers and surveyors through to contractors, expert witnesses and lawyers will have to face the difficult task of preparing or assessing a delay claim from time-to-time but few have received any significant training in how to go about the task.

By describing the methodologies used to consider time issues on construction projects and by pointing out the pros and cons of each method, this book will assist those having to deal with the difficulties and complexities of the analysis and evaluation of delay claims.

This book is not a protocol or guidance note but it does offer practical advice to construction professionals on evaluating delays, with a jargon-free commentary on construction delay issues, particularly:

- programming and delay analysis techniques commonly used in the industry;
- requirements of standard forms of contract relating to time issues; and
- judgments in the lead UK court cases concerning construction delays.

Stephen Lowsley
Christopher Linnett

Analysis quick reference

There are a variety of different approaches for analysing delay, but this book focuses on the five main methods – as-planned v as-built, as-planned impacted, collapsed as-built, windows analysis and time impact analysis. Chapter 5 discusses each of these methods in detail, but the table below provides a quick reference guide.

Most delay analysis techniques have their critics and all should be used in the light of their weaknesses and limitations as well as their strengths.

Analysis	Features	Pros	Cons
As-planned v as-built Straightforward comparison between planned programme and as-built programme (section 5.1)	Bar chart format to create a graphical comparison. Requires planned programme and as-built records Often delivered with narrative explaining the results	Simple to prepare Easy to understand Helps to focus on areas of probable delay Widely recognised	Full as-built records may not be available Provides little more than an indication of where delay occurred Planned programme is theoretical so as-built may be completely different Difficultly displaying intermittent works
As-planned impacted Adds delays onto the planned programme (section 5.2)	Requires planned programme with sufficient detail in linked bar chart or critical path format	Can be used during works to consider prospective impact on planned programme as 'what if' method One of the most commonly used retrospective critical path-based method Works well with sequential and logic-driven activities` Does not need as-built records	Results can be unreliable because planned programme often lacks certainty May require significant assumptions in respect of the contractors planned intent Excludes consideration of what actually happens – no account taken of contractor delay, mitigation or acceleration Often gives completion date later than actual

Analysis	Features	Pros	Cons
Collapsed as-built Removes delays from the as-built programme (section 5.3)	Requires as-built records Logic links are added to create dynamic critical path As delaying events are removed programme is time analysed to view delaying impact	Method measures both cause of delay and impact on completion Easy to understand Can be relatively simple Inexpensive once as-built programme has been produced Based on what actually occurred	Full as-built records may not be available Needs evidence of logic links or any link will merely reflect analyst's assumptions Reliability is questionable Does not take into account concurrent delays or resequencing Problems associated with different working periods and calendars may be encountered Conclusions about contractor performance can be distorted if activity slows down to fill available time created by a delay Often produces a completion date earlier than the planned programme
Windows analysis Breaks the project down into slices of time before viewing the state of progress (section 5.5)	Delaying events are analysed in sequential periods Impact of delaying event at the end of one window acts as the start of the next window Important that selected time period is not too long and not too short Utilises a networked as-planned master	Programme reflects actual status of project at beginning of a window Acts as a reasonable planned programme through to anticipated project completion Looks at delays on a real-time basis Splitting the project into shorter periods makes it easier to analyse	Although delay is quantified the cause is not demonstrated without additional analysis Detailed as-built information may not be available Can be time consuming and costly to prepare

Analysis	Features	Pros	Cons
Windows analysis *continued*	programme updated with as-built information Delay detailed at end of a window reflects likely delay at that point in time not necessarily the full delay associated with the events	Enables different methodologies to be used in each windows so analysis is relevant to activity	Planned programme simply reflects what was planned and does not take history of project into account Problems can occur when the project has been significantly resequenced
Time-impact analysis Takes a 'snapshot' of programme status immediately before a delay and then impacts the event onto the updated planned programme (section 5.6)	Based on a reasonable planned programme Must be a linked bar chart or critical path network to act dynamically Essentially a prospective technique, but can be used retrospectively	Shows current information Provides detailed and robust retrospective analysis because as-built status is tracked through project	Shows an indication of 'likely' further delay Time consuming and costly Can be difficult if there are many delay events Cannot be used if progress records are not available

1

The construction industry's propensity for delays

Delays happen on most construction projects, whether small or large, simple or complex. Factors such as the weather, material shortages, labour problems, unforeseen ground conditions, interruptions by others and variations during the works can cause delays to projects as small and simple as relaying the patio at home or as large and complex as a new major international airport.

Construction delays are not a modern phenomena. The delays on some of the UK's most famous landmarks, such as St Paul's Cathedral, the Houses of Parliament and the Clifton Suspension Bridge would make the delays on more recent high profile construction projects look distinctly trifling.

Given the number of things that could go wrong on a site, it is not surprising that few, if any, construction projects go perfectly to plan. The organisation and operation of a construction site is a complex undertaking and even on a relatively simple project, such as the construction of a new house, the contractor has to attend to many tasks, including:

- liaising with designers and statutory bodies;
- ordering, accepting delivery and sometimes storing hundreds of different items of materials;
- organising different tradesmen;
- entering into agreements with and co-ordinating subcontractors;
- arranging for plant and equipment to be available when needed;
- protecting the works against weather and vandalism;
- observing health and safety requirements;
- complying with regulations and laws; and
- incorporating changes into the works.

All of these tasks are usually undertaken against a backdrop of tight commercial and contractual constraints.

Many other industries would be able to produce a list similar in nature, but the construction industry has to carryout most of its work exposed to or affected by the elements, with heavy reliance on a changeable workforce and relatively little reliance on automation. In addition, although most projects adopt traditional methods of construction, many are effectively prototypes using one-off designs.

The particular difficulties faced by the construction industry means that the likelihood for things to go wrong is high and as a result works will often be delayed. Everyone who works, or who has ever worked, in the construction industry will understand the propensity for events to conspire to cause delays and every construction professional will, at some time, have to either make or assess an application for the completion date for a project to be amended due to delays.

How bad is the problem?

In 1998 the UK government funded Egan report, *Rethinking Construction*, pointed out that construction projects were 'widely seen as unpredictable in terms of delivery on time, within budget and to the standards of quality expected'. Following this a report by the National Audit Office in 2001, entitled *Modernising Construction*, indicated that 70% of projects undertaken by government departments and agencies were delivered late.

Three years later BCIS published detailed research in a *Guide to Building Construction Duration*, which found that nearly 40% of all projects monitored had overrun the contract period.

The BCIS research broadly indicated that overruns occurred in about 40 per cent of projects whether the work was new build or refurbishment, whether the client was from the public or private sector, and whether the project was house building or another form of construction project. There were some regional variations around the UK with only 31% of projects in the Yorkshire and Humberside region overrunning, compared to 42% in London and the South East. However, on any analysis, the perception that a large number of construction projects finish later than planned appears to be entirely justified.

1.1 But what is a delay?

When people talk about 'delay' to a construction project, they generally mean delay to the planned completion date, but delay may also mean delay to a particular activity or sequence of activities.

The word delay can be used as a verb, meaning to make late, to be slow or to defer; or as a noun, referring to the duration that something is made late, slowed down or deferred. Delay could, therefore, be described as lateness or slowness, but these are comparative terms and, by definition, must be measured against some form of benchmark.

This benchmark could be the planned timing of an activity or the timing based on standard industry outputs/production rates, or even the timing that would have been achieved had the delay event not occurred. Depending on which of these benchmarks are used the period of delay may vary considerably.

Disruption

In the construction industry disruption is often referred to at the same time as delay with claims often made for 'delay and disruption'.

Disruption is an interruption to the flow or continuity of something and in the construction industry the term delay is generally used to refer to an activity that cannot proceed, whereas disruption is used to refer to an activity that can proceed but not as quickly as ought to be the case. For example, a plasterer may be delayed if the internal walls have not been constructed on time but disrupted if progress is hampered by working in rooms with poor access for materials, by poor lighting, or by working in close proximity to other trades.

Delay and/or disruption to a project will slow the progress of particular parts of the works and may cause the original completion date to be missed. Timely completion of some activities is critical to the completion of the overall project, while other activities may be less critical – delays to non-critical activities will not necessarily lead to a delay to the completion date.

1.2 The purpose of delay analysis

The primary reason for analysing delays is to ascertain whether the contract completion date should be adjusted or, put another way, to see whether an extension of time should be awarded.

An extension of time provides the contractor with a longer period to complete the contract works and defers the date from which the employer can claim or deduct damages for late completion.

In the majority of cases the employer estimates the cost of late completion before commencement and this estimate is included in the contract as liquidated damages – meaning that the contractor knows at the outset the amount that may be deducted if the project is completed late. If damages have not been liquidated and inserted into the contract agreement, the employer can still make a claim against a contractor for costs incurred due to late completion but, in this case, damages for breach of contract would have to be proven.

This means that the primary effect of an extension of time clause is to provide the contractor with the possibility of relief from liability for liquidated damages. The employer also benefits because the liquidated damages clause remains 'alive', even if the original completion date has become unachievable due to employer delays – the start date for the right to deduct liquidated damages is simply deferred to a later date.

It is a common misconception that an extension of time automatically leads to monetary compensation (prolongation costs or loss and expense), but this is not the case under most forms of contract. For example, there is no automatic link between extension of time and loss and expense in JCT standard forms, as pointed out by Judge Fox-Andrews QC in *H Fairweather & Co Ltd v London Borough of Wandsworth* (1987) (see chapter 8 for more information). However, in this case the judge recognised the inevitable link made in practice between time and money claims – in reality, if awarded an extension of time, a contractor will not only avoid liquidated damages, but will often recover prolongation costs.

1.3 Difficulties of delay assessment

Given the history of construction delays it might be expected that the industry would, by now, have developed ways of accurately analysing the cause and effect of delay events. A few years ago some people thought that computer-aided critical path analysis techniques would herald a breakthrough, but while it is true that computers have revolutionised the way in which delay claims are made and reviewed, they certainly have not reduced the number of disputes, or made delay analysis any simpler.

As stated above, delays can occur to many activities for many reasons during a construction project, but not all delays cause the overall period for the work to be prolonged. Therefore, assuming a benchmark has been established for measuring delay, the first difficulty is sorting out the significant from the insignificant delays, which is not as easy as it sounds.

In theory significant delays are to critical path activities and insignificant delays are to activities that are not on the critical path but, there are many problems with this simple theory. For a start, non-critical activities will not stay non-critical if delayed excessively, so there is only a certain amount of delay that can be absorbed before non-critical activities become critical.

Another difficulty with this simple theory is that parties will often find it difficult to agree which activities are critical and which are not. The critical path is determined, in part, by the programmer's logic, and so the critical path may vary depending upon who prepares the analysis.

The route of the critical path is also likely to vary depending on when it is carried out. Prospective analysis has to make assumptions about what will happen in the future whereas retrospective analysis can use as-built data. It is likely that assumptions made in a prospective analysis will be different to information used retrospectively.

Even if a critical path can be agreed, there is likely to be a problem with concurrent critical delays (some caused by the contractor and some by the employer). There may then be disagreement about mitigation of delays by the contractor or, perhaps more to the point, the lack of it.

For these and many other reasons the assessment of delays to completion of a project is not, by any means, straightforward.

1.4 The black art

The analysis of delays on construction projects is complicated and difficult, not least because of the large number of individual activities that have to be dealt with, even on a relatively simple structure. Powerful personal computers and sophisticated computer software appeared, at least superficially, to offer a solution, because they are ideal for handling and sorting large amounts of data. The programming software is able to produce precise answers at the click of a button.

In particular, the introduction of computers has effectively allowed the use of the operational research technique known as 'critical path analysis'. This technique, which was too complex for practical use without the aid of computers, not only sounded right (in that it suggested that the critical delays to a programme could be identified) but it was supported by the ability to produce voluminous, high quality, coloured programmes and charts. Critical path analysis also brought about a perception that delays could be analysed scientifically so as to produce precise and reliable results.

However, the multiple difficulties of construction delay analysis were not to be so easily tamed. People are naturally suspicious of things they do not understand and many of those in the industry did not understand the computer delay analysis techniques used by programmers. In fact the delay analysts themselves were sometimes at a loss to understand the results of what they had produced. Suspicions about the techniques inevitably increased when analyses produced results that flew in the face of commonsense and when it was discovered that results were, apparently, capable of manipulation by the programmer. These suspicions have led to the analysis of construction delays to be seen as something of a 'black art'.

Summary

Time is an important aspect of any construction project and so it is normal at the beginning of a project for the parties involved to set a timeframe in which the various tasks required to complete the works are to be undertaken.

This construction period is usually based on an estimate of how long a project will take but may simply be determined by the date that the employer wants the project to be completed.

Delays are a relatively common occurrence on a construction site, not least because of the sheer complexity and to some extent uncertainty involved in any project.

Delay analysis is used to determine the cause or causes of delay to ascertain whether the construction period needs to be extended to allow the contractor more time to complete the project.

The cause or causes of delay to a construction project are often complex and although computers have made the analysis of data so much easier, they have not provided a simple or foolproof solution to all the problems of delay analysis. In fact, many people are suspicious about the results produced by delay analysis carried out on computers.

2

Planning for the project

As soon as anyone starts to seriously consider having construction work carried out they will have to think about issues relating to time. For example:

- What is the earliest start date?
- Would it be better to start on site at a particular time of year?
- How long will the works take to design?
- How long will the works take to build?
- Is there a date by which the works must be complete?

As a construction project moves forward, from being an idea, to a definite proposal, to an actual event, questions about 'when' and 'how long' will become more specific and more detailed – from beginning to end, time is an issue. With this in mind most projects will include programmes setting out target dates by which each element of work must be (or should be) complete.

2.1 The pre-commencement period

In most cases before work can commence on-site funding has to be secured, professionals have to be appointed, planning approval has to be obtained, tenders have to be sought and received and contracts have to be placed.

On medium to large developments a developer's professional advisors are likely to prepare a strategic programme incorporating these pre-commencement activities and the construction period. The amount of time available to undertake each phase of work may well be dictated by the project completion date. Projects such as sports stadiums, schools and supermarkets, usually have to be ready for use by a certain specific date – completion of sports facilities may be driven by the first event of the season, schools by the start of the academic year and commercial developments by the desire to commence trading by a traditionally busy period such as Christmas. In these cases, programming for the project will, from the start, be constrained by the fixed end date.

The amount of time available in which to carry out the various stages of work will affect considerations about the procurement route to be adopted as there may be insufficient time available to follow the traditional method of procurement, whereby the design is fully developed, bills of quantities are produced and competitive tenders are invited. In these cases other methods of procurement must be considered.

It is not the purpose of this book to discuss different methods of procurement of construction projects but, as a matter of commonsense, it is suggested that the risk of delays and disputes is increased, if time does not allow for a project to be planned carefully and sensibly at the outset. Professional advisors will have a duty to ensure that clients understand all the alternative procurement routes available and the risks involved with each.

Understandably all clients want the highest standards of work for the lowest price in the least time, but if time really is the employer's priority, compromises may have to be taken on other issues, such as cost and/or quality.

Setting the construction period

The time period to be allowed for the construction works may be calculated in distinctly different ways:

- on the one hand, an analytical assessment may be made of how long it would take to undertake a project of the size and complexity of the one under consideration, using industry norms; or
- the period may be set simply by adding up the number of weeks between the earliest start date and the completion date demanded by the employer.

The first approach has the merit of allowing a reasonable time to the contractor to carry out the works. One way of establishing a reasonable time period based on industry norms would be to engage a construction programmer to draft an outline construction plan. Alternatively, the BCIS construction duration calculator CD, supplied with the *Guide to Building Construction Duration*, could be used – or, more likely, the professional teams engaged by the developer will have a good idea of what constitutes a reasonable time based on past experience of similar projects. In general it is the employer's team who assess the contract period, but occasionally the enquiry document invites the contractor to include the time period required to complete the works in its tender.

The benefits of allowing a reasonable period of time for the construction works include an increase in the likelihood of obtaining a competitive price at tender stage and a decrease in the likelihood of an overrun to the project, with the inherent risk of claims and disputes – however, this approach may produce a period that does not suit the developer's needs.

In contrast, the second approach only takes the developer's needs into account. If, for operational or financial reasons, a developer requires a particular completion date or contract period, that timing can be incorporated into the construction contract, but this is not without risks.

If the construction period is too short it may lead to qualified tenders and/or higher tender prices – tendering contractors may include the direct costs of any anticipated prolongation in their bids, including perhaps the cost of liquidated and ascertained damages for a period of time. In this case the developer may well lose out twice – once because the project is completed late and again because the damages have effectively been cancelled out by the additional cost of the works.

Saving time

In circumstances where the end-date is fixed by the needs of the developers it might be possible to shorten the pre-commencement time period. The saving can be used to allow more time for the works to be carried out on site, but this too comes with risks.

If the pre-commencement period is shortened there is a risk of poorly or incorrectly detailed tender documents, an inadequate tender period and insufficient construction information being available once works commence.

Poor tender documentation containing a lack of detail and poorly specified works might be taken as signifying an undeveloped design. In this situation a contractor might consider that the prospects of securing additional time and costs through claims for incomplete and/or late construction information are highly favourable. Similarly, anomalies in any measurement items or discrepancies in the contract documentation may lead the contractor to consider that he will be able to recover significant costs by making contractual claims.

In reality few contractors these days are naïve enough to think that claims can be used to generate profits. In the vast majority of cases a contractor faced with having to make contractual claims will find it very difficult to recover what is due, let alone make a profit out of the situation. However, the undesirable possibility that a contractor might adopt this approach still exists.

2.2 The main contractor's tender programme

When invited to tender for construction contracts most contractors will review either the time to be allowed and/or the time required to carry out and complete the works. For all but the smallest of jobs a contractor will produce at least a basic outline tender programme to assist in developing the estimate. This programme will help the estimator form views about the resources needed to undertake the works, particularly time-related preliminaries items, such as supervision, scaffolding and major plant items.

In some contracting organisations the tender programme is prepared by the planning engineer who will be involved with the works should the contract be secured, whilst other organisations employ planning engineers to work exclusively on tenders. On relatively straightforward projects the tender programming may be undertaken by the estimator or by a contracts manager.

As well as simply preparing the programme the planner will usually have some involvement with:

- the site visit;
- preparation of a scaffolding schedule;
- temporary works design;
- temporary services requirements;
- liaison with subcontractors in respect of attendances and time requirements;
- staffing requirements;
- plant requirements;
- buildability issues;
- site establishment;
- health and safety plan development; and
- the method statement preparation.

The above list is not exhaustive and the overall role of the planning engineer will vary from organisation to organisation.

The level of detail on the programme will depend on many factors such as the size of job, size of company, policy of company, nature of job and requirements of the tender enquiry. It is not unusual for an enquiry document to call for a simple bar chart programme to be submitted with the tender – this programme is unlikely to be presented in any great detail and will simply show the key activities and illustrate the overall project timing, build philosophy and strategy.

As with any planning exercise, the tender programme should not be prepared in isolation and input from other members of the contractor's team is likely to be invaluable, particularly if they are likely to be involved if the contract is secured. Unfortunately, it is often the case that such staff are involved on other projects and so their available time and input is likely to be limited.

Preparation

There is no prescribed format for the preparation of a tender programme, but tender programmes for medium-to-large contracts will generally be prepared in some detail. Typically the planning engineer, estimator or other person assigned with the task of producing a tender programme, will start by identifying appropriate programme activities from the tender documentation. This person will then calculate durations for each activity based on standard or estimated labour and plant outputs and apply these to the chosen resource levels.

Standard outputs are readily available from commercially available trade pricing publications as well as various planning related web sites. Alternatively, most contractors' estimators and planners maintain their own library of estimated outputs. Labour and plant outputs are generally based on average outputs for working in all conditions and the tender programmer will adjust these average outputs to reflect the conditions likely to be found on site, in the same way that the estimator adjusts his outputs when pricing.

The tender programmer may also need input from specialist subcontractors and suppliers in respect of design and manufacturing periods, installation times, attendances and general methodology for non-standard construction operations.

In the preparation of any tender programme there is a degree of uncertainty. Any programming or planning of construction work cannot be an exact science and a precise period for the execution of the works cannot be estimated with certainty. However, the tender programmer is not expected to determine the timing and interaction of all of the elements of the works with complete precision – what can be provided is a reasonable assessment based on experience of the construction process. At times the planning process relies on an intuitive feel of the likely and appropriate time periods required.

Often the first draft of the tender programme will show the works being undertaken in what is considered as an optimum period, which represents a period that can be achieved with relatively high outputs and relatively few problems. This optimistic assessment can then be reviewed in the light of any periods for the works stated in the tender, the level of risk the contractor's directors are prepared to take in order to secure the work, the risk allocation in the proposed terms of contract, the proposed level of liquidated damages for late completion, the market conditions, the company's workload and any other relevant factors. These factors are matters that many contractors will discuss at their tender adjudication/settlement meeting.

2.3 Subcontractor's tender programme

Some subcontractors are of similar size and composition to main contractors and for these the production of tender programmes for major projects will be similar to those set out in section 2.2. In the case of particularly complex or large subcontract projects – such as services installations or works that require subcontractor design input – it is good practice for the main contractor to provide full details of the required timings on which the subcontractor can base his bid and submit his own tender programme.

In these situations the main contractor often includes a 'constraints programme' with the tender enquiry, which details the overall time for the subcontract works, the general required sequencing, windows of time for the execution of specific sections of work, concurrent works being undertaken by other subcontractors, and key dates for areas to be completed and handed over to the following trades. A constraints programme is usually presented in the form of a bar chart or even a simple schedule of dates abstracted from the contractor's tender programme and from this basic information the subcontractor can produce his own detailed tender programme demonstrating if and how the main contractor's requirements can be achieved.

However, most subcontractors, whether large or small, will not submit a programme with their tender. This is because:

(a) they are not requested to do so;
(b) they are not prepared to do so; and/or
(c) there is insufficient time.

Very often, the only programme information provided to a subcontractor at tender stage is a duration within which the subcontract works will be required to be completed. On other occasions not even this level of information is provided – the subcontractor is simply told that work will have to be carried out to meet the main contractor's programme (if and when one is produced and issued).

Even if a main contractor wished to have a tender programme from subcontractors, many would be unable or unwilling to provide one. The majority of subcontractors in the construction industry are small businesses competing in a market where overhead costs are kept low. Such companies cannot incur significant costs preparing tender programmes for work that may not come their way even if they are the lowest tenderer.

If a subcontractor was asked to provide a tender programme and did have the resources to do so there may still be difficulties due to a short tender period. The time period allowed to contractors to prepare and return a tender is rarely generous and so it may be wholly unrealistic to expect a subcontractor to provide a programme as well as a price in the time allowed.

Given that large parts of most construction works are carried out by subcontractors their lack of programming input at tender stage may be considered a concern, but due to the problems outlined the situation is unlikely to change in the foreseeable future.

2.4 The planned programme

In general, following the award of a contract, one of the contractor's key tasks will be to produce a planned programme for the execution of the works. This programme is sometimes referred to as the construction programme, the master programme or the contract programme. (The term contract programme is used by some contractors regardless of its significance under the terms of the contract agreement.)

Sometimes the tender programme is adopted as the initial planned programme. Dependent on the contractor's management structure, this programme may then be developed by the same planning engineer who dealt with the tender or alternatively the tender planning information may be handed over for development by the contractor's construction planning engineer and construction team.

To some extent, the contract documentation is likely to prescribe the format of the planned programme, as well as the timing for its submission. What is actually required will vary from project-to-project and in some cases the requirements are highly prescriptive, dictating particular computer software to produce the planned programme and requesting a full copy in an electronic format, while on other occasions the contract specifies the details of particular activities that are to be included in the programme and/or the maximum permissible durations for each activity. The one thing that is invariably the case is that the programme is required to be produced in the form of a bar chart that ought to be readily understood by all of the parties.

Maintaining the programme

Once works get underway it is usual for the employer to require the contractor to use the planned programme for monitoring purposes. Contractors are required to update the programme to reflect actual progress achieved on site as well as any changes to the course and sequencing of the works. On many projects the planned programme is submitted to the employer's team for comment and, in certain cases, formal acceptance.

Planned programmes are key documents in the management of projects but often they are insufficiently detailed and do not comply with the requirements set out in the contract. Equally, response to the programme from the client is not always forthcoming. It is not until the project is running into difficulty that comments are made and, by this stage, they tend to be adverse.

Given the importance of the planned programme it is perhaps surprising that both sides are so often guilty of a casual disregard of their obligations. When disagreements crop up it can often even prove difficult to identify:

• the contractor's original planned programme;
• the date on which it was submitted to the employer; and
• any comments made by the employer's team.

This situation could be simply resolved by contractors ensuring that all programmes issued to the employer are formally recorded, with the reasons for issue fully explained, and for all employers to acknowledge receipt and make or confirm comments in writing – this is particularly important if a series of programmes are issued around the start of the works.

2.5 Preparation, problems and solutions

The contractor's planned programme should demonstrate the basic concept for the execution of the works within the contractually required timings, thereby reflecting the contractor's overall strategy. Greater detail can be shown in short-term programmes, which set out the project sequencing and implementation of the works within the overall parameters of the main planned programme and tend to be more tactical than strategic.

The main planned programme is often described as representing the contractor's best guess. This is probably a little unfair as the programme will be based on the available information and the contractor's experience. It is however well recognised and accepted that the planned programme can only represent the contractor's reasonable view and, in reality, it is most unlikely that the works will be undertaken strictly in accordance with this programme.

This uncertainty in the planned programme is due to many factors. For example, at the commencement of the project the information used for the production of the programme will, in certain respects, be largely undeveloped (e.g. the contract might contain provisional sums and provisional quantities; the architect may not have carried out detailed design for the finishing elements; specialist subcontractors may not yet have been appointed; and certain elements of the works might be awaiting development of design by the contractor). Therefore, the original planned programme illustrates one of many possibilities of how the work may progress and even in the unlikely event that there were no major uncertainties at commencement stage the plan could still change if the contractor found that his original intent was unworkable or could be improved.

Revised programmes

At various points throughout the project the contractor is likely to submit revised programmes. After even a relatively short period of time the planned programme may bear little resemblance to the timing and sequence of works actually being carried out, making the planned programme of little use to mangers of the project.

There are many different reasons for the changes to the planned programme – there may have been delays to the works; there may have been changes to the sequencing and timing of the works; additional works may have been instructed; or a more detailed programme may be required. Generally, progress will then be monitored against the revised, as opposed to the original planned, programme.

Some contracts require contractors to provide revised programmes on a regular basis and/or when variations have been instructed that will impact progress.

Anyone familiar with a construction project will understand that it is not practical to plan too far ahead, at least with any degree of detail, and in most cases it is not really necessary to do so. At the start of a new building project of say two years overall duration, the actual timing of the ceramic wall and floor tiling to new toilet and kitchen areas at the end of the project is, not unreasonably, unlikely to be considered a great priority. Therefore, such work might well be represented on the planned programme by no more than a single all embracing activity entitled 'Toilet and kitchen fitting out'.

This is not to say a contractor would or should disregard the timing of such works – not least because advance requests for design information, appointment of subcontractors, ordering of materials and organisation of labour, will all have to be kept in mind – but at the outset, such works are not a priority. This situation will, of course, eventually change and in the last four to six months of the same project the tiling works may become the priority, with the planning, co-ordination and execution of these works being critical to the overall project completion. When this stage is reached the level of detail in the planning will be much greater , which is where short-term tactical programmes can be produced to demonstrate the timing and detailed sequencing of how works are to be implemented.

Therefore, the planned strategic programme is supported on most projects by tactical planning over short periods and between key milestones. By way of further illustration, the key priority when works first commence might be to undertake the site clearance and complete the foundations to enable the key activity milestone of structural steel erection to commence at the designated time. Once this milestone or key date has been achieved the construction team will focus on the next priority and milestone, which might be the construction of the external building envelope and roofing to provide a weather tight environment for following trades.

The fact that the works are only planned with any degree of detail over these short periods is often reflected on the initial planned programme, which may show the substructure works in some detail, the superstructure and envelope works in a little less detail and the service installations and final fitting out as one all embracing activity.

Some contractors produce separate internal planned programmes and other specific programmes that are not forwarded to the client. These may show activity timings and an overall project completion date in advance of the contractual date, representing the contractor's target programme for completion. In theory, setting such a target and giving subcontractors targets ahead of the external planned programme, will help maintain an element of 'float' and contingency. However, whether this dual approach really produces any benefits to the contractor is a moot point.

2.6 Subcontractors' programmes

The planned programme of works produced by subcontractors for main contractors and the processes adopted are really little different to those adopted by the main contractor for the employer but, with simple trades packages, requiring only a single visit to site, a planned programme of works may not be required. In any event, the subcontractor may not possess sufficient knowledge in respect of the release of work areas and/or of the planned work by others, to produce a worthwhile programme.

Generally, it is for the main contractor to co-ordinate the works and to ensure that work is released and undertaken by the subcontractor in compliance with the terms of the subcontract.

Summary

When completing a tender for a construction project, contractors will consider the time available and usually produce a basic outline tender programme, detailing the anticipated construction activities and sequence.

The level of detail included in the programme will depend on the size and nature of the job and could be little more that a simple bar chart, but on medium to large contracts the tender programme may be produced in some detail.

There will be some uncertainty to any tender programme as it is produced to indicate the expected sequence and timing of the works as well as the anticipated duration of the main project elements within the required construction period. It will not be produced with the intention of defining the project activity timings with complete precision.

During the main contractor's tender period subcontractors may submit their own tender programme, but because of the time limits such programmes are the exception rather than the rule.

Following the award of a contract one of the contractor's initial tasks is to produce a planned programme for the execution of the works. This will sometimes be initially no more than a revised version of the tender programme.

The contract documentation may well stipulate the format of the planned programme and sometimes such requirements may be highly prescriptive. Once work has commenced it will be expected that the planned programme be updated to reflect progress achieved.

Good forward planning is key to the success of a project but planned and updated programmes are too often neglected by both sides, which can cause difficulties if a dispute arises.

Revised programmes may be or may have to be submitted at various points throughout the project. These will take into account such issues as any delays, further required enhancement and detailing, any variations, and general resequencing – progress will then usually be monitored using the new programme.

3

Planning techniques

As discussed in the previous chapters, construction projects are inherently complex, which makes effective planning key to a project's success. There are many project planning and programming methods, but basically they all strive to provide a system of management for the co-ordination of construction projects.

In addition to laying out an overall strategy the planning technique chosen for any project will allow the project team to measure progress, quantify impacts and adjust to changes.

The main delay analysis methodologies rely on the technique known as critical path analysis and for this reason a little more detail has been included under this heading. Given the importance of computers in modern planning and programming, the chapter also includes a brief commentary about the use of computers.

While this chapter discusses the techniques available for project planning and programming, it is not intended as a fully comprehensive guide – the aim is to provide a general overview of the techniques and the appropriateness of their application.

3.1 Computers

Prior to the personal computer becoming widely available, the majority of construction planning was undertaken manually. The use of computer-assisted analysis was restricted to those companies having access to mainframe computers. This has all changed and now programmes that have not been computer generated may well be frowned upon.

Most of the available computer software for planning applications is based on critical path analysis, although some rely on a linked bar chart format and others allow the production of a simple graphical bar chart. The network diagram associated with critical path analysis is not particularly easy to follow and therefore the software packages usually allow the option to display results of such analyses in the form of a bar chart.

The key purpose and function of the planning of any project is to inform and communicate the intended forward plan to the project team and to provide a means of monitoring the project progress status. In this respect planning software is a most valuable tool and the advantages of its use include:

- activities can be coded or categorised enabling a user to apply filters and view a discrete selection of activities, such as all of the services activities or all of the activities relating to the first floor;
- alternative activity sequences or 'what if' type exercises can be easily and rapidly performed;
- groups of activities can be summarised to produce 'high-level' strategic programmes;
- histograms and 'S' curves can be produced, which enables resource levels and expenditure to be illustrated graphically; and
- programmes can be updated and amended promptly, allowing real-time progress reporting.

Each individual brand of computer software for programming has its own particular features – some have better graphics and display features, whilst others offer more powerful processing, customisation and sorting capabilities. Despite these variations, the software does, generally, allow for the exchange of data with other planning packages, as well as with standard spreadsheet and database applications.

Having said that, care is needed when transferring data between different computer software applications as the different packages may interpret and process the information in slightly different ways resulting in potential anomalies.

Rubbish in, rubbish out

The actual process of calculating the project activity timings with critical path analysis is very simplistic, consisting of a basic addition and subtraction exercise. However as with any computer operation the commercially available planning software does no more than process the information it is given.

It should not be forgotten that planning software is only a tool and in this context the well-used adage 'rubbish in, rubbish out' is worth repeating. If the data input is flawed the computer cannot and will not rectify those flaws – making any computer software only as good as the data input allows it to be.

Computers have revolutionised construction programming and planning but it should not be forgotten that the real skill or art in successfully and realistically undertaking any planning analysis involves:

- understanding the project scope;
- considering potential alternatives;
- breaking down the works into the relevant activities;
- defining the likely activity durations; and
- identifying the relationships between the considered activities.

This is not a matter of producing programmes that are precise, but is more about considering what is reasonable and achievable. The process of producing reasonable and achievable programmes in the construction industry cannot be simply taught or achieved by the press of a button on a computer; it requires experience of construction projects and an understanding of the overall construction process.

3.2 Bar charts

Bar charts have been, and are still, extensively used in the construction industry. There is no specific set layout for a bar chart but the usual and recognised format is for the activity descriptions to be listed in a vertical column on the left hand side of the chart, with activities represented by bar lines plotted against a timescale on the horizontal axis.

Historical development

The development and introduction, in the 1920s, of the Gantt or bar chart is accredited to American industrialist and management consultant Henry Laurence Gantt. Its potential for utilisation in the planning and monitoring of construction projects was soon recognised and it was used in the US on such major projects as the construction of the Hoover Dam.

Bar charts also have a long history of use within the UK construction industry and, before the introduction of the personal computer, bar charts were prepared manually by contractors who often had standard pro-forma templates and associated stationery. Production of any large-scale bar chart was a major drafting exercise with activity descriptions and general lettering being applied manually, sometimes with the help of plastic stencils. The activity bars and other graphics shown on the charts were also drawn by hand or with the use of commercially available graphic transfers.

As can be imagined, amendments to such programmes were difficult, time consuming and not always practical – relatively minor revisions to the programme often necessitated a complete redraw.

Progress updating on such charts was achieved by means of shading the activity bars, using a different colour to differentiate between the progress achieved each week (the choice of colours could become quite creative after a time). Progress was also commonly depicted by means of map pins, strategically positioned in each activity bar. These pins were then connected by a piece of string or elastic to represent the traditional 'time now', drop down, progress line.

Pros and cons

The main advantage of the bar chart is its simplicity – the format effectively displays and communicates the necessary information and it also has the benefit of being well recognised, accepted and understood.

Modern programming software enables critical path analysis to be displayed in bar chart format, but in order to produce a bar chart it is not always necessary to input critical path data. Some of the available programming software allows the programmer to simply draw the activity bars onto a pro-forma sheet, replicating the manual creation of a bar chart. However, unlike the manual exercise, the computer exercise can be carried out with great speed, corrections are easy to make and the printed image is superior to the one produced manually.

As well as all members of the project team being able to understand the bar chart's simple format, it does not have to be produced by a specialist programmer. For example, construction managers can produce their own tactical programmes to communicate their short-term planned intent to the various subcontractors and/or simple summary programmes to report overall project status to senior management or clients.

However, the advantage of being able to create a bar chart with relative ease can also be a drawback. Because production of a bar chart is easy it may mean that, unlike critical path analysis, the activities are drawn with insufficient thought or consideration of the logical dependencies and interfaces between the various planned activities. Likewise this relative ease of production may lead to the activity bar simply being pasted across the chart to suit the time available, with little consideration of realistic durations or the level of resources required.

Also if too many different updated bar charts are issued on a project, some of which prove to be flawed and unrealistic, it will eventually lead to what might be described as 'bar chart fatigue', so it is best to have controls on production and the update process.

Another drawback with simple bar charts is that they do not react dynamically when changes are made, in the way programmes with linked activities do. Therefore, there are limitations to the use of such bar charts when it comes to recording site progress, assessing the overall project progress status and identifying the causes of project delay.

The linked bar chart

Showing logical dependencies between the activity bars to form what is referred to as a 'linked bar chart' can alleviate some of the problems associated with the simple bar chart. These dependencies help to reinforce the planned intent and will force the programme author to consider the activity relationships and durations more carefully.

The big advantage of the linked bar chart is that the use of commercially available software will allow the chart to be scheduled in much the same way as a critical path analysis. It will also graphically show the activity 'float' as well as those activities that are critical. When a bar chart is linked in this way it can be rescheduled utilising the computer software by inputting progress data. Unlike the simple bar chart, the linked bar chart will react dynamically, adjusting the timing of the remaining work activity bars and demonstrating any variation to the overall date for completion.

Most linked bar chart software will only represent logical links between the activity bars graphically (there is no separate analysis to show how links have been made, as there is with critical path analysis software applications). Links shown graphically are likely to be difficult to follow on all but the simplest programme and so, even with the data in an electronic format, it may prove difficult to cross-check the logic links applied in order to confirm them.

3.3 Critical path analysis

Critical path analysis is a technique that defines the shortest theoretical route through the sequence of programme activities, from project commencement to completion. A critical path is established by linking the various work activities on the programme and applying estimated timings to these activities and relationships.

The importance of the technique is that it distinguishes between those activities that are critical to the completion date and those that are not – delays to critical activities will affect the end date, whereas delays to non-critical activities may not.

History of critical path analysis

The programming technique now known as critical path analysis (often abbreviated to CPA) was developed in the late-1950s, in both the US and Europe.

In the US research was led by the E. I. Du Pont de Nemours Company in respect of the development of a technique that they called the 'Critical Path Method' (CPM) for implementation on major complex projects.

One of the better-known early uses for this type of programming was by the US Navy Special Projects Office, who developed and utilised a critical path based technique referred to as the 'Programme Evaluation and Review Technique' (PERT). This system is credited by some with saving two years in the development and delivery of the Polaris missile.

The critical path analysis technique has been the subject of much academic discussion. When first developed the methodology was portrayed in what is referred to as 'a circle and arrow' or 'activity on the node' diagrammatic format, which necessitated that the relationships between the project activities were generally sequential. More flexibility regarding activity relationships was provided with the introduction of the 'precedence diagram format', which forms the basis for the majority of modern planning software packages used in the construction industry today.

Critical path analysis was also developed in the UK in the 1950s by the ICI Group and the Central Electricity Generating Board (CEGB) for use in connection with the overhaul of major generating plants. As in the US the utilisation of the technique is credited with substantial reductions in the required project periods. In the early 1960s the Building Research Establishment (BRE) undertook further development work on the technique for the construction industry.

The fundamental principle of this technique is relatively simplistic but the time and effort required to draw the networks and undertake updates and revisions manually dictated that its use throughout the 1960s and 1970s was mainly restricted to companies with access to mainframe computers. The introduction of the personal computer in the 1980s has meant that commercially available planning software using critical path analysis is now commonplace.

The basic concept

In order to understand the strengths, weaknesses and limitations of critical path analysis it is necessary to understand the basic principles.

In broad terms a critical path analysis is developed by identifying programme activities and then linking the activities. Therefore, the first thing to consider is the relationships between activities (such as whether activity B can be started before activity A is completed). In the explanations below a standard format is adopted, which is to show project activities as rectangular boxes and the inter-relationships as lines or arrows.

There are four basic relationships, or 'logic links', between project activities: 'finish-to-start', 'start-to-start', 'finish-to-finish' and 'start-to-finish'. These are generally represented in a standard 'precedence diagram format' as follows:

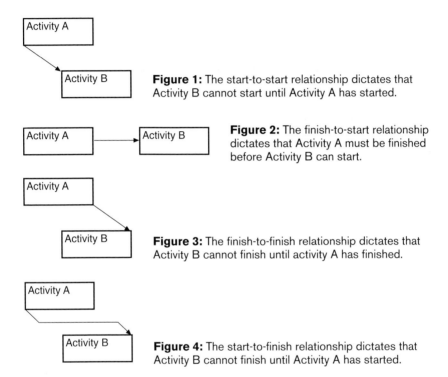

Figure 1: The start-to-start relationship dictates that Activity B cannot start until Activity A has started.

Figure 2: The finish-to-start relationship dictates that Activity A must be finished before Activity B can start.

Figure 3: The finish-to-finish relationship dictates that Activity B cannot finish until activity A has finished.

Figure 4: The start-to-finish relationship dictates that Activity B cannot finish until Activity A has started.

It is important to understand that, in all cases, these relationships are firm and positive. Therefore, in the finish-to-start example, Activity B *cannot* commence until Activity A is complete.

In general all activities within the programme (other than the first and last) will have at least two logic links; one from an earlier or predecessor activity to the activity start, defining the time at which the activity can commence, and one linking the activity to later or successor activities. An example network is considered in detail later in this chapter.

Leads and Lags

The various logic links referred to can have periods of time assigned to them, to dictate a period between the start and/or finish of one activity and the start and/or finish of the succeeding activity.

In figure 5 there is a lead-time from Activity A of two days prior to the commencement of Activity B. This type of restraint on the programme is known as a 'lead'.

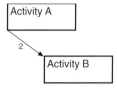

Figure 5: Activity B cannot commence until two units of time, usually days, have elapsed following commencement of Activity A.

Activities with 'finish-to-finish' relationships can also have time constraints.

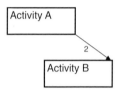

Figure 6: Activity B cannot finish until two days after Activity A has finished.

In this situation Activity B lags behind activity A by two days – giving this type of restraint the name 'lag'.

Most computer software does not specifically differentiate between the terms 'leads' and 'lags'

Some of the commercially available software also allows negative times to be assigned to the logic links. Figure 7 shows a negative lag.

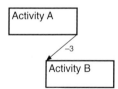

Figure 7: Activity B can commence three days before activity A is complete creating a negative lag.

Most programmers do not use a 'negative lag' between activities when preparing a critical path analysis, as they prefer to view a progressive programme. In theory a negative lag may accurately define a relationship between two activities but in reality it is more likely that Activity B in figure 7 will be driven by the start and progress of Activity A, not by its completion, making it more logical to use a 'start-to-start' relationship. Some consider negative lags to be flawed or false 'backwards' logic.

Calculation of activity start and completion times

The logic links shown in figures 1–7 were represented as very simple precedence diagrams. Generally, the precedence diagram format shows start, duration and completion information about each activity and usually represents an activity as a rectangular box containing spaces for the activity description and timing information, as set out below:

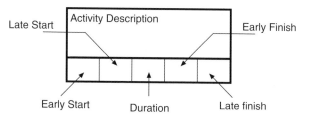

Figure 8: A typical activity box from a precedence diagram.

As figure 8 shows the duration is displayed in the centre of the activity box; the early and late start times are to the left and the early and late finish times to the right (some software packages display the layout of the early and late times differently).

Once the activities within a project have been defined they can be linked together to form a network (this is why critical path analysis is sometimes referred to as 'network analysis').

Figure 9 overleaf represents a small network for typical substructure works, with activities linked together by logical constraints and the estimated activity durations shown in numbers of days.

Constraint dates

The logic driving the project activity timings can be overridden by imposing constraint dates on the starts and finishes.

As an example, the employer may wish to handover an existing building to a demolition contractor in stages. It may be a term of the contract that demolition of certain structures cannot commence until four working weeks after handover of the site. In such circumstances a constraint date may be applied to the start of the demolition activity dictating that it can commence no earlier than four working weeks after commencement of the works.

It is important that only essential constraint dates are added, as they prevent the network from acting dynamically when it is re-scheduled.

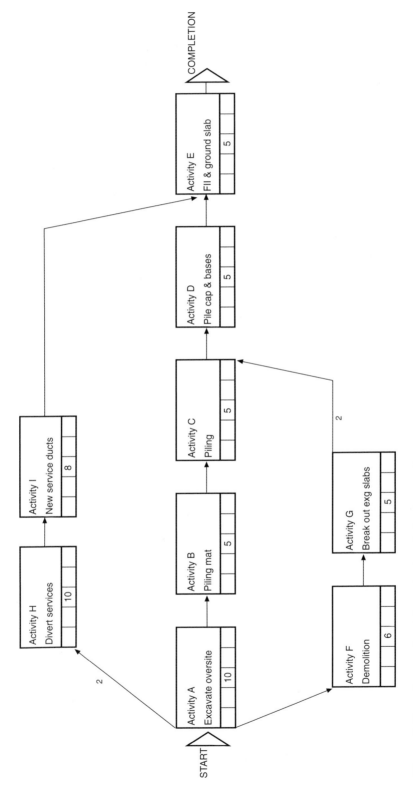

Figure 9: Precedence network for a simple substructure package

Once this network has been produced the earliest start and earliest finish of each activity can be calculated. Programmers usually refer to the calculation process of the earliest times as the 'forward pass' and the latest time as the 'backward pass'. The process of calculating both the earliest and latest activity start and finish is known as time analysis or scheduling.

The forward pass

As discussed, the precedence diagram provides for the earliest start date to be entered in the box on the lower left hand side. In figure 10 the substructure package network is reproduced with the earliest start and earliest finish times calculated on the basis of the logic and lead times previously entered.

In figure 10, overleaf, the commencement of the project is represented by Activity A, which has an early start at day zero, the start of the project. It has already been estimated that Activity A has a duration of ten days – making an early finish at day ten.

The start of activity H is constrained by the 'start-to-start' link with Activity A, which has a lead-time of two days – meaning that Activity H can only start at day two. This activity also has an estimated duration of ten days and so the earliest it can finish is day 12 (early start of two plus duration of ten).

This simple process of adding the durations, leads and lags is carried out for all activities and in this illustration it can be seen that the earliest that the project can finish is day 30, which is determined by the early finish of Activity E.

The backward pass

Once the forward pass has been completed and the early start and finish times have been entered onto the network the latest starts and finishes can be entered – this is known as the backward pass.

As established, Activity E is the final activity for the project. Therefore the earliest date Activity E can finish is the same as the earliest date the overall project can finish – day 30. Because activity E represents the final activity the latest finish is the same as the earliest finish. It has already been estimated that the activity E duration will be five days, so the latest start is day 25 (latest finish of 30 less duration of five).

Figure 11 shows the backward pass – the reverse of the forward pass – with activity durations being deducted rather than added.

Even with a very simple network it can be seen that the network diagram is not simple to follow. However, this data can be converted into a linked bar chart by giving the activity timings day numbers, which can be related to a project calendar and converted to dates.

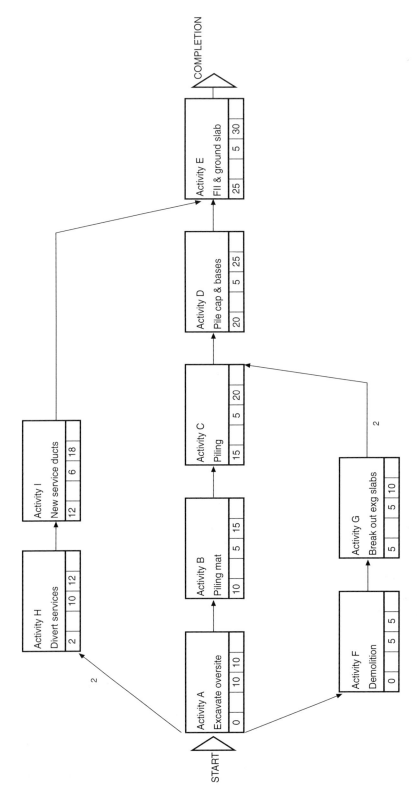

Figure 10: Precedence network for a simple substructure package – the forward pass

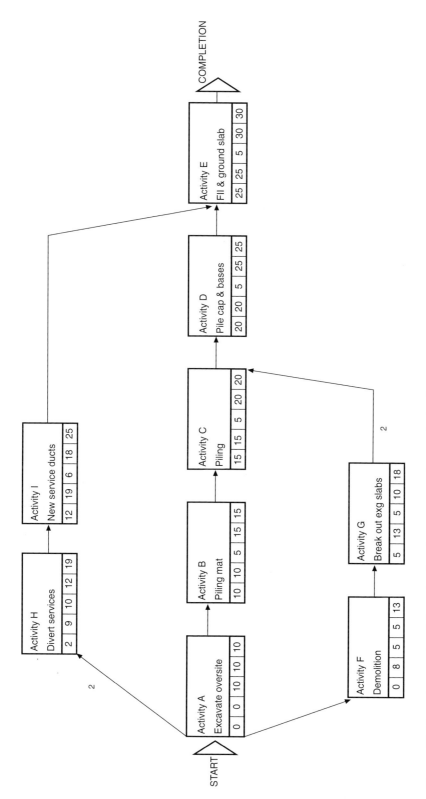

Figure 11: Precedence network for a simple substructure package – the backward pass

In any project differing calendars can be applied to the activities, for instance some activities may be planned to be carried out five days per week, with Saturdays and Sundays being designated as non-working days. Other activities may be planned to be worked on six or seven days per week – Likewise differing holiday periods can be applied to the project calendars and project activities.

Conversion of critical path network into bar chart

Modern computer programs are able to convert critical path networks, like those shown in figure 11, into traditional bar charts. This is illustrated by figure 12, which shows a linked bar chart based on the same substructure project information used to construct the network in figure 11.

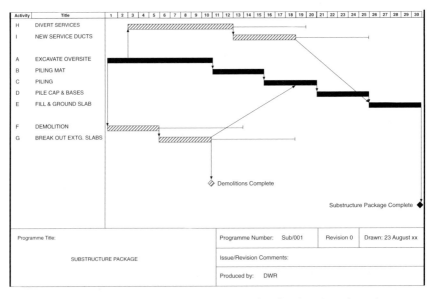

Figure 12: Linked bar chart of the substructure using the data from the substructure package network described in figures 9–11. (For the sake of simplicity, in this example, days have been left as numbers rather than being related to a calendar.)

Float and the critical path

'Float' can be described as the difference between the total time available in which to undertake a particular activity and the total estimated time of the activity duration. Effectively, float is the 'spare' time available in which an activity can be delayed or prolonged without it causing any impact on following activities and/or the completion date.

For example, the substructure package network, illustrated by figure 11, indicates that Activities F, G, H and I have float. There is a difference between the earliest and latest start and finish times of these activities indicating that a limited delay will not affect the overall programme.

Taking activity I ('New service ducts') as an example, it can be seen that the earliest that this activity can finish is day 18 and that the latest it can finish, without causing the overall project to be extended beyond day 30, is day 25. Therefore this activity can start later than planned or it can be prolonged but, provided it does not finish beyond day 25, it will not cause the project completion to be delayed. The linked bar chart (figure 12) illustrates the extent of the float on the various activities by means of a trailing line following the activity bar lines.

There are two basic types of float:

- 'total float' refers to the time by which an activity can be delayed or prolonged without affecting the project completion date; and
- 'free float' refers to the time by which an activity can be delayed or prolonged without affecting the timing of any of the succeeding activities.

When an activity containing an element of 'total float' is progressively delayed, the amount of float will reduce. When the entire 'float' has been utilised and the activity has zero 'total float' it will have become an activity that is critical to the original planned completion date. If delay to the activity continues, the float will become negative. Negative float indicates delay and as such two days negative float reflects a two-day delay to the original planned completion.

Milestones

'Milestones' are usually represented on a programme by a small diamond to simply identify a key point in time such as the date by which the roof is to be made weather tight, the 'power-on' date or a sectional completion date – these are activities with zero duration. These milestones can be linked to the start and finish of project activities utilising the previously described logic. Figure 12, the substructure linked bar chart, shows two milestones: one linked to the completion of demolition activities; and the other identifying the completion date of the substructure works.

3.4 Practical difficulties with critical path analysis

It may come as a surprise to those unfamiliar with sophisticated critical path analysis, which relies upon such precise and detailed data and advanced modern computer hardware and software, so that the results produced can be misleading or even plain wrong – and this is not a reference to data input errors or computer flaws.

Critical path analysis can be wrong simply due to the level of detail used to prepare the analysis. There would appear to be an obvious solution to this problem – make sure the level of detail is correct. However, it is not this simple.

Level of detail – global activities

Sometimes the work scope to a particular area may be uncertain when the planned programme is being produced (for example perhaps the work to a basement of a building to be refurbished). In cases of uncertainty the contractor is likely to depict the various work tasks to be undertaken in the basement simply with one activity bar, called 'works to basement'. Given the uncertainty about the scope of the work there would not really be an alternative, but these activities of long duration are often pushed onto the critical path.

Some of the work in the basement of a building to be refurbished may well be critical but, in reality, there are likely to be many separate discrete tasks to carry out and it is unlikely that all will be critical. Therefore, in this case, the critical path shown on the programme may well be incorrect, simply due to the length of a global activity bar.

In this type of scenario the updated programme may indicate that the project as a whole is in delay, because of delays to the basement, when in reality the completion date is not actually under threat.

Level of detail – composite activities

On many construction projects key trades, such as the electrical and mechanical services installations, are on the critical path. This being the case, the entire first-fix services activity will be shown as being critical. However, on a typical project, the services first-fix activity will consist of many different tasks and elements – including pipework, ductwork, electrical containment, panel boards, wiring, testing and insulation – and not all of these works will be critical.

These subactivities could be further divided, with electrical containment and wiring being broken down into the various systems, such as low voltage power, lighting, controls, fire alarm, CCTV, security and communications. Likewise, pipework could be divided into activities relating to chilled, low-pressure hot water and domestic plumbing.

First-fix service elements could then be separated into locations within the building, such as under floor, high level, walls and risers, and further split to identify different floor levels, zones or specific rooms.

If this level of detail was provided, the critical path would run through certain elements of the services installation works but it would not run through the entire activity, meaning in the more simplified programme, which shows first-fix services as one activity, the critical path may be misleading.

However, to provide the level of subdivision referred to above would result in a huge programme, which would prove difficult and impractical to follow and implement. A balance must be struck between the level of programme detail and the need to exactly define the critical path. In striking this balance it is likely that some level of accuracy will have to be compromised, so the results of any analysis should be considered in this light.

Overlapping activities

When critical path analysis networks were first developed they were displayed graphically as circle and arrow diagrams. This format meant that it was difficult to show overlaps between the activities. To simulate the effect of overlapping activities it was necessary to create 'dummy' activities, but this complicated an already difficult exercise.

As a result, most early critical path analysis was based on activities being undertaken sequentially, with the commencement of one activity being dependent on the completion of the preceding activity or activities.

The use of the 'precedence diagram format' introduced a lot more flexibility as it enabled activity timings to be overlapped. This was a significant improvement because it allowed the programmes to reflect the construction process where most project activities do overlap. However, this does introduce certain problems.

In figure 13 it can be seen that the relationship between the internal blockwork partitions and the following activity, of plastering, is a 'start-to-start' link. The constraints specify that plastering cannot start until ten days after blockwork has commenced. This relationship may seem logical and reasonable but it makes an assumption that in the ten-day period between the start of blockwork and the start of plastering, sufficient blockwork will be built to allow the plastering to commence. Therefore, it would be more accurate to show the relationship between these two activities as a 'finish-to-start' relationship, dictating that plastering cannot commence until sufficient blockwork has been constructed.

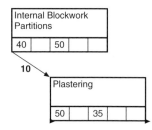

Figure 13: Part of a network in which plastering works overlap with the construction of internal blockwork partitions.

To show this relationship accurately would require the blockwork and plastering to be subdivided into short discrete activities, with start-to-finish relationships, relating to small areas, or even individual walls or rooms. But as discussed too much programme detail results in a prescriptive programme, which may well prove impractical to implement.

This example also raises another issue relating to detail and the critical path. If the blockwork had commenced on time, and good progress had been made in the first ten days, the works would appear to be on programme and no warnings would be given when the rescheduling was carried out. But what if the block layer had progressed all of the fair-faced blocks or all of the low-level work and there were no completed areas ready for plastering? In percentage terms progress of blockwork may be 20% in accordance with the planned programme but plasterwork would not be able to commence and a critical delay would be about to occur.

From this example it can be seen that, in respect of the commencement of the plastering work, not only are the first ten days of work to construct the internal partitions critical but it is equally important that, within this ten-day period, the blockwork is suitably sequenced. As with other areas of work, in respect of the block partition operations some of the work elements or areas of work may be more critical than others.

There is no simple answer to these types of problems. A balance has to be struck between sufficient detail and accurate logical relationships, but if a programme is to remain simple enough to use it will often mean a compromise on the precision of the data input. Such a compromise will affect the accuracy of the programme and any rescheduling. Therefore, some caution should be exercised when making critical decisions on the basis of information produced by critical path analysis.

Overlapping activities with start and finish constraints

Figure 14 shows the relationship between blockwork partitions and plastering. In this example plastering is planned to commence ten days after the start of the blockwork and logically cannot be completed until five days after finishing the blockwork.

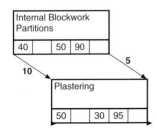

Figure 14: Simple illustration of the problems associated with overlapping activities.

In the previous examples the activity earliest finish times have been generated, when carrying out the forward pass, by adding the activity duration to the earliest start. In figure 14 the plastering can commence at day 50 and has a duration of 30 days meaning that the earliest finish would be day 80. However the plastering cannot be completed until five days after the blockwork, thus the earliest completion of the plastering is constrained until day 95.

Based on these times the 30 days of plastering will be undertaken within an overall period of 45 days between day 50 and day 95. In reality the plastering contractor would probably visit the site on a number of occasions as and when sufficient areas of blockwork become available. The works would be undertaken in a discontinuous manner, which is illustrated by the bar chart example at figure 15.

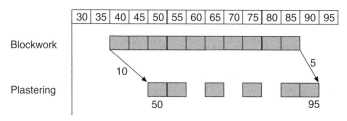

Figure 15: Plastering activity discontinuous

Some of the available programming software includes a feature that would reflect discontinuous work and the earliest times given in figure 15, however, software without this feature would only be able to consider the plastering as a continuous activity of 30 days. This being the case the earliest completion of the plastering would be constrained by the completion of the block work until day 95 and the software would set the earliest start of plastering at day 65 (earliest completion of 95 less duration of 30) – 15 days after the earliest possible start.

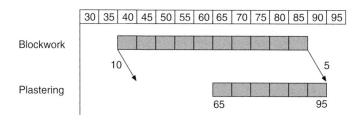

Figure 16: Plastering activity continuous

This may have obvious implications for any following activities that have a logical link with the start of the plastering operations (such as painting). Programmers often overcome this problem by increasing the activity duration to 'fill' the total time available (in the case of this example the duration of the plastering activity would be increased to 45 days to reflect the earliest start at day 50). In this type of situation the activity duration will reflect the period *available* rather than the period *required* to undertake the task.

The overlapping of activities employing start-to-start and finish-to-finish relationships introduces an element of programme flexibility and alleviates the need for very many highly prescriptive activities having finish-to-start relationships. Figures 15 and 16 illustrate that some care is needed in the use of such overlaps and that the potential problems require some consideration. Again this demonstrates that in any programming exercise there must be a compromise between the level of detail and the need to try and apply precise logic.

Overlapping activities – wholly or partly critical

In general all activities within a critical path network must either be critical or must contain an element of float. Prospective planning generally assumes that activities are continuous and therefore critical activities have both critical starts and finishes. This is basically how the available planning software reacts, with activities being indicated as wholly critical. Notwithstanding this, as discussed, some of the software packages will allow the activity duration to become split or discontinuous.

Figure 17 shows a precedence diagram where each activity is linked by both a start-to-start and finish-to-finish relationship – creating what is often referred to as a 'ladder'.

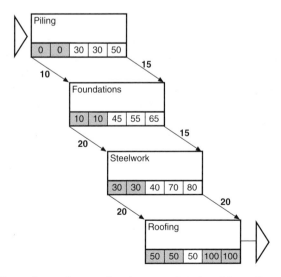

Figure 17: Precedence format showing a project involving piling, foundations, steelwork and roofing. (The shaded entries denote critical start and finish times.)

As with the previous example of the substructure package network (figure 10), the 'forward pass' in figure 17 means that the early finish times are derived from the early start plus the activity duration (for example, the earliest finish for steelwork is 70 days, which is derived from the early start of 30 days plus the activity duration of 40 days).

However, the backward pass process used in the substructure package (figure 11), which produced latest start times by deducting the activity duration from the latest finish, does not work in the case of figure 17, except for the final roofing activity.

If timing were calculated in a similar way to the substructure network at figure 17 then the latest start time for steelwork would be the latest finish of day 80 minus the duration of 40 days to make a latest start of day 40 but, as can be seen, the latest start for steelwork is day 30. The reason for this ten-day difference is that the latest start of the steelwork activity is derived from the latest start of roofing less the start-to-start lead time (roofing latest start of 50 less the lead of 20).

In figure 17 the start dates are critical for all activities but, because of the overlap created by the start-to-start and finish-to-finish relationships, the finish dates for the first three activities of piling, foundations and steelwork contain float. In other words once an activity is sufficiently progressed to allow the following activity to commence there is an element of float.

This type of situation is not difficult to imagine. With many construction operations, once a certain amount of work is complete the following trade can commence (for example on multi-storey buildings the lower floors may be painted before some of the upper floors have even been constructed).

In the situation illustrated by figure 17 it is logical to presume that once sufficient piling had been completed and the piling rig moved, the initial foundation works could commence. The network shows, by the 'start-to-start' link, that the estimated time period for this to happen is ten days. Therefore, although the piling is expected to take 30 days overall, it is only a critical operation for the first ten days and at that point the critical work becomes the start of foundations.

Providing that it is advanced far enough ahead of the foundation works, the piling could (in theory) take up to a total of 50 days to carry out without the overall project completion date being under threat. Similar relationships exist between the foundations and steelwork as well as between the steelwork and roofing.

The way earliest and latest timings have been calculated in figure 17 is probably a little academic and programming software will generally be unable to portray such activities as 'partly' critical. In reality the activity relationships are finish-to-start (for example, a certain amount of the piling must be finished before the foundation works can start).

If the foundation activity were to start at day ten as planned and progresses for the planned duration of 45 days then by implication it would be complete by its earliest finish of day 55, so to utilise any of the float the actual duration would need to be prolonged or be discontinuous.

Measurement of progress

Perhaps the most fundamental problem associated with the updating of progress is quantification – the measurement of progress will inevitably be based partly on the subjective impression of the person undertaking the exercise.

For example the activity of roofing may appear to be close to completion when tiling is largely completed, but at this point there may still be much outstanding works, for example, fixing of ridge tiles, cut tiles, flashings and the like. Superficially the works may appear to be 90% complete when in fact in terms of overall time only 50% has been completed. This illustrates the difference between the measurement of progress based on visual observation and progress based on man-hours required to complete the task.

Measurement of progress will also prove difficult to quantify where an activity comprises of many separate tasks and/or trades such as first-fix service installations. For example it may be found that ductwork is largely complete whereas electrical and pipe work installations have only just commenced. In these circumstances it would be difficult to quantify an overall progress figure for first-fix services. (Progress monitoring is discussed in more detail in Chapter 4).

Resource-driven logic

In some instances the activity relationships and timings may be driven by resource availability rather than by any necessary activity sequencing. As an example, on a project to strip out and refurbish a ten-storey office block it would be possible to commence the strip out on all floors on day one. However, it would obviously require a very large labour resource to do this and in practice one would expect the work to commence on the tenth floor and work down. In this case the start of the ninth floor strip out would be dependent on when the resources from the tenth floor strip out become available. In other words the ninth floor strip out would have a 'finish-to-start' relationship with the tenth floor works.

In the office block situation the logic is resource driven – the planned sequence and duration of strip out works is governed not by physical restraints but by resource utilisation

Such resource driven logic may well lead to problems when delay is considered. Using this same ten-storey office block example the programme would be set up with restraints that would show that the ninth floor could not commence until the tenth floor works were fully complete. But imagine that unforeseen conditions on the tenth floor put works at this level 'on-hold'. The programme would suggest that the ninth floor could not commence and the whole project was in delay but, in reality, the labour resource would simply be relocated and the works would be resequenced.

In this case any delay would be kept to a minimum or possibly entirely mitigated. Similarly if unforeseen additional works cause the tenth floor works to be prolonged there may be an opportunity to introduce an additional resource to commence the ninth floor as planned rather than wait until the tenth floor is complete.

This example is simplistic and it may be that the resource driven logic applied to the programme is more complex and more difficult to trace and evaluate. In these instances some care is required, particularly when applying progress and assessing delay.

Identifying the critical path

As discussed, the critical path through a project is the sequence of activities that represents the shortest possible time to complete that project, but on any planned project it may be possible for there to be more than one critical path.

In the substructure package example (detailed in figures 9–12) it can be seen by reference to the dark shading on the linked bar chart (figure 12) that the critical path runs through activities A, B, C, D and E. These activities have an earliest and latest start as well as an earliest and latest finish, which implies that the critical activities must commence and end at these times, or earlier, if delay to the overall project completion is to be avoided.

As the project progresses the critical path or paths can change. As an example, take a project to refurbish both the ground and first floors of an existing office block. Both floors are planned to commence at the same time, with the ground floor to be carried out in 20 weeks and the first floor in 18 weeks. This being the case the project critical path would be shown through the ground floor activities (simply because the ground floor has the longer duration), while there would be two-weeks of float for the first floor works.

However, the situation might change after the works have commenced. If the progress report at week four of the project indicates that progress to the ground floor has gone according to the programme but the first floor has suffered delays and only one week's progress has been achieved, then the critical path would change.

In this scenario there is still an estimated 17 weeks of work to carry out on the first floor but only 16 weeks work left on the ground floor. Therefore, by week four of the project, the first floor would become critical and the ground floor would have one-week of float.

It is not only delay that will cause the critical path to change – it might also change if:

- the contractor finds a better way of doing things and re-sequences the works;
- progress is better than anticipated in the programme; and/or
- work is omitted, added or varied.

On a fast-track or complex project the critical path can change frequently and, at certain times, it may be in an almost constant state of change, which makes it exceptionally difficult if not impossible to define. Judicial notice has been given to these problems. In the judgement of Royal Brompton Hospital NHS Trust v Frederick Alexander Hammond & Others (see section 8.17) it was noted that the establishment of the critical path can be difficult and that during the course of the works it is likely to change if progress is affected by an unforeseen event.

3.5 Application of critical path analysis to construction

Critical path analysis is a relatively simple process, but it is highly deterministic, producing precise results reliant on the availability of precise and exact information. A technique requiring precision and certainty would clearly be suitable for a factory or production type of environment, where outputs and activity timings can be tested and their accuracy verified, but even though commercially available planning software is widely used in the construction industry is it suitable for the planning of construction work?

The initial planned programme for a construction project is often based on undeveloped design information and provisional sums, and many activities require input from specialist subcontractors. The unique nature of construction projects, as well as the many elements of uncertainty and risk, means that activity durations can only ever be best estimates, in most cases.

Furthermore, the logical relationships between the activities required for critical path analyses, particularly the use of 'leads' and 'lags' to produce overlaps, can only be, at best, reasonable assessments of logical restraints. In many instances it would be difficult to consider such assessments as definitive.

Therefore, critical path analysis will produce apparently precise and exact timings for a construction operation but these may well be based on imprecise or 'best-guess' information.

If 'best estimate' information is used to produce a critical path analysis, the results of that analysis should only be considered to be a best estimate, not a precise representation of the planned intent. It is therefore important to consider the results of critical path analysis in the light of the data on which it is based.

This is particularly the case when reviewing the input of the progress achieved and progress updates of the planned programme. Utilising the input progress data the software will recalculate the timing and sequencing of the activities through to overall project completion. The reliability of the results of this analysis will again be dependent on the accuracy of the data used. The potential difficulties of interpreting progress updates are considered in more detail in chapter 4.

Construction project logic

Critical path analysis operates most accurately where the activity sequence is largely linear and where the options in respect of the logical relationships is limited, such as in a production process in an environment where the sequence of the activities and logic is usually rigid and well defined. Within the construction process the logic can be best described as being either 'prescriptive' or 'preferential'.

Prescriptive logic applies to activity sequencing that must be adhered to. For example, placing of structural concrete must follow the erection of formwork and reinforcement, plastering must follow wall construction, cladding must follow erection of the structure, and so on.

However, a contractor may have some scope to choose and dictate a desired sequence in respect of certain areas of a project. In these circumstances the imposed logic can best be described as preferential, that is the sequence and logic is what the contractor desires rather than a sequence that is imposed. For example, fitting out works may proceed from the bottom floor working up or alternatively from the top down; and certain finishes can be fixed early and protected or left until towards the end of the project when the danger of potential damage is limited.

The extent of the prescriptive and preferential logic will depend on the nature of the works. A contract to construct a multi-storey concrete frame will, by its very nature, dictate a prescriptive sequence and logic. Some degree of choice may be available to the contractor in respect of whether the works at each floor level progress from north to south, or south to north; there will also be some choice in respect of the overlap of activities, such as how many columns are constructed prior to commencing the formation of the next level of floor. However, the contractor has no choice other than to commence the structure at the lowest floor level and work up to the roof level. The logic and sequencing on this type of project is largely prescriptive and sequential and the application of critical path analysis is likely to produce reliable results.

On many projects there is a mix of both prescriptive and preferential logic. During the construction of the building frame and envelope the activity sequencing may be largely linear and sequential and the logic prescriptive but once the building is watertight, and the internal walls and first-fix trades are being executed, the logic may well be a mix of both prescriptive and preferential logic. When the second-fix and finishing trades are being undertaken the logic may become more preferential than prescriptive.

As an example, once the traditional wet trades of plastering and screeding are complete the works are 'opened up' for the commencement of many of the following trades (such as suspended ceilings, doors, general joinery, second-fix services, floor and wall tiling). Although there are some prescriptive interfaces between these works in reality they, together with the other finishing elements such as decorations, soft floor coverings and the like, may all progress with an element of concurrency through to final snagging and handover. How these are sequenced is a matter of what the contractor prefers and on a large project it may be found that due to various differing circumstances works on one part of the project are sequenced differently to identical works in another location.

Therefore, the suitability of critical path analysis for construction work may be dependent on the type of work – it is likely to be more suited to a project or series of activities where the sequencing and logic is largely prescriptive.

Interpretive caution

The examples above represent an overview of just some of the operational problems associated with critical path analysis. These are not intended to disparage the technique, but rather to emphasise that a degree of caution and understanding is required when interpreting results.

As explained, if the logic and sequencing is largely prescriptive and sequential, the application of critical path analysis is likely to produce reliable results. When a progress update on such a project is carried out the results are likely to be reasonable and will reflect the sequence of work that must be undertaken.

On a project where the logic tends to be more preferential than prescriptive the results of a progress update are likely to be less reliable. The sequence and timing of the remaining activities following an update will be based on preferential logic and will represent just one of a number of sequencing permutations that could or may be undertaken. In this sort of situation the logic dictating the timing of the remaining works will need to be revisited to ensure that the planned intent through to completion is realistic and reflective of what is likely.

Perhaps in most cases it will be prudent to apply a broad interpretation of the information provided by critical path analyses and on a construction project it may be beneficial to take the view that all activities containing float (up to a certain level) are to be considered as being equally critical.

Pros and cons of critical path analysis

Critical path analysis is highly deterministic – it produces precise results that necessitate the availability of precise data – and as a result it can struggle to deal with the variables and subtleties of construction operations. However, critical path analysis programming can still provide construction managers with an effective tool for co-ordinating, executing and monitoring a project.

The critical path or paths on a project may well change from time to time but the advantage of computer generated critical path analyses is that the impacts of delay and progress can be readily and quickly identified and the programme rescheduled. The rescheduled programme should provide a warning to management that recovery measures are required in certain areas, but, having said that, there is also a danger that practitioners become more involved in maintaining the programme and electronic data, than in co-ordinating, planning and managing the project.

Because the process is not transparent it is considered, by some, to be a 'black art', but on the other hand, some people are so bedazzled by the ability of the computer to process so much data and to produce such neat and colourful programmes that they accept the results too readily.

The flexibility and user-friendly features of modern computer software not only allow easy updating and beneficial alterations to programmes, but also provide the opportunity for data to be manipulated to produce contrived results. In addition to this, network diagrams are usually complex and difficult to follow and the methodology combined with the software means that the raw data is difficult to interrogate and practically impossible to follow without access to the electronic data.

The problems with critical path analysis outlined in this book are not exhaustive but neither are they intended to undermine the technique. They do however demonstrate that the methodology and the results that it provides should not necessarily be accepted without some caution. Critical path analysis is prospective and any results following its application may only represent a likely or probable outcome. How likely or probable these results are is dependent on many things including the certainty of the information available and the nature of the works in question.

3.6 Line of balance

Line of balance is a production technique used for the planning of work involving repetitive tasks or the production of multiple units. In the construction industry it is particularly useful in the planning and co-ordination of projects such as housing, the fitting out of multiple apartments or hotel rooms, erection of repetitive structures such as electricity pylons, multiple foundations or plant bases and the like.

The fundamental principle of the technique is to establish the balance of resources such that the rate of progress of the individual trade activities do not delay or impact on each other. Taking the fit-out of a new apartment block as an example the first activities in each of the apartment units may include:

- metal stud partitions and plasterboard one side;
- first-fix services;
- plasterboard partitions second side and ceilings; and
- plaster and skim.

Fig 18 shows the first two trades of metal stud partitions and first-fix services. The stud partition works in this illustration start at apartment 1 and progresses sequentially to apartment 10 with the start for each apartment determined by completion of stud partitions in the preceding apartment (this implies that the works are undertaken by one gang working progressively through the apartments).

The linked bar chart has only been included in figure 18 to illustrate the principle of the line of balance technique. When using the line of balance technique it should be developed independently, from first principles, utilising estimated man-hours for each trade activity, the gang size and the required buffer time. This will produce an estimate of the time from the start of the first unit, in this case apartment 1, to the completion of the last unit. The basic principle is to apply sufficient labour to each trade to ensure that all activities progress at around the same rate. As shown in figure 19.

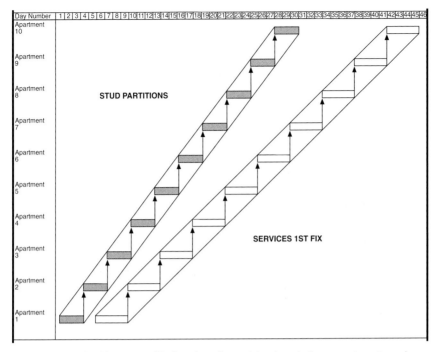

Figure 18: Linked bar chart. (Rather than the activity descriptions apartment numbers are shown on the left and the activities are shown against the various apartments.)

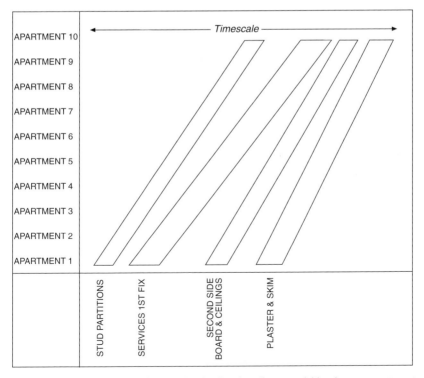

Figure 19: Line of balance diagram for the first four fit-out activities for ten apartments

The actual duration of each activity for each apartment and thus the steepness of the sloping lines is determined by the labour allocated to the activity. It is ideal, although not usually practical, to 'balance' the labour and thus the production of each of the trades so that all of these lines run in parallel.

It is also worth noting that it is usual to make an allowance, or to insert a 'buffer' time, between the completion of one trade in each apartment and the start of the next trade. This represents an element of contingency but it also reflects reality, as it is unlikely that the first-fix services installations will commence at the very moment that the stud partitions are completed.

3.7 'Time chainage' diagram

The 'time chainage' technique, as the name implies, relates to the planning of works of a linear nature where activities are related to, or identified by, a geographical location. In the construction industry these types of works include projects such as road and motorway construction, railway works, pipelines and tunnels (the technique is, therefore, usually associated with civil engineering projects).

The time chainage diagram is very similar to both the bar chart and line of balance but, rather than simply relating an activity to a timescale, time chainage relates activities to both time and location.

In figure 20 the chainage, in kilometres, is shown along the horizontal axis and the time, in weeks, is shown along the vertical axis. The activities are graphically represented by lines or boxes.

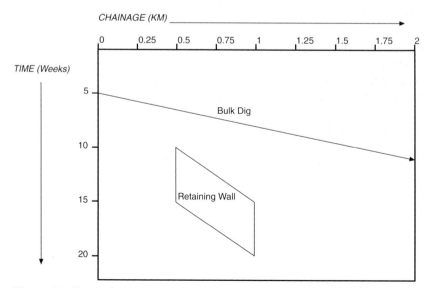

Figure 20: Simple time chainage diagram.

The activity of bulk dig is indicated by a single line that represents commencement at chainage zero on week five, with progress to chainage two and completion on week ten. Likewise the activity for the construction of the retaining wall commences at chainage 0.5 on week ten, with works at this chainage planned until week 15. These works are indicated as progressing towards chainage one and being completed at week 20.

As well as showing what activity will be worked on at one time, the time chainage diagram shows where on the construction site a team will be working at any given time. This can be useful in showing where a potential clash may occur (which in turn could delay the completion of the project).

The example at figure 20 is very simple and the diagrams used in practice are more detailed and complex. However, this makes them difficult to understand. As such, this technique requires a little practice and experience to become familiar with the layout and the overall philosophy.

3.8 PERT/Risk analysis

In the late 1950s the US Navy Special Projects Office developed a methodology for use on the Polaris missile programme, which they referred to as the Programme Evaluation and Review Technique (PERT). The development of Polaris involved works by a great number of differing contractors and subcontractors and, because it was a unique project with little or no historical data, in respect of the required and likely timings, forecasting with any degree of certainty was difficult.

The PERT technique allows an average duration estimate to be used taking into account three types of estimate for each task: optimistic, most likely and pessimistic. These estimates are weighted to quantify an average duration and are applied to a critical path analysis.

To what extent this technique and other 'probabilistic' risk analysis techniques are used in the construction industry is not clear but there is no reason why they should not be used as there are some parallels between the development of Polaris and major works in the field of construction. Like Polaris, some major construction projects rely on many specialist subcontractors carrying out a large spectrum of trades and disciplines.

Although it may be difficult to argue that all construction project tasks are totally unique, it is generally accepted that, to some extent, every major construction project is a prototype with certain unique features. These factors, together with such considerations as environmental conditions, mean that there is always an element of uncertainty and risk in respect of the project timings. This being the case the application of 'probabilistic' techniques such as PERT may be appropriate in certain instances.

3.9 Phasing diagrams

The use of simple 'phasing diagrams' is another very effective tool used to supplement the formal project planning.

Marked up architectural plans and elevations used in conjunction with a bar chart can often provide great assistance in communicating the proposed planned sequence as reference to locations such as gridlines may be difficult to envisage when simply incorporated within an activity description on a bar chart.

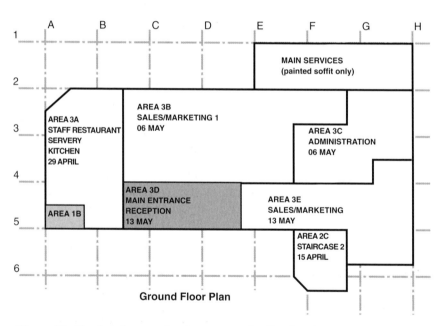

Figure 21: Phasing diagram showing proposed ceiling handover sequence

These graphical presentations can be used to indicate such things as the proposed phasing and timing of the external brickwork construction; release of areas by a particular subcontractor to allow the following trades to commence (including final snagging and handover of completed areas). Figure 21 indicates a very simple phasing diagram relating to the proposed timings and handovers of ceilings to allow the commencement of final-fix services.

3.10 The choice of technique

The choice of the technique to be used on any particular construction project is dependent on the nature of the works, personal preference, available expertise and, in some cases, on what is required by the terms of the contract.

The simple bar chart is adaptable, easily produced and understood and its use may be beneficial on most projects, whereas the use of the time chainage diagram is very much restricted to works of a linear nature.

On certain projects a variety of techniques may be appropriate, for instance on the construction of a large hotel critical path analysis may be used to plan and monitor the works associated with the substructure, frame and envelope, with a line of balance technique being employed during the repetitive fitting out of the many bedrooms.

Above all it must be stressed that there are many formal and informal techniques available and there is no single format that is appropriate to all circumstances.

Summary

There are many project planning methods available and with the growth of computer technology it is increasingly common (and desirable) that programmes be computer-generated.

However, care should be taken with computer programming because poor data entered into even the most expensive and sophisticated computer system is still poor data.

The main methods used for construction planning are:

- **Bar charts**, which are well recognised and understood with the format effectively displaying the necessary information;
- **Linked bar charts,** that show logical dependencies between activity bars and can alleviate some of the problems associated with the simple bar chart;
- **Critical path analysis,** used to define the shortest theoretical route through the sequence of programme activities establishing relationships between the activities on the programme and applying estimated timings;
- **Line of balance,** used generally in work involving repetitive tasks to establish a balance of resources so that the progress of individual tasks will not impact on each other;

continued

- **Time chainage,** relating to the planning of works of a linear nature where activities are connected to a geographical location – helping to prevent any potential location clashes on site;
- **PERT/Risk analysis**, using an average duration estimate to find the critical path, which is then plotted on a network diagram; and
- **Phasing diagrams**, with marked-up architectural plans and elevations used in conjunction with a bar chart to view the proposed planned sequence in relation to location.

The choice of technique is dependent on a number of factors including personal preference, type of project and on what is required by the contract. There is no format that will be appropriate to all case.

4

Monitoring progress

Monitoring progress is carried out regularly on most, if not all, construction projects for the purpose of identifying problems areas, if any, and to provide the latest estimate of likely completion date of the works. In practice, it is very difficult to be precise and clear about the level of progress achieved at any given moment on a construction site but the level of detail and accuracy of progress reports do not, in general, have to be to the level of precision and accuracy that would be required if making a formal claim under the contract.

Progress is frequently monitored these days by simply entering data into the planned programme and setting the computer to reschedule using the updated information and this task does not require further commentary here. In this chapter consideration is given to monitoring progress in other ways and to the dangers or relying upon the results of updated planned programmes.

4.1 Record keeping

Most contractors maintain various contemporary records on construction projects as a matter of company policy, a management tool, due to contract requirements and/or to comply with statutory duty, and many of these provide information about the progress of the works, for example:

- progress meeting records;
- programme progress updates;
- contemporaneous short-term programmes and updates;
- marked up drawings;
- progress photographs;
- general correspondence;
- concrete pour records;

- daily site diaries and labour allocation sheets;
- quality control inspection sheets;
- daily weather records;
- general meeting minutes; and
- formal subcontractors' handover and inspection sheets.

In practice many of these records turn out to contain insufficient detail, are inaccurate or are incomplete – in some cases they are not kept at all.

It is inevitable that some of the contractor's site staff will be more conscientious than others when it comes to record keeping and, as a result, the quality and detail of records is likely to vary considerably for different sections and time periods of the works.

What is often seen is that record keeping tends to improve as the risk of a dispute increases and in this case there is likely to be a great contrast in the available data – with little or poor information being available for the first part of the project when things were going well, and detailed records for the remainder of the works as things start to go wrong.

The likelihood of finding a full set of accurate site records may be increased if the client has a full-time records-keeping representative on site but this is not always going to be the case. Therefore, if a client wants records to be kept it is of great importance that the contract documentation is prescriptive about record-keeping requirements.

This is still no guarantee that records will be kept and it is not unusual to find that the client's team has made no formal requests for records required by the contract or, for that matter, any formal complaints when they do not appear. Once again, the focus tends to shift when a problem occurs and a dispute is brewing and it is at this stage that parties tend to look more closely at the terms of the agreement and seek to enforce them.

When records are actually submitted by the contractor, some form of independent auditing and verification should be undertaken so that any complaints in respect of anomalies or lack of data are made at the time rather than some time later when a dispute has arisen.

Of course most construction projects, even those where the works have been delayed, will not be the subject of a formal dispute, in which case there will be no need to keep records specifically for the purpose of retrospective analysis but the type of records referred to above will be of assistance if the need arises to compile an as-built programme after the works have been carried out.

4.2 The as-built programme

An as-built programme provides a means of both monitoring progress and, if necessary, providing evidence to substantiate an assessment of liability for any delays. As implied by the name, an as-built programme provides a record of when the various project works were actually undertaken.

It can be useful when compiling programmes for tender purposes or for new projects to use as-built programmes from previous projects to help with calculating likely activity timings. It is, however, more likely that as-built data will be used when a dispute has arisen either to demonstrate the delay being claimed or to rebut allegations based on theoretical methodologies (by showing what actually occurred as well as by indicating areas of culpable delay).

It is helpful if the as-built programme is compiled as the works progress, with the data being agreed between the contracting parties. Some of the planning computer software will allow actual start and finish dates to be recorded as part of the updating process and thus an as-built programme is compiled simply by regularly updating the planned programme with the progress achieved. Such updating will produce a programme that provides a comparison between what was planned and what actually occurred.

The planned programme often lacks certainty, with some of the activities embracing a number of separate operations. Therefore, if a direct comparison is made between the planned and as-built programmes the differences between activity timings and durations in such cases will only be illustrated in broad terms.

4.3 Histograms, 'S' curves and planned progress monitoring

Histograms and 'S' curves are used in the construction industry for a variety of purposes and are particularly useful for progress monitoring purposes.

In figure 22 the solid line or 'S' curve indicates the cumulative quantity of concrete planned to be poured. The dotted line represents the actual cumulative total of concrete poured up to week 16. It can be seen that initially the rate of the actual concrete pours was slightly better than that planned, however as from around week 8 the weekly quantity began to fall behind that planned. From looking at the actual trend it would seem unlikely that the shortfall in progress will be recovered and the completion of the concrete pouring activities will be later than planned.

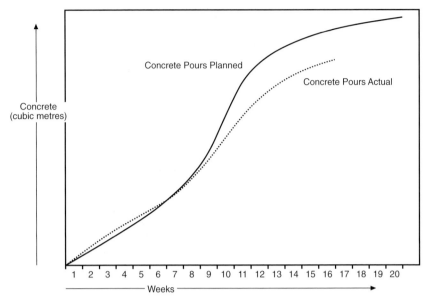

Figure 22: Simple 'S' curve relating to the pouring of concrete.

In the early 1980s the Property Services Agency (PSA) produced a more formalised approach to the use of 'S' curves, which they called 'Planned Progress Monitoring'.

The PSA's technique was introduced just prior to the introduction of the personal computer and prior to sophisticated planning software becoming available and so the 'S' curve was produced manually and was often superimposed on top of the bar chart. The introduction of the personal computer and planning software has meant that it is far easier to generate histograms and 'S' curves for progress monitoring purposes than the manual method envisaged by the PSA.

This method initially relies on the production of a traditional bar chart, then for each week of the project the number of activity bars occurring in that week is counted and recorded, usually on the bottom of the bar chart (for this reason, planners often refer to it as 'counting the squares'). Once this exercise has been completed the cumulative total of these 'activity weeks' can be plotted as a simple line graph depicting planned progress – producing an 'S' curve. Figure 23 shows a typical layout for the planned progress method.

As works proceed the progress achieved each week is recorded by shading the relevant activity bar lines. At each progress update the number of 'activity weeks' actually achieved can be counted and the cumulative total plotted to produce a line showing progress achieved. The difference between the planned progress 'S' curve

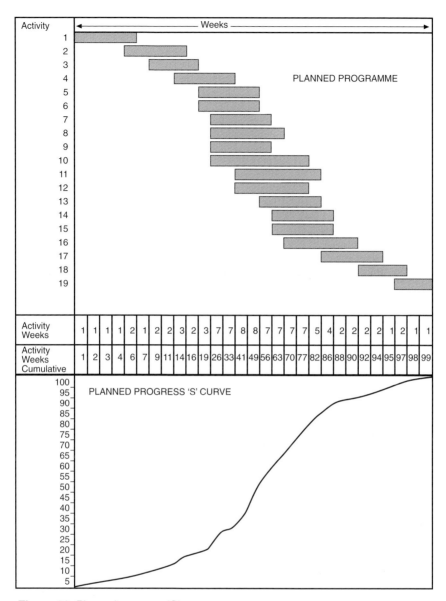

Figure 23: Planned progress 'S' curve

and the progress-achieved curve can be compared and any shortfall in overall progress noted.

Figure 24 compares the planned progress layout illustrated at figure 23 with the actual progress achieved recorded. The progress achieved is represented on the bar chart by dark shading and on the cumulative graph or 'S' curve as a dotted line. It can be seen from comparing the two curves that the progress achieved to date is somewhat less than that planned. The tables also show that 63 activity weeks were planned but only 43 achieved.

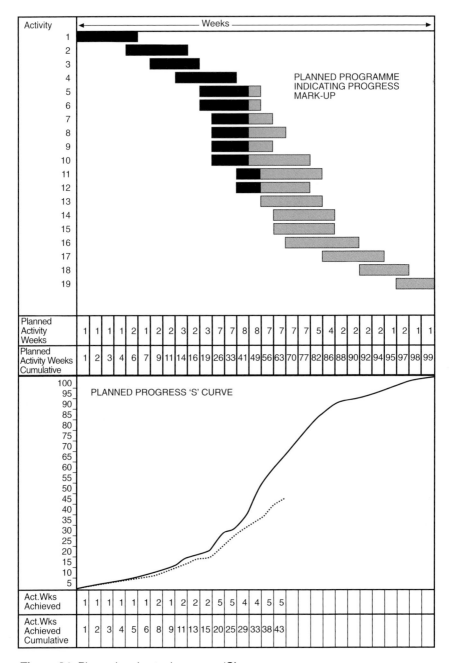

Figure 24: Planned and actual progress 'S' curves

This methodology overcomes one of the disadvantages of the simple bar chart, in as much as it indicates progress in the context of the overall project progress. However, it must be stressed that the planned progress technique is by no means exact, with the achieved progress curve simply representing the cumulative total of all of the progress recorded. It takes no account of the required progress of the critical activities and implies that all general progress is valuable progress.

To illustrate this problem, imagine that after a certain duration the works are assessed and it is found that the cumulative progress actually achieved totals 250 activity weeks, which is close to the planned total. The conclusion, at face value, is that the project is on programme. However, if the contractor has taken advantage of recent exceptionally mild weather to progress the non-critical external works ahead of programme, while the critical structural works have fallen behind, this assessment of overall project progress will be entirely misleading.

Conversely the recorded cumulative progress achieved may be less than that planned, with the cumulative total indicating that the project is behind programme, but this may simply be because non-critical activities have failed to progress as planned. Providing the critical activities have progressed there is probably no immediate cause for concern.

Sole reliance on the results of the planned progress monitoring technique is likely to prove misleading. The results can give a good indication of a problem area, particularly if the shortfall in progress continues to deteriorate at every progress update. Therefore, the methodology should be considered as a useful indicator of ongoing trends rather than as a definitive measure of progress and project status.

Other uses

Histograms and 'S' curves are used for a variety of purposes and are not restricted to progress curves based simply on activity weeks. Progress can be monitored by comparing interim valuations with the estimated cost of the planned activities or progress can be illustrated by outputs of major activities, such as by the volume of concrete placed or the number of bricks laid. On a large project it may prove beneficial to produce separate progress curves for discrete areas, such as individual floors or specific trades such as the brickwork activities.

4.4 Earned value analysis

'Earned value analysis' is a sophisticated version of the 'planned progress monitoring' technique utilising planned and actual progress curves. As well as measuring and comparing the work planned with the work carried out, it also utilises measures of budgeted costs, actual costs and earned value.

Whereas the 'planned progress monitoring' technique produces a cumulative 'S' curve based on 'activity weeks', an 'earned value analysis' generates various curves by reference to cost or budget. Figure 25 illustrates the basic principle of earned value analysis.

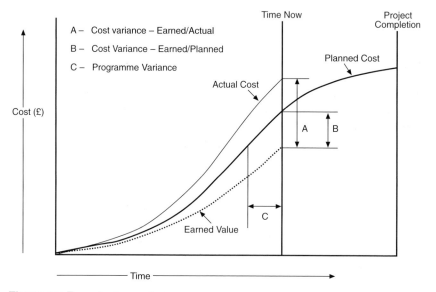

Figure 25: Earned value analysis

The base line is the 'planned cost' curve. This is produced by weighting the planned programmed activities in terms of estimated cost or budget. In 'earned value' terminology this is referred to by the acronym BCWS, which is short for budgeted cost of work scheduled.

In much the same way as 'counting the squares' for the 'planned progress monitoring' technique, a progress curve is generated when the programme is regularly updated. This curve is the 'earned value' or budgeted cost of works performed (BCWP).

As can be seen in figure 25 the actual cost of work performed ('ACWP') can also be monitored and plotted.

Therefore, an 'earned value analysis' provides a comparison of target progress and cost against actual progress (measured in terms of earned value) and actual cost. This enables progress and cost projections to be made to the completion of works based on historical project performance and it also allows trends to be monitored.

British Standard 6079:1, 2002, Project Management, places much emphasis on this technique and it has been credited with providing accurate estimates of the anticipated completion dates.

However, 'earned value' is dependent on and particularly sensitive to the accuracy of the utilised base data, namely the planned programme and planned budget. Together with this the project progress and cost reporting need to be realistic for the information generated to be of use.

4.5 Milestones

The use of 'milestones' in programmes was explained during the review of critical path analysis in chapter 3 (detailed with figure 12), but it is also possible to produce a complete chart of milestones to provide a useful 'high level' illustration of project progress.

These charts consist of a bar chart or simple schedule of key dates relating to elected project milestones, which represent the achievement of key project events such as the commencement of structural steel, getting the building weather-tight, having the permanent power supply connected or perhaps achieving handover of a section. Actual progress towards and achievement of these milestones can then be recorded and reported.

The milestone chart is really limited to this high level reporting and monitoring role and the progress of the works between these milestones will also require a more detailed 'day to day' planning and monitoring approach.

4.6 The old-fashioned way

Even in an age where sophisticated planning software is common-place, when it comes to recording site progress, planners are still reliant on coloured pencils and marker pens. Simply using the planning software to record the activity percentage complete may fail to illustrate the exact areas that are being worked on or whether areas are being completed in the correct sequence. The easiest solution to this problem can be to make separate notes.

For instance on a project consisting of many small rooms it may be that the suspended ceiling grid is recorded as 50% complete, as planned. An annotated and marked up architectural plan will define this progress and help determine if the individual rooms are actually being progressively completed, to allow commencement of the second fix services to the ceilings. Marked-up drawings will also provide a good contemporaneous record that may prove invaluable in the event of a time-related dispute.

4.7 Updating the programme

As the project progresses a planned network can be updated to reflect the progress achieved to enable projects to be monitored and managed. When carrying out a progress update, a critical path analysis will utilise the applied logic to produce activity timings and a projected sequence for the remaining works through to completion.

For each activity against which progress is updated the computer can recalculate the remaining duration, which will represent the estimated duration of works left to be done. An activity identified as 50% complete, with an original duration of ten days, will be shown to have a remaining duration of five days. The network can then be 'time-analysed' utilising these remaining durations, starting from the time of the progress update.

If the actual progress achieved is different to that planned, activity timings will be reset. This will result in the earliest completion of the project being recalculated and any predicted changes being identified.

There can be problems with physically assessing progress in respect to certain elements of the works. For example, the progress of blockwork partitions may be simply based on measured quantity, whereas the assessment of the progress of first-fix services may be a little more difficult.

In theory, detailed measure of all of the various elements of the services fixed could be undertaken and by applying some form of output rate or labour loading, but in reality the progress measure is likely to be based on a broad overall assessment rather than a detailed measure. This generally provides sufficient accuracy for management of the project.

Summary

Monitoring the progress of a construction project may create vital evidence should delays occur. Good record keeping is key to this so that contractors can prove what occurred throughout the project.

In practice many records are not kept in sufficient detail or they are inaccurate – in some cases records are not kept at all.

One of the key methods for monitoring progress is to create an as-built programme, which can also be helpful as evidence to substantiate a delay assessment.

As the project progresses a planned network can be updated to reflect work achieved. Some of the methods used for progress monitoring are:

- histograms and 'S' curves;
- earned value analysis; and
- milestones.

There are some practical problems to successfully monitoring progress on a construction site, such as the need for interpretive caution in determining progress (just because a job looks almost finished does not mean it is).

5

Analysis of delays

There are many different ways in which delays can be reviewed but most construction delays will be analysed using one of the following methods:

- as-planned v as-built;
- as-planned impacted;
- collapsed as-built;
- windows analysis; or
- time impact analysis.

The titles of these different methodologies may sound like programmers' jargon but, in fact, they accurately and succinctly describe what is involved with each type of analysis.

The first technique, the **as-planned v as-built**, is as it says a comparison of the planned programme for the works against the as-built programme. Therefore, this form of analysis is based on a simple graphical comparison of what was expected to happen and what actually happened. It is a method widely adopted by contractors and construction professionals to identify delays and is also used as an invaluable first step when undertaking a delay analysis using one of the other techniques.

The simple identification of delay may not, in itself, be sufficient to determine which factors actually caused the project to finish late as some delays cause individual tasks to take longer but do not affect the end date because they are not critical to completion. Therefore, most delay methodologies try to identify the critical delays. The 'as-planned impacted', collapsed as-built, 'windows analysis' and 'time impact analysis' use critical path analysis to determine the effect of delay. These critical path-based methodologies are the main recognised scientific methods of evaluating delays to construction projects and in practice all critical path analyses these days rely upon computer models.

The **as-planned impacted** method operates by adding, or 'impacting', changes onto a planned programme. By adjusting the planned programme to account for the effects of omissions from or additions/delays to the works a revised programme is produced showing the impact of changes. Of all the critical path analysis techniques this is probably the most popular.

The **collapsed as-built** technique is, in some respects, the reverse of the 'as-planned impacted' method. It operates by removing changes to the as-built programme causing it to 'collapse'. The aim is to produce a programme showing what would have happened 'but for' the effects of the delay events.

Windows analysis is a review of progress at certain periods of time. By compiling data about the progress during each window of time, delays can be identified and explanations sought.

The **time impact analysis** technique is similar to 'windows analysis', but rather than looking at delays within defined windows of time, the actual timing and duration of the delaying event itself forms the period for analysis.

Each of these five methodologies is described and commented upon in detail in this chapter and it will be seen that there are difficulties with and advantages to each approach. There is also some guidance as to the basic procedure to be adopted in the production of these various types of delay analysis. This guidance is based upon a review of the procedures generally adopted by delay analyst practitioners but it should be noted that there are no fixed guidelines about how these methodologies should be implemented and in many cases variations will be found.

5.1 As-planned v as-built

This is the most simple and probably the most commonly used form of delay analysis. It involves a straightforward comparison between the original planned intent, represented by the planned programme, and what actually occurred, the as-built programme. A typical 'as-planned v as-built' programme is shown opposite.

As can be seen from figure 26, the 'as-planned v as-built programme' is prepared in a bar chart format, to produce a graphical comparison. In conjunction with this, someone with knowledge of the project may

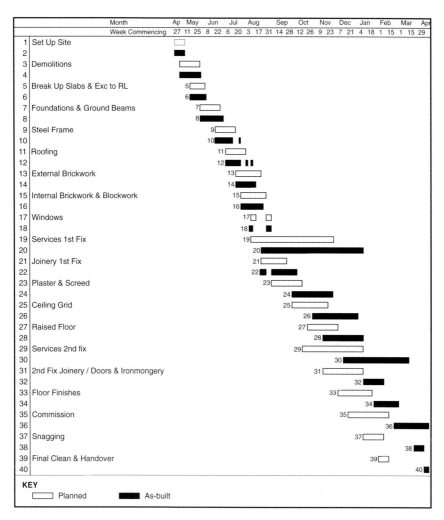

Figure 26: As-planned v as-built programme

be able to produce a narrative to explain why the planned intent was not achieved and why the planned activity timings changed.

On simple projects, or on projects where there were few differences between the planned programme and the actual sequence and duration of activities, it is likely that such a narrative could be produced relatively easily and may prove sufficient in demonstrating the cause and effect of delay.

Figure 26 shows that the works were undertaken very much as planned until the start of activity line 19, the first fix services, and activity line 23, the plaster and screed works. Therefore, any interrogation of and narrative about the causes of delays is likely to start at these points.

Process involved

To produce an 'as-planned v as built' analysis obviously requires a planned programme and appropriate as-built records. Planned programmes are produced for all but the smallest of construction projects and so this is rarely a problem, but full and accurate as-built progress records may not be quite as readily available.

Generally someone will have either produced regular progress schedules, issued regular progress reports, kept site diaries and/or have a set of dated photographs from which an as-built programme can be produced, or better still, some contractors mark-up a planned programme as work proceeds, so the information to undertake this type of analysis is usually available in one form or other.

As stated earlier, this method is widely used in the construction industry, but what does an 'as-planned v as-built' programme actually tell you? A comparison of planned against actual provides no more than an indication of where delay occurred against a theoretical plan for the project. As commented in chapter 2, the original planned programme is likely to be based on undeveloped information and it is far from certain that it will be strictly adhered to. For this reason alone, any differences between the planned and actual activity timings need to be considered with some care.

If a contractor has adopted a different sequence or made changes to the amount of operatives used on various operations (thereby changing the duration for the tasks) the actual as-built programme may look very different to the planned programme, regardless of whether any delaying events occur or not. In such circumstances it may reasonably be asked, what is the point of comparing the 'as-built' programme with a theoretical programme that bears no resemblance to the way the project has been carried out?

Even if the planned programme is accepted to be an appropriate baseline for reviewing delays there is still the problem of as-built records. There is no guarantee that records will be suitable for this type of delay analysis even if they have been kept accurately throughout the project. To be of use the as-built records must enable a like-for-like comparison to be made with the planned programme, so if, for example, the as-built records describe the progress of the superstructure, as a whole, whereas the planned programme shows brickwork, roof caressing, roof tiling, windows and external doors as separate items, no detailed comparison can be made for this part of the works.

As with all forms of planning and programming the number of separate activities used for this methodology needs to be restricted in order to keep the analysis meaningful and manageable – a large number of activities contained on several sheets of paper will result in a blur of information making it difficult to draw any meaningful conclusions. If the planned or as-built information is subdivided into a large number of activities, it will have to be summarised into relevant key activities.

An accurate as-built programme is produced by recording activity start and completion times for each activity and producing a continuous as-built bar line on the programme, stretching from the time of the actual commencement through to the time of actual completion. However, a solid bar linking the activity start and completion of an activity may not be sufficient to explain a delay and it may be necessary to use a broken line to reflect works that have been undertaken intermittently – the stops and starts of the activity may be important when it comes to analysing the project.

An intermittent line may, however, still be inadequate to enable conclusions to be drawn about delay events. For example, works to a roof may have been carried out during two separate time periods (and an intermittent bar used to reflect this on the as-built programme) but, in order to analyse the impact of delays, it may be necessary to know which sections of the roof were being carried out during each period of work.

It could be that an instruction had been issued during the first period to undertake work on the south side of a roof and an intermittent line on an as-built chart against 'Roof' does not reveal whether the instruction was issued before, during or after the south side was commenced. In this case, without separate evidence, it will be impossible to gauge the effect, if any, of the instruction.

Another problem with as-built records is defining when an activity is complete. Based on available data an as-built programme may be drawn to show that a particular activity took 15 weeks to carry out, but progress records could reveal that the activity was 95% complete after ten weeks. It is probable that, in most respects, the activity was substantially complete after ten, not fifteen, weeks and that the final five per cent of the work, carried out between the tenth and fifteenth weeks, may have been minor, non-critical work, of no real significance to the project as a whole.

This may appear to be a minor difficulty that can be resolved by a little bit of common sense because, if work was essentially complete after ten weeks in this example, the as-built bar could show a ten-week duration and the minor finishing could be discounted. However, who is to say the final five per cent is minor non-critical work? In a dispute the other side are likely to consider the final five per cent as critical.

This can become quite a problem because the nature of the construction process, particularly in respect of architectural finishing works, means that in many cases activities are progressed until they become substantially complete (say 90–95% complete) and the last five to ten per cent of the activity is often undertaken over an extended period, in an intermittent fashion.

For example, second fix joinery on a building project will commence after plastering and may well progress in a timely manner up to a point where the next critical finishing trades can start. However, it may be that the fixing of the last few doors, outstanding items of ironmongery and other miscellaneous items, such as notice boards and access traps, continue through to the end of the contract period. In this situation a subjective view needs to be taken as to when, in programme terms, joinery works can be considered to be complete – the problem with this is that disputing parties rarely share the same subjective views.

Production of an as-planned v as-built analysis

The key to this method is the as-built information. Ideally, an as-built programme will be compiled as the works proceed but, more often than not, an as-built programme is either not produced at all or is not prepared in detail and with accuracy. Therefore, detailed as-built programmes generally have to be compiled retrospectively, using available written records. The analysis and interpretation of an 'as planned v as-built' analysis will be assisted by:

- technical queries, showing the date of issue and the subsequent timing of the answer;
- manpower and plant histograms comparing the planned levels and actual labour and plant levels; and
- cumulative 'S' curves plotting financial expenditure, general overall progress or specific progress such as quantities of concrete poured or number of bricks laid.

Annotated layouts and drawings are also very useful and can be effectively utilised to show the impact of delay by graphically comparing the planned and actual phasing and sequencing of the works.

The detail that can be included on any as-built programme will obviously be dependent on the quality of the records available. Actually establishing the level of this detail, identifying and abstracting the necessary information and compiling the programme requires some skill and experience and is not without its difficulties. An example of a detailed as-built programme is included at figure 38 in chapter 6.

Summary

The **as-planned v as-built** method is simple to produce and, as a result, it is relatively quick and easy to prepare. It also has the benefit of portraying the facts in an easy-to-understand format and so, unlike some of the more complex delay methodologies, is easy to interrogate and verify, even if you are not an experienced delay analyst.

When more complex forms of analysis are undertaken a simple review of planned and actual progress can be invaluable in helping to focus on the areas of probable delay, as well as identifying areas that can be discounted.

However, for this form of analysis to be an option, there has to be an agreed planned programme and as-built records. If one party considers the planned programme sequence and durations were unreasonable and unachievable, the whole basis for this form on analysis is in dispute. Also, if the as-built records are incomplete or inaccurate or inconsistent with the planned activities then no meaningful comparison can be made.

5.2 As-planned impacted

'As-planned impacted' is probably the most commonly used of the retrospective critical path-based methodologies. In basic terms it consists of adding or 'impacting' the considered delays onto the planned programme.

A similar technique is often employed during the course of the works to consider the prospective implications on the planned programme – a 'what-if' analysis. This enables the effects of various scenarios to be considered and for this reason this methodology is often referred to as the 'what-if' technique.

Figure 27 represents a simple planned programme consisting of critical activities 1–3, which have an overall duration of 16 weeks.

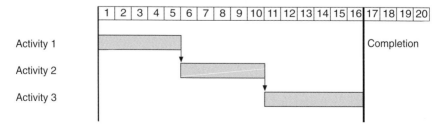

Figure 27: Planned programme

Figure 28 shows this same planned programme but with an added delay of three weeks to critical activity 2. Once the delay is added, the programme is rescheduled and the activity timings re-calculated. The resultant revised programme demonstrates the impact of this delay to the overall completion date – in this case a delay of three weeks.

Figure 28: As-planned impacted programme

In figure 28 the impact of the delay is simulated by increasing the duration of activity 2. This approach would be suitable if, say, there was a simple increase in the scope of the work of the planned activity. However, variations instructed during the course of the works will, in some cases, represent works that are not covered by the planned programme activities; in these instances additional activities will need to be included on the impacted programme. Figure 29 shows the inclusion of a delay activity to represent such additional works.

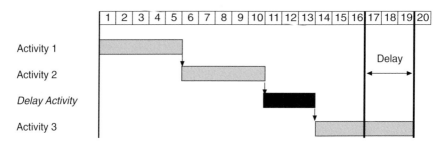

Figure 29: The inclusion of a delay activity to the planned programme.

In figure 29 the additional work is shown as a three-week period following activity 2 and prior to the commencement of activity 3. As with figure 28 the additional work or delay activity falls on the critical path and so the impact results in a delay to overall completion of three weeks.

Process involved

Unlike the 'as-planned v as-built' method, the 'as-planned impacted' method does not require as-built records to be maintained and the results plotted, in order for comparisons to be made. All that is needed is a planned programme and someone who can evaluate the effects of changes/delays to the contract, incorporate them into the programme and then reschedule the programme, to produce a revised completion date.

The planned programme will have to be in sufficient detail to enable the changes and delays to be impacted. For example, it may prove difficult to reasonably simulate the effect of a variation relating to say the first-fix services, in a specific room, located on the second floor, if the only relevant planned activity is a single all embracing activity line on the planned programme entitled 'services installations', which covers all rooms on all floors.

Similarly without access to the person responsible for the preparation of the original planned programme it may be difficult to define exactly what the activities encompass – for example does the activity described as 'Precast concrete floors' also include the precast concrete stairs and structural concrete topping? Or, what work items were envisaged as being included within the activities 'Second-fix services' and Final-fix services'?

Therefore, the use of this technique and the validity of the results it produces are dependent on the adequacy and clarity of the selected planned programme. There are a wide number of reasons why the planned programme may lack certainty and produce results that are unreliable, including the facts that the original planned programme is often based on undeveloped information and that, as the works progress, the contractor refines his methodology and generally finds different ways of undertaking the works to suit the circumstances. Having said this, a simple comparison between the as-built activity timings and the timings predicted by the 'impact analysis' may be all that is required to demonstrate that the approach is sound and reasonable.

Problems will be encountered if the original planned programme, used as the baseline to impact the delays, has been substantially amended and re-issued during the course of the works. If this is the case, although the original planned programme represents the contractor's planned intent at the outset of the project, later amendments and re-issues may demonstrate that this planned intent changed. In such circumstances it may be argued that the use of the selected programme is inappropriate.

As stated, with the 'as-planned impacted' approach, the changes or delays are progressively added and the planned programme is rescheduled. The idea is that the programme responds dynamically to simulate the effect of these delays and to show any impact on the completion date.

To work in this way, the planned programme has to be in the form of either a critical path analysis or a linked bar chart. In practice programmes are frequently not linked or it is found that the logic applied to the programme is insufficient to enable it to properly react dynamically, once the delays have been added. For this reason the logic used in the planned programme will usually need to be added to or enhanced retrospectively.

The logical relationship between certain of the planned activities may be self apparent but a major criticism of this retrospective application of logic is that it requires significant assumptions to be made in respect of the contractor's original planned intent.

It is normal practice to impact the delaying events individually, thereby quantifying the extent of the delay arising from each event. However, it should be borne in mind that this quantification will be dependent on the order in which the events are impacted. It is usual practice to impact changes sequentially, in chronological order, and this would appear to be the fairest and most reasonable approach to adopt. This approach has the benefit of identification of the cause and effect of the delay to the completion date.

Criticism

This technique is possibly the most widely used form of critical path-based delay analysis, but it is probably fair to say that it also attracts the most criticism. Some commentators go as far as to describe the method as 'suffering from a fatal flaw'[1] because it deliberately excludes consideration of what actually occurred on the project. It is inevitable that a simple reliance on the planned programme will mean that no account is taken of the contractor's own delay or, for that matter, any mitigation and/or acceleration measures undertaken.

The other major problem associated with the 'as-planned impacted' technique is the fact that the effects of the impacted delaying events are theoretical and often bear little relation to what actually occurred. A simple comparison between the as-built activity timings and the timings predicted by the impact analysis can be undertaken and if this shows a large discrepancy the entire analysis may begin to resemble a meaningless academic and theoretical exercise.

The dislocation of reality from what the analysis shows is frequently revealed by major differences between the actual completion date and the completion date produced by this methodology. The completion date predicted by the 'as-planned impacted' analysis is often later than the completion that actually occurred, which tends to be explained by claims that acceleration or mitigation measures were introduced in order to finish 'early'.

In some cases such claims are, no doubt, true and can be supported by factual evidence. However, more often, significant differences between the actual completion date and the much later estimated date produced by the impacted planned programme cannot be attributed to any action or revised measures employed by the contractor – in these cases the difference is more likely to be the by-product of the theoretical nature of the methodology.

In the majority of cases, for a contractor to have any hope of regaining lost time on a project, great effort or exceptional measures will be required. Such effort or measures are likely to be of such significance that they will be easily identifiable. If acceleration measures have been put in place it is recommended that the effects of these are shown separately to the 'as-planned impacted' delay analysis.

As discussed in chapter 3 the logic applied to any programme is either 'prescriptive' (meaning that which creates an activity sequence that must be adhered to) or 'preferential' (representing an activity sequence that the contractor chooses).

The 'as-planned impacted' technique works particularly well when the activities are largely sequential and the logic is prescriptive. For example with the construction of a high rise concrete frame (a largely prescriptive sequence of activities) the structural works must commence at the foundations and lowest floor level and progress up to the roof level and impacting a delay onto the planned programme relating to say the first floor columns is likely to produce a result which closely simulates what is likely to have actually occurred. In this case the contractor will have little, if any, opportunity to mitigate the delay by resequencing the subsequent structural works and therefore the results produced are likely to be reasonable.

On the other hand, a project to refurbish a number of houses may involve preferential logic, in as much as the sequence of undertaking the individual houses is one that the contractor prefers to adopt rather than one which must be adhered to. So impacting a delay on the planned programme relating to a lack of construction information to the first house planned to be refurbished is likely to show a consequential delay to all of the succeeding houses. And yet, in reality, once the delay to the first house becomes apparent, labour will be diverted to carryout work to one of the succeeding houses earlier than planned. In this case the work to the first house will be re-scheduled and will commence once information becomes available.

Providing the construction information for the first house is not too late, the actual impact of the delay is to merely change the sequence of working, not to cause delay to overall completion. In this type of scenario the 'planned impacted' technique will produce a result that is somewhat different to what actually occurred and so the analysis may prove to be unrealistic and unreasonable.

Production of a planned impacted delay analysis

A 'planned impacted analysis' is produced as follows:

1. Establish and select the 'planned programme' that is considered to represent the contractor's original as-planned intent.
2. Ensure that, once the delaying events are impacted, the selected programme can be rescheduled using programming software and that it will produce a dynamic reaction (this may mean adding required logic links, adapting existing logic and restraints or re-creating the planned programme in the form of a critical path network).
3. Particularise and quantify the delaying events to be impacted.
4. Add (or impact) the first delay onto the selected planned programme. (It is recognised good practice to impact the delaying events chronologically starting with the first event that occurred.)
5. Reschedule the programme so that it acts dynamically, simulating the effect of the impacted delaying event (note the delay, if any, to the overall completion date).
6. Repeat the process for each event, sequentially impacting the subsequent delaying events (note the delay to the overall completion date associated with each event).
7. Once all of the delays have been impacted, establish whether the results are fair and reasonable (use a common sense approach and cross check with what actually happened, if records exist).
8. If the overall completion date produced by the analysis is beyond the date when actual completion occurred, ask yourself whether it is reasonable to suggest that this demonstrates acceleration on the part of the contractor. (If so, can acceleration be independently demonstrated?)
9. If the results appear unreasonable the only recourse is to revisit each delaying event and check the way they have been impacted and linked into the programme. (As stated in chapter 3, critical path analysis is a precise technique and is certain to produce a precise and definitive result, but it is not certain to produce a result that stands up in the face of common sense.)

Summary

The 'as-planned impacted' methodology has simplicity and basic theoretical fairness, but it works best when used on projects where the works must be carried out in a particular sequence, as opposed to those where the sequence can be easily varied.

The technique has the benefit that it can be used when suitable as-built records have not been kept or are no longer available. It is also relatively easy and inexpensive to prepare and, subject to the presentation skills of the analyst, relatively simple to follow and understand.

However, it is a theoretical exercise requiring subjective input and no account is taken of what actually happened on the project. As a result, this methodology can produce results that defy reality or common sense logic, and, as discussed, a methodology that relies on subjective opinion and/or theoretical data is likely to be the subject of significant disagreement between disputing parties.

5.3 Collapsed as-built

The 'collapsed as-built' technique is, in some respects, the direct opposite of the 'as-planned impacted' process – the 'as-planned impacted' technique uses a planned programme and adds particularised delaying events, whereas the 'collapsed as-built' technique uses the as-built programme and removes delaying events.

As delay events are removed in the 'collapsed as-built' method, the overall completion date becomes earlier. Once all of the considered delays have been subtracted the technique seeks to portray how and when the works would have been undertaken and completed 'but for the delays' – for this reason the technique is often referred to as the 'as-built but for' technique.

The 'collapsed as-built' methodology is illustrated by figures 30–33.

Figure 30 indicates a simple as-built programme consisting of three critical activities with an overall duration of 20 weeks. The dark shading represents activity delay and in the case of activity 1 a one-week delay is shown occurring in week four and in activity 2 a three-week delay is shown occurring in weeks eight, nine and ten.

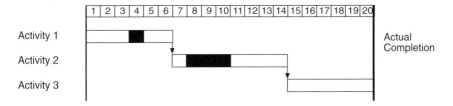

Figure 30: Simple as-built programme

Figure 31 illustrates the same as-built programme with the delays to activities 1 and 2 removed. Rescheduling the programme causes it to collapse indicating that, 'but for' the delays identified, the works could have been completed in 16 weeks. Therefore, the impact on overall completion of the delays to activities 1 and 2 is four weeks.

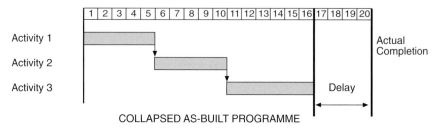

Figure 31: As-built programme with delays removed from activities 1 and 2

In figure 30 the delays were simply represented as prolongation to activities 1 and 2. However, it is common practice, when compiling the as-built programme, to represent the delays as discrete activities. Figure 32 shows an as-built programme with delays A and B represented discreetly.

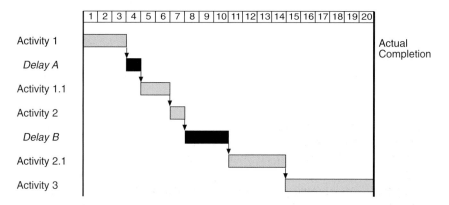

Figure 32: As-built programme with delays A and B represented discreetly

Using programmes like figure 32, it is common practice for delay analysts to simulate this deletion of discrete delay activities by reducing the delay activity durations in the network to zero rather than actually deleting them, to produce a programme as illustrated in figure 33.

By allocating a zero duration to delay events A and B and rescheduling in figure 33, the programme has collapsed to show an overall completion in 16 weeks. Therefore, the critical impact on overall completion of delay activities A and B is again shown to have been four weeks.

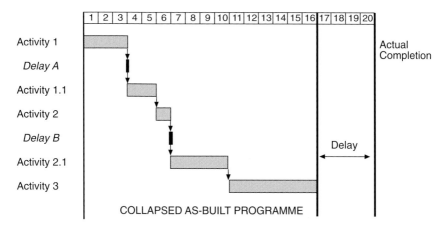

Figure 33: As-built programme with discrete delays set to zero

Process involved

In order to adopt this technique it is essential to have a suitably detailed as-built programme, but as discussed in section 5.1 it may prove to be difficult to produce such a programme, even if accurate detailed records exist. One particular problem outlined is that it may prove difficult to establish, with any degree of certainty, when particular activities were finally completed.

Critical path analysis is a precise process producing precise results and as a result it requires input of precise information – any uncertainty in respect of the activity timings will produce a result that is equally uncertain.

Assuming that the problems with producing an as-built programme can be overcome and the data has been entered on a computer, the next task will be to add logic links to enable the programme to collapse dynamically when the delaying events are removed. For this to happen, the as-built programme must be produced in the form of either a linked bar chart or in a critical path format and in order for the exercise to remain truly an analysis of the as-built situation, these logic links will have to be applied to maintain the as-built activity timings.

For example, if the start of the plastering activity is found to have been fifteen days after the start of chasing to blockwork partitions and installation of conduits for services, a start-to-start link should be made between these two activities, with a time lag of fifteen days. This would then produce a programme that accurately reflects the actual time lag between the commencements of these two activities. However, such links should be made with care as it may appear to be logical and sensible to link certain activities but, without some form of independent verification from contemporaneous documentation or witness of fact evidence, any link will merely reflect a delay analyst's assumption.

In the example given, there may have been sufficient progress to allow the plastering to commence on site earlier, and the only reason the actual start was fifteen days after commencement of chasing and conduits was that this was the date when the plastering subcontractor actually turned up on site. In this case the logic of a fifteen day 'start-to-start' link is a fiction. And whether accurate or artificial, once a fifteen day lag has been inserted as a link into the programme, it will remain constant as the delaying events are removed and the programme collapses.

At the time the site team may not have 'chased' the plastering subcontractor to commence earlier due to the fact that the start was not considered critical in the light of the delays that were occurring at that time. However as delays are removed and the programme collapses the plastering works may move onto the critical path making the commencement critical. After the event, the fact that these works could have commenced earlier will not be recognised.

There will be many similar situations and, in practice, the as-built programme used in this form of delay analysis is likely to contain logic links that are dependent upon the delay analyst's subjective views. In this respect the methodology is open to criticism in respect of its validity. As indicated above, this criticism can be addressed by relying on contemporaneous documentation or witness of fact evidence to form logic links.

Once the as-built programme has been compiled and the logic links added, the events considered to have caused delay can be removed or, as explained earlier, the duration of the activity representing the event can be set as zero. When commenting on the 'as-planned impacted' technique it was noted that it is good practice to add the delaying events in the chronological order in which they occurred. The same is true with the 'collapsed as-built' method but in reverse – it is good practice to remove the delays sequentially starting with the latest event that occurred.

After each delaying event is removed the programme is time analysed. If the delaying event in question is critical to completion this process will cause the programme to collapse and the overall completion date to become earlier. The extent of the variation to the completion date between each subtraction represents the delaying impact of the event removed. Therefore, this method identifies both a cause of delay and measures the effect that delay has on the completion date.

There is a view that the revised programme produced by the removal of each delaying event should be checked and reviewed, to ensure that the activity sequencing and timings are reasonable and valid. If any anomalies are found it is suggested that the applied logic should be reconsidered and, if necessary, altered. The thinking is that this will ensure that the removal of further delaying events will produce more reasonable results.

There be may some benefit in this approach but, if some links are to be adjusted, it calls into question the reliability of the whole analysis. If the logic first applied to the as-built programme has to be fundamentally adjusted to make the result 'look right' it rather begs the question, why put links into the programme in the first place? In formalised disputes concerning delays to construction projects this type of 'tinkering' with the logic is likely to be the subject of much disagreement between the parties.

Collapsed as-built and concurrent delay

The 'collapsed as-built' technique involves the removal of employer delays from the as-built programme to produce the theoretical end-date that the contractor would have achieved had it not been for the delays. However, sometimes there are two delays occurring at the same time, one of which is an employer's delay and the other a contractor's delay. If only the employer's delay is removed from the programme when concurrent delays were occurring, the programme is prevented from collapsing by the contractor's delay.

In this case the end date will not change and would indicate that the contractor has no entitlement to an extension of time due to the particular employer's concurrent delay. This outcome might not reflect the law and the terms of the contract upon which the delays occur and it may be that, under the contract, certain concurrent delays or concurrent delays in general entitle the contractor to an extension of time.

Perhaps, and more likely, the legal position as to how to deal with concurrent delays is unclear and/or it is difficult to be sure whether the delays were truly concurrent. As discussed later in this chapter, most project task durations tend to expand to fit the time available and so it can be very difficult to identify and quantify a contractor's culpable delay. Only by removing all of the delays could a view of any concurrent delay be undertaken.

Calendar issues

Problems can arise when the period of the working week varies – perhaps part of the project under review commenced by working a standard five-day week but later moved to a five and half, six or seven day week. In such cases, as the delaying events are removed and the programme collapses, various activities may move from a period when weekends (or part of the weekends) were worked, into a period when no weekend working occurred – so a seven-day delay may show up as a 1.4 week delay on a programme based on five-day working weeks. Further problems arise when deciding how to represent periods, such as Saturday mornings, when only minor operations were carried out with a much reduced workforce.

Programming software does allow many different calendars to be used, enabling the various work patterns and the working and non-working periods to be simulated, but if different calendars are mixed it will cause the programme to become complex and difficult to follow. Because of this complexity a seven-day calendar is often applied to all activities. In this case an activity that commenced on a Wednesday of one week and finished on the Tuesday of the following week, would have a 7-day programme duration even if the working week was only Monday to Friday.

Time available

Activity durations on a construction site often expand to fill the time available, so if four men can complete a task in the time available there is little point employing eight men to carry out the work in half the time – as Wickwire and Ockman ask, 'why hurry up and wait?'[2]. The consequence of this understandable behaviour is that it can distort the conclusions being made about the as-built performance of the contractor, which will affect the logic used to draw up the as-built programme, and, in turn, this will affect the results produced when the programme is rescheduled and collapsed.

The problem can best be explained by an illustration of a possible scenario occurring on a site. Imagine the construction of the foundations lies on the critical path and the contractor plans to undertake these works in a period of four weeks. Immediately upon commencement of these works the proposed start of the erection of the structural steel frame is deferred by two weeks, perhaps due to late issue of information and/or variations, meaning that there is now a period of six weeks between the start of foundations and the start of steelwork. In the light of this change, the plant and labour resources are reduced by the contractor and redeployed elsewhere. The contractor can see no reason to 'hurry up and wait' and as a result the foundations take five weeks to complete.

When viewed retrospectively, using the 'collapsed as-built' technique, the two-week employer delay associated with the late information and variations to the steelwork would be removed from the as-built programme and should then show that 'but-for' the delay to the steelwork the work would have commenced two weeks earlier. However, because the contractor slowed down and took five weeks to do the foundation work, the collapsed programme will only indicate a one-week delay.

In a simple scenario like this it may be possible to identify the reasons why the additional week was taken to construct the foundations and a compensatory adjustment could be made to the as-built logic. However such circumstances are likely to be lost in the complexity of events and activities occurring on a typical construction project – delays are rarely straightforward single issues – and the contractor may not recover a full period of delay caused by the employer.

In the foundation example the time taken for the foundation construction was measured against what was planned. If the planned programme had not specifically identified this period it would be difficult to say whether the contractor would always have required five weeks or whether it was simply a case of making adjustments so as to make use of the time being available.

Contingencies

Putting these difficulties to one side, is it safe to say, in any event, that the collapsed as-built programme produces a date upon which the contractor would have completed 'but for' delay events?

Often this form of analysis produces a completion date earlier than the one on the contractor's planned programme. This may be because the original plan allowed contingencies for contractor delays that did not materialise but contractors usually explain that the difference is evidence of acceleration.

This may be a valid explanation in some cases but, in reality, it is probably more likely to be due to inaccuracies and anomalies associated with the 'collapsed as-built' methodology. Any acceleration claim ought to be reasonably apparent and should be demonstrated independently and supported by evidence.

Collapsed as-built – the basic procedure

A collapsed as-built analysis is produced as follows:

1. Establish and compile an as-built programme in sufficient detail, including relevant activities to reflect the alleged delaying events.
2. Apply appropriate logic links to reflect the as-built sequencing and to ensure the as-built activity timings will be maintained when the programme is re-scheduled using programming software. Ensure that the logic applied will enable the programme to act dynamically once the delaying events are removed and the programme is rescheduled – to allow this to happen the as-built programme will need to be created as a linked bar chart or in the form of a critical path network.
3. Particularise and quantify the delaying events and ensure that the as-built programme contains appropriate discrete activities to allow these delaying events to be removed.

4. Remove the first delay from the created as-built programme. (It is recognised good practice to remove the delaying events in reverse chronological order – starting with the last event that occurred.)

5. Reschedule the programme so that it acts dynamically. If the considered delay had any delaying impact to overall completion the programme will collapse (the overall completion date will become earlier). Note the difference between the overall project completion prior to and subsequent to removal and programme rescheduling – any difference represents the impact of the delaying event in question.

6. Review the collapsed programme to see if it still represents a valid and realistic programme (if not some adjustment to the logic may be required – any such changes should be minimal and could be considered to be manipulation of the technique).

7. Repeat the process, sequentially removing the delaying events and noting the effect each event has to the overall completion date.

8. Once all of the delays have been removed establish whether the results are fair and reasonable. (If the overall completion date produced is somewhat earlier than the original planned date for completion is it reasonable to suggest that this demonstrates acceleration on the part of the contractor? And, if it is considered reasonable, can any acceleration be independently demonstrated?)

Summary

The 'collapsed as-built' method has the benefits of being relatively simple to understand, and inexpensive to prepare once an as-built programme has been produced.

One of the undoubted strengths of the 'collapsed as-built' technique is the fact that it is based upon what actually occurred and as a result it can produce an apparently compelling argument, especially when used by contractors.

It can be said that even allowing for the contractor's own culpable delay the results of the collapsed as-built methodology represent the situation had the employer not caused delay. The 'collapsed as-built' method also has the benefit of identifying both a cause of delay and producing a measure of the effect of that delay on the completion date.

However, this method relies on the ability to produce a sufficiently detailed as-built programme and it may be argued that the application of logic to this programme is subjective and fails to portray the planned intent at the time the delays occurred. Also the fact that it seemingly represents a compelling argument, may lead to results being too readily accepted, without critical appraisal.

As with all of the recognised delay analysis methodologies, the 'collapsed as-built' technique is not without its critics. One view is that the use of this method is restricted by its inability to identify concurrency, resequencing, redistribution of resources or acceleration, particularly when the nature of the as-built logic is complex. In fact, the Society of Construction Law, *Delay and Disruption Protocol*[3] notes that where acceleration, redistribution of resources, or resequencing has taken place the results obtained may be unreliable.

The one problem highlighted more often than others is the fact that the removal of delays will only produce results when removed from the longest path (this is the path or string of activities that form the critical path at the end of the project and by implication will include the last activity to finish). The disadvantage of always looking at this longest path is that it only portrays the final critical path and may not represent the critical path earlier in the project or the critical path at the time the alleged delays occurred.

Like other delay analysis techniques, if 'collapsed as-built' is to be used, it should be used in the light of its weaknesses and limitations.

5.4 A comparison of 'as-planned impacted' and 'collapsed as-built'

The 'as-planned impacted' and 'collapsed as-built' techniques have a number of similarities but, in other respects, are opposites – the 'as-planned impacted' technique involves the addition of delaying events onto the planned programme, whereas the collapsed as-built involves subtraction from the as-built programme. In this section the two methods are contrasted, by showing how each would deal with similar background facts.

Figure 34, overleaf, represents a simple planned programme for construction works to project areas A and B. These areas are not subject to sectional completion dates – the contract allows one date for completion of the entire project. In the planned programme the contractor intends to complete the works in a period of 16 weeks.

During the execution of the works detailed in figure 34, activities 1 and 2 in Area A and activity 4 in Area B are delayed by events attributable to the employer. Using an 'as-planned impacted' technique the contractor produces the programme in figure 35.

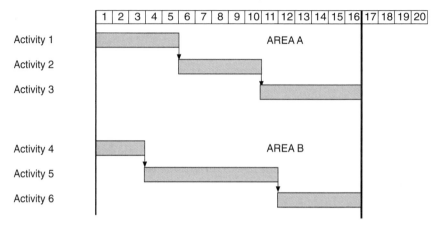

Figure 34: Planned programme for construction works to project areas A and B

As can be seen in figure 35, area A, activity 1 was delayed by one week, at week four of the project and Activity 2 was further delayed by three weeks, at weeks eight, nine and ten, while area B, activity 4, was delayed by a period of one week in week two.

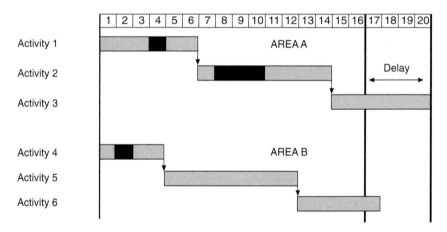

Figure 35: As-planned impacted programme for areas A and B

The overall result of impacting these employer delays is to push the overall projected completion date back to week 20, a delay of four weeks. Figure 35 shows that the delay is being generated by the delay to area A, because although area B was delayed beyond the original date for completion, the delay was not critical to overall project completion.

Relying on the above results it can be concluded that the contractor has an entitlement to an extension of time of four weeks.

However the results are different when considering a similar scenario using a 'collapsed as-built' approach. In figure 36 the as-built programme for the same project works shows that the project was actually not completed until week 21 largely due to contractor delays to activity 5 and 6. The programme includes the same employer delays as figure 35 but as a result of the contractor delays the actual completion was determined by the completion of Area B.

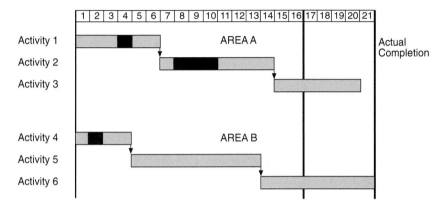

Figure 36: As-built programme for areas A and B

A 'collapsed as-built' analysis is set out in figure 37 with the employer delaying events removed.

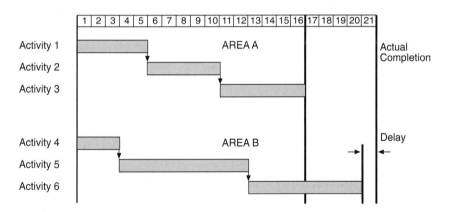

Figure 37: Collapsed as-built programme for areas A and B

The total four weeks of employer delay that occurred to Area A has been removed causing this section of the as-built programme to collapse, indicating a 'but-for' completion of area A at week 16.

Likewise the one-week employer delay to area B has been removed, causing the as-built programme for this section of the as-built programme to collapse by this period. Because of the contractor's own culpable delay to Area B, completion of this area is shown by figure 37 at week 20 'but-for' the employer delay.

As can be seen, this produces a conclusion that the contractor has an entitlement to an extension of time of only one week.

The simple scenarios illustrate how the choice of methodology can produce significantly different results. The 'as-planned impacted' example demonstrates an entitlement to an extension of time of four weeks simply because it makes no allowance for what actually occurred – it does not recognise the contractor's own culpable delays in area B.

In contrast the 'collapsed as-built' example demonstrates a delay of one week because it has only considered the delays that lie on the longest path, that is the one for project area B, which was ultimately critical simply because it was the last to finish. Removing the area A delays had no impact because of the contractor's own culpable delay to area B.

These two scenarios are exceptionally simple and it is very easy to see how differing results can emanate from similar facts. In reality the situation on a construction site is likely to be far more complex than this example and understanding the reasons for the results will be very difficult to determine. Neither of the techniques is particularly transparent and interrogation of the results will not be possible without access to the underlying electronic data.

5.5 Windows analysis

'Windows analysis' is not so much a technique in its own right, but is more of a way of breaking the project down into manageable slices (or windows) of time and viewing the state of progress. Because this method involves slicing the project duration into regular intervals, it is also known as the 'time slice' method.

With this method, rather than analysing delaying events in the context of the whole project period, the project is broken down into a number of sequential periods. The effect of the delaying events are then analysed within these periods with the impact at the end of one window forming the start of the following window.

Process involved

With 'windows analysis' it is important that the selected time period for each window is not too long because, otherwise, it may prove difficult to assess and analyse each activity and any delay. On a typical construction project a window period of around four weeks or one calendar month is often used so as to coincide with the frequency and timing of the monthly progress meetings and the programme progress updates.

Although this time period is generally appropriate for each window it may vary dependent on the overall project period and the nature of the works being analysed. For example, during the early substructure stages of a typical construction project the operations being undertaken and the trades present on site are likely to be relatively limited.

The initial activities might comprise activities such as site clearance, excavation for foundations, construction of foundations, backfilling excavations, drainage and ground floor slabs. These operations and the logical relationships between them tend to be relatively simplistic and linear in nature and it may be more appropriate for this section of the project to be analysed as a period greater than four weeks. In this sort of scenario there may be some merit in timing the windows to suit key milestone events, for example the first window may comprise of all works from commencement through to the start of the erection of the superstructure.

Conversely during the latter stages of a typical building project, when there are likely to be many activities being undertaken, with complex interfaces, then a four-week window or shorter is probably more appropriate (subject to the availability of detailed information).

The basic principle is to utilise a networked as-planned master programme and to update it using as-built information to reflect the actual progress status of the project at the start of the window. This will include any delay up to that date as well as any mitigation and/or acceleration. The start of the window effectively represents 'a line in the sand' with the activities prior to this time representing what actually occurred and the activities following this point representing a reasonable planned sequence of activities through to overall project completion.

All activities and events planned and actually occurring within the window are considered and updated. Actual activity starts and finishes occurring within the window are logged and any required additional activities are inserted with relevant activity omissions made. The programme is then updated to reflect the actual project status at the end of the selected window. Again, the sequence of activities following the end of the window represent a reasonable planned sequence through to overall completion.

This exercise will produce:

- a programme reflecting the actual status of the project at the commencement of the window and a reasonable planned programme through to anticipated overall project completion;

- an as-built programme for the activities and events occurring during the course of the window;
- a programme reflecting the actual status of the project at the completion of the window and a reasonable planned programme through to anticipated overall project completion.

Any difference between the timing of the anticipated date for overall project completion at the start of the window with the anticipated completion at the end of the window will indicate whether any delay or saving in time occurred during the course of the window.

The windows are looked at sequentially with the status at the end of one window forming the status for the start of the following window. Assuming that the end of the last window is at the actual completion of the project then the sum of the delays occurring in each window, after taking into account any gains will correspond with the actual overall delay to completion.

It is important to note that any delay quantified at the end of the window does not necessarily reflect the full delay associated with the events occurring within that window. It only reflects the likely delay at that time. The effect of the events may continue into the subsequent windows and so the delay may increase. Conversely the impact of the delays may be reduced, due to mitigating measures and events occurring within the subsequent windows.

As an example a delay may occur to the early part of the project during the construction of the foundations. The contractor may then be able to resequence some of the later works to the envelope, maintaining the critical 'building weathertight' date and allowing the services and fitting out works to start much as originally planned. To some extent it will not be until the end of the last window that the full effect of all of the delays can be assessed.

Although the status at the start and end of the window will allow any delay to be quantified it will not in itself demonstrate the cause or causes of that delay. Analysis of these delaying events can be carried out using any method that is applicable, dependent on the activities and events in question. It may be appropriate to use a 'collapsed as-built' technique or an 'as-planned impacted' methodology. Alternatively, if the events and activities occurring within the window are not too complex, a simple 'planned v as-built' comparison may be sufficient.

Strengths and weaknesses

One of the main strengths of the 'windows analysis' is that it looks at the delays on an actual or 'real-time' basis – the start and finish of the window reflects the actual status of the project works at those times.

Generally when applying critical path-based delay analysis methodologies to the whole project, the process can become highly complex and the practitioner will have great difficulty assessing the validity of the results and identifying any anomalies, while also giving consideration to such issues as mitigation and concurrency. The benefit of looking at the delays and progress of the works within short windows of time, rather than looking at the whole project, is that there will be fewer activities and events and less information to consider. The short timescale and limited number of events and activities means that the analysis can be undertaken with a little more objectivity and probably more pragmatically.

When applying a single methodology to the whole project it might be found that it is more applicable to some areas of work than others (the inherent problems with both the 'as-planned impacted' and the 'collapsed as-built' methodologies have already been discussed). However, the use of short windows of time means that differing methodologies can be used dependent on which is considered the most relevant to the events in question.

One of the main problems with the 'windows analysis' is the extent of the detailed as-built information that is required to re-create and simulate the project status at the start and end of each window. The 'windows analysis' will be easier to implement and will work better when a detailed as-planned master programme has been regularly updated with progress throughout the project. That is not to say that it will be impossible to recreate this information retrospectively but this will be dependent on the availability of some form of progress records to demonstrate the project status at the timing of the desired windows.

Compilation of this data is likely to be a time consuming and costly task and updating of the planned master programme and the maintenance of progress records during the course of the works is a fairly fundamental requirement in the planning and management of any project. In *Delay and Disruption in Construction Contracts* Keith Pickavance suggests that, in his experience where regular progress updates have not been kept, it is unlikely that general detailed records of the progress of the planned work will be available.

Therefore, it seems reasonable to conclude that if a regularly updated programme is not available, the likelihood of the availability of sufficient other progress and as-built records to retrospectively recreate such a programme is likely to be limited in practice.

Difficulties may also occur if the planned master programme has been heavily amended. For example, in the latter stages of the project the master programme may be replaced with a detailed 'completion' programme. At the time of this change problems are likely to be found in reconciling the activities at the start of the window, which relate to the as-planned master programme, with activities at the end of the window that relate to the new 'completion' programme. It is therefore important to incorporate any programme amendments to ensure that the prospective as-planned programme is reasonable through to completion and reflects the intent at the time.

Commenting on both the 'windows' and 'time impact' analyses, Jon Wickwire and Stuart Ockman warn that:

> '... care must be taken to ensure that the as-planned schedule for completion is reasonable and reflects the parties' intention at the time of the delay.'[4]

The analysis and quantification of the delay within each window will be based on the critical path and the extent of the delay to project completion at both the start and end of each of the windows. This will be directly dependent on the progress updates as well as the sequence of the works yet to be completed, as dictated by the 'as-planned' programme through to project completion. Therefore the accuracy of the quantification of the delays within each window will be directly dependent on the accuracy of these progress updates, as well as the reasonableness of the as-planned programme.

As previously discussed, the planned programme may be unreliable for many reasons and there are difficulties with forward planning of construction projects over long periods. As such, the prospective as-planned programme associated with a window at the early part of the project, where the works still have some time to run, may be considered less reliable than a window occurring at the latter stages of the project. In any event, the prospective nature of the programme will only display a possibility of what may occur – it is not a record of what will actually occur.

Another frequent criticism of the planned programme to completion is that it simply reflects what was planned and does not take account of the history of what has actually been achieved to date. So, if for example, it has taken twice as long as planned to construct the brickwork up to the first time slice or window, it seems reasonable to suggest that the remaining brickwork will also take longer than planned. Conversely better progress than that planned will also not be reflected because this form of analysis projects forward on the basis of the original plan.

A further problem can arise when works prior to the programme update have been sequenced and progressed in a manner differently to that planned. When the planned programme is updated with progress and rescheduled, the future work will generally be scheduled based on the logic and sequence set previously for the planned programme. Thus the prospective plan will reflect the original planned intent rather than how the works have and will be undertaken.

Notwithstanding the above, and as previously noted, the results of one window are carried forward into the next window on an incremental basis, so the end of the last window will reflect when completion was actually achieved and the aggregate of the delays will equal the actual total delay that occurred. On this basis, although the overall delay may reflect the actual delay, because of the points raised, the quantification of the individual delays may be unreliable. It is therefore recommended that after analysing all of the windows, the results are tested and some view of the project delays as a whole is taken to ensure that the quantification of individual delays is fair and reasonable.

Points for consideration

1. When compiling the master as-planned programme the contractor is likely to include additional time within certain activities, to cover potential risks such as adverse weather conditions. This additional time preserves an element of 'float' and provides a contingency period if things go wrong. In the initial 'as-planned' context these activities may not be critical and will have little bearing on the planned completion date. However, as the programme is updated, these activities may form part of the critical path and will then have a direct relationship with the overall completion. A view will have to be taken as to the validity of the remaining activity durations when considering whether the updated as-planned programme realistically reflects the planned intent through to completion, otherwise the completion date may be being driven by an excessive contingency allowance.

2. During the project, as the as-planned programme is updated, the contractor is likely to amend the programme logic and activities to ensure that the updated programme reflects the contractual date for completion. These amendments might be a genuine attempt to show reasonable mitigation measures to overcome any delay following the progress input but may also reflect a desire to simply maintain the required end date and to 'mask' the impact of the contractor's own culpable delay. When using the windows analysis consideration of such amendments will be required.

---

3. It is not always easy to accurately assess the progress of some activities. The progress of say, the construction of blockwork partitions may be relatively easy to assess whereas the progress of services installations, even with a great deal of effort, is unlikely to be quite as straightforward to establish.

The level of accuracy of complex activities, such as services installation, could be increased if the contractor painstakingly marked up drawings to indicate the extent of the wiring, pipework and ductwork installed. In reality the time taken to undertake such an exercise is often limited and the main contractor (for both progress and valuation purposes) may rely on information provided by the services subcontractor, making only a cursory assessment to test its general overall reasonableness. It may also be argued that contemporaneous progress updates may be sufficient for project management purposes but insufficient for the accurate and precise determination of delay.

Windows analysis – the basic procedure

A 'windows analysis' is produced as follows:

1. Establish the number and timing of the windows to be used for the analysis. It is desirable that if the planned programme has regularly been updated, the timing of the windows should coincide with these updates.
2. Locate the original planned programme as well as all amendments. If the planned programme has been regularly updated then copies of the regular updates will be required – it may be that, although the contractor undertook regular and detailed progress updates, the planned programme was only prepared as a simple bar chart and in these circumstances the planned programme will have to be converted into a linked bar chart or critical path network. (As previously commented, the retrospective addition of programme logic may attract some criticism, in as much as it presupposes the contractor's original planned intent.)
3. If the planned programme was not updated with progress during the works, locate progress records to enable the programme status at the start and end of each window to be established.
4. Locate as-built records to enable the events occurring within the window to be plotted.
5. Determine the programme status at the start of the first window. This will usually be the commencement of the project (if this is the case then the programme status will simply be represented by the planned programme).

6. Determine what activities were to be undertaken within the timeframe of the first window and, using the as-built records, plot the actual start and finish dates of these activities. The as-built data may indicate that additional activities occurred, which were not shown on the planned programme (if this is the case then they will have to be added).
7. Determine the programme status at the end of the window.
8. Compare the planned dates with the actual dates and quantify any delay or advancement.
9. From the as-built documentation establish the cause of any delay or advancement and, from the documentation, determine responsibility.
10. Using the programme status at the end of the window, as the start of the following window, again review what activities are planned and repeat the above.

When a contractor carries out a programme progress update contemporaneously, a review of the impact on the prospective planned programme through to project completion will be undertaken to ensure that the planned sequence and timing remain reasonable, which may necessitate the need to re-sequence activities, make amendments to the programme logic and review activity durations.

If the programme has not been updated during the life of the project and the programme status is being recreated retrospectively, the planned programme will need to be checked at each update to ensure that it predicts a reasonable and workable sequence.

Summary

'Windows analysis' has the advantage of simulating the project status at the time of the delay and reviews delays on a 'real-time' basis. The analysis of delays is easier to undertake and to understand compared to other methods because it is restricted to consideration of a limited time-period and a limited number of activities.

However, it can be time consuming and costly to prepare and may prove difficult, if not impossible, to create retrospectively if progress updates have not been undertaken during the life of the project. It is also reliant on the reasonableness of the as-planned programme and the accuracy of progress updates.

5.6 Time impact analysis

'Time impact analysis' effectively involves taking a 'snapshot' of the programme status immediately prior to the occurrence of the delaying event, and then impacting the event onto the updated planned programme. The technique is often referred to as 'snapshot' analysis and is not dissimilar to 'windows analysis'. Whilst 'windows analysis' concentrates primarily on incremental periods of time and then looks at the delays within the windows, 'time impact analysis' starts with the identification of the timing of delaying events.

As with 'windows analysis' the basis for 'time impact analysis' is a reasonable planned programme. This programme will be required to act dynamically once the delaying events are impacted and therefore it must be in the form of either a linked bar chart or a critical path network.

Process involved

Time impact analysis is essentially a prospective technique, in that it predicts likely future delay, however it can be used retrospectively. When used prospectively an isolated programme is prepared representing the likely sequence of events associated with the delaying event. This programme should include the necessary logic so that it will react dynamically when integrated into the main planned programme and will be in the form of a linked bar chart or a small critical path network. This programme is often referred to as a 'subnet' or 'fragnet'.

The extent of this isolated programme will be dependent on the particular delay being simulated. If the event relates to a variation to the structural steel frame, then the programme may need activities for:

- issue of the instruction;
- placement of the variation order;
- preparation of new or revised design drawings;
- date of approval of drawings;
- procurement of any specialist elements;
- fabrication period; and
- installation period.

The extent of the programme required to simulate a very simple delaying event such as an increase in the quantity of brickwork will be much more limited and may only require a single activity to reflect the additional time needed.

Once the likely sequence and timing of the delaying event activities have been considered the 'subnet' simulating the delaying event can be incorporated into the current as-planned programme. This will be the programme updated with the progress achieved at the time of the event, which represents the current status of the project. The activities that have been progressed will represent the as-built history of the project, whilst the prospective activities represent the work that has still to be undertaken providing a realistic programme through to overall project completion.

Logic links are applied to activities to simulate the relationship between the activities within the 'subnet' and those in the main 'as-planned' programme. The as-planned programme with the added delay 'subnet' is then time analysed and the overall project completion date is re-calculated. The difference between the calculated project completion prior to the inclusion of the delaying event 'subnet' and any later completion after inclusion represents the likely delay.

However, this will only indicate likely 'further delay'. Retrospective analysis may indicate a greater entitlement to an extension of time. Consider a situation where the project consists of the construction of two independent offices, block X and block Y, and the contract allows for a single date for completion. The as-planned programme is regularly updated and immediately prior to an employer generated delaying event, the predicted completion of block X is ten weeks after the contract completion date, whilst block Y is predicted to finish on time.

The employer delay event relates to a major variation to block Y and it is simulated by means of a 'subnet', incorporated into the 'as-planned' programme and the predicted contract completion recalculated. It is found that the completion of block Y is now likely to be nine and a half weeks late. However, the overall date for completion remains unchanged at 10 weeks late due to the delay to block X. In this case the delaying event has caused no further delay to the predicted contract completion and, despite the major employer delay, it may be argued that no extension of time is due.

The difference in this example between the contractor and employer delay events is small but the impact of the difference could be huge. If the liquidated damages for late completion of the contract were £100,000 per week, the contractor in this scenario could be looking at a £1 million deduction from the final payment certificate.

There are great problems predicting and recording with precision the durations of construction activities and yet a great deal can turn on such analysis. In the example, it may be possible to show that the employer delay is ten weeks and the contractor delay is nine and a half weeks, in which case perhaps there is no liability for liquidated damages. This type of scenario is also likely to raise the issue of concurrent delay. Concurrent delay has been the subject of consideration in legal cases and is also addressed in some forms of contract (see chapters 7 and 8) but it remains an intractable problem in delay analysis.

When 'time impact analysis' is used retrospectively a much more detailed and robust approach can be taken, with the as-built project status being tracked and analysed throughout the course of the occurrence of the delay. The actual extent of this 'tracking and analysing' is difficult to quantify and it would largely be dependent on the nature of both the project works and the delaying event in question. In some cases it may necessitate a very detailed analysis reconstructing the project history using contemporaneous records.

The status of the as-planned programme is recorded at the end of the delaying event. Therefore, a comparison can be made between the planned completion prior to and after the onset of the delay event. If the delaying event occurred in isolation, any difference in the projected completion will represent the impact of that event. It must be noted that where other delays overlap or are concurrent, some consideration must be given to the impact associated with each of these individual events.

Time impact analysis – the basic procedure

The following procedure relates to the simple, rather than the more detailed forensic, application of time impact analysis:

1. Locate the original planned master programme, as well as all amendments (if this programme has been regularly updated with progress then copies of the regular updates will be required). It may be the case that although the contractor undertook regular and detailed progress updates the planned master programme was only prepared as a simple bar chart. In these circumstances the planned programme will have to be converted into a linked bar chart or critical path network. (The retrospective addition of programme logic may attract some criticism in as much as it presupposes the contractor's original planned intent.)
2. If the planned programme has not been updated during the works, locate progress records to enable the programme status immediately prior to the event to be ascertained. If the programme has been regularly updated then the update nearest the start of the delay is usually chosen. (When used prospectively the planned programme should theoretically be updated at regular intervals as the works proceed. Therefore the updated planned programme as described in steps 1 and 2 should be readily available.)

3. Compile a 'subnet' of activities to simulate the effect and sequence of the delaying event being analysed.

4. Incorporate the 'subnet' into the as-planned programme and reschedule. If the predicted project completion date is extended then this represents the likely delay.

In the case of the retrospective use of the 'time impact' methodology, it can be applied very simply, much the same as when applied prospectively. This involves incorporating a 'fragnet' representing the delaying event into a planned programme that has been updated with progress at the time immediately prior to the delaying event occurring. As with its prospective use this will simulate the likely delay associated with the event in question.

When used retrospectively, 'time impact analysis' can be used much more forensically, with a detailed review of progress throughout the course of the delaying events being undertaken.

Even when used in this detailed forensic way the overall impact on completion will be determined by the reasonableness of the planned programme, that is the likely sequence of works from the time that the delay ceased to have an impact through to completion. The validity of this sequence and the projected effect on completion will be dependent on the nature of the project and the activity logic. As previously described if the logic is prescriptive then the actual outcome may not be too different to that projected. If the logic is largely preferential it may be found that in the event the remaining works, following the event being analysed, were actually undertaken somewhat differently than those projected by the planned programme.

The validity of this sequence may also be dependent on the timing of the delaying event. If the delay being analysed occurred at the start of the project there may be some uncertainty in the planned programme representing the remaining period through to completion. A delay occurring towards the end of the project period will mean that the remaining planned period will be relatively short and therefore certainty is more likely.

As with the 'windows methodology', events are required to be impacted and analysed chronologically. The extent and detail of the analysis will be dependent upon what the analyst considers to be appropriate but it is suggested that, in addition to the above procedure, the project history throughout the course of the period of the delaying event should be analysed and tracked with the 'as-planned' programme status being set at the point when the delaying event ceases to have an impact.

The status of the as-planned programme, prior to the onset of the impact of the delaying event and after it has ceased to have an effect, can be compared and the delay can be quantified. Great care will be needed to ensure that all concurrency and any overlap in the timing of the events are considered.

It has been suggested that 'time impact analysis' is one of the more robust and thorough techniques. In fact, the Society of Construction Law *Delay and Disruption Protocol* (the Protocol) recommends that 'time impact analysis' should be used both for the analysis of prospective and, where the necessary information is available, retrospective delay.

In recommending 'time impact analysis' the Protocol adopts the principle that retrospective delay and subsequent entitlement to extension of time should be assessed in the light of the contractor's planned intent and the progress achieved at the time of the occurrence of the delaying event. The ultimate conclusion of the Protocol in respect of the guidelines on retrospective delay analysis states:

> 'The Protocol recommends that, in deciding entitlement to EOT [extension of time], the adjudicator, judge or arbitrator should so far as is practical put him/herself in the position of the CA [Contract Administrator] at the time the Employer Risk Event occurred.'[5]

In making this recommendation the Protocol duly recognises that results may not match the as-built programme because the programme's performance may have been influenced by the effects of attempted acceleration, resequencing, redeployment of resources, or other delaying events.

To truly simulate the Protocol recommendation – and on the basis that extension of time should be dealt with as close to the occurrence of the delaying event as possible rather than adopting a 'wait and see' type approach – the time impact analysis technique would need to be applied in a very simple form. This would involve a retrospective application very similar to that adopted prospectively.

Notwithstanding this the Protocol acknowledges that 'time impact analysis' can also be used to assist in resolving more complex delays involving concurrency, acceleration and disruption. It also comments that time impact analysis is the most thorough method – although it can be the most time-consuming and costly when performed forensically.[6] Such a detailed approach would move the determination of delay away from the position of the contract administrator at the time and make it much closer to an analysis of the as-built status and what actually occurred. This is confirmed by the Protocol itself where, at section 4 under the heading of 'The terms of the contract', it includes 'time impact analysis' as a technique that can be used to determine actual delay as well as a technique that can be used to determine likely effect.[7]

The Protocol's guidelines on exactly how 'time impact analysis' should be applied is, therefore, a little difficult to ascertain. It does, however, seem to recognise that the retrospective application of 'time impact' analysis, can be undertaken in a manner similar to its prospective use. Alternatively, a much more robust and thorough forensic approach can be used entailing a detailed analysis of the project history throughout the period from the initial occurrence of the delay through to the time that it ceased to have an affect.

Although the Protocol considers 'time impact' analysis as the most thorough method, it is probably fairer to say that the extent of its thoroughness is dependent on the detail and quality of the records available, as well as their application and interpretation. The nature and likely impact of the delaying event in question, as well as issues of concurrency and mitigation will also dictate to what extent a thorough analysis is required and merited. Therefore, it is suggested, this technique, like all others, has merits and weaknesses and these should be kept in mind when using the approach.

Summary

'Time impact analysis' simulates the project status at the time of the delay and therefore looks at the delays on a 'real-time' basis. It also allows for a robust and detailed analysis of actual events. As Jon Wickwire and Stuart Ockman noted, time impact analysis provides 'a chronological and cumulative method to analyse delay[8].'

However, it can be very time consuming and costly to prepare. On a project with limited and sequential delaying events each event can be looked at discretely but if there are many events, some of which overlap or are concurrent, then the process will be considerably more difficult and will require a high level of detail.

Due to the complexity involved, the technique often needs to be undertaken by a skilled delay analyst, particularly when applied retrospectively and forensically. This may put the use of the technique out of the reach of most ordinary construction professionals.

'Time impact analysis' relies on the availability of detailed contemporaneous records and the reasonableness of the 'as-planned' programme. If records are not available the technique cannot be used and if the as-planned programme is not reasonable the technique may produce absurd results.

continued

Data can be produced retrospectively from contemporaneous records but this is likely to prove time consuming and exceptionally difficult. Furthermore, as commented under the 'windows analysis' section, if the contractor has not updated the 'as-planned' programme with progress it is unlikely that he will have kept good records making it impossible to employ this technique.

It is interesting to note that, generally, only the prospective application of 'time impact analysis' is referred to, not its retrospective application. However, 'time impact analysis' can be used retrospectively to reflect what actually happened on a project, in particular what happened relating to the progress of a delay event. The use of retrospective time impact analysis can actually be quite useful to simulate what extension should have been awarded at the time.

In some circles there would appear to be confusion between 'time impact' or 'snapshot' analysis and 'windows' or 'time slice'. In principle 'time impact' analysis is not dissimilar to 'windows analysis', in that the project status is recorded at the end of the occurrence of the delaying event in a similar way to the status being recorded at the end of the window. As with the 'windows analysis', the method is chronological and cumulative, with the project status at the end of the delay representing the status at the commencement of the subsequent delay. Also, like 'windows analysis', 'time impact' analysis relies on an as-planned programme being regularly updated with progress throughout the works.

6

Preparing and evaluating a claim

When preparing a delay claim any one of the five main delay analysis techniques discussed in chapter 5 might be used, providing the necessary data exists and providing the technique suits the circumstances. Other than the 'as-planned v as-built' technique, these forms of delay analysis rely on critical path analysis. In this chapter further comments are made about the weaknesses lurking within each form of analysis and suggestions are made about when particular methods can be used and how the results should be viewed.

Some delay analyses are prospective (concerned with or applying to the future) and others are retrospective (having application to the past) and this distinction is drawn when considering the preparation and evaluation of claims below.

6.1 Prospective claims

Most forms of construction contract (including the JCT standard forms) require contractors to notify the employer of delays, within a prescribed period, and to estimate the effect, if any, that these delays are likely to have on the completion date for the project. The employer's agent then has to review the claim, again usually with a prescribed time period, and make any relevant award. These claims/awards are prospective – they are estimates of what might logically occur as a result of present or past delay events. Therefore, any award of extension of time to be based on the 'likely' effect of the relevant events rather than the actual delay that transpires.

The Society of Construction Law Protocol advocates that applications and awards of extension of time should be dealt with as close in time as possible to the occurrence of the delay event and discourages a 'wait and see' type of approach.[9] However, under most forms of contract the employer's agent is unable to subsequently reduce any extension of time awarded and this could, in theory, lead to an extension being given where one is not ultimately needed.

Imagine, for example, the employer wishes to upgrade the specification of a key element of the works, maybe the windows or suspended ceilings. Following investigation the contractor provides a quotation from the manufacturer indicating an extended procurement period and as such the contractor notifies and demonstrates that the additional requirements will result in a delay of eight weeks. The employer's agent duly issues the variation for the new specification and as required under the contract reviews the contractor's notification, accepts that the eight weeks delay is 'likely' and awards an extension of time of eight weeks. Following this award the manufacturer contacts the contractor saying that due to the cancellation of a major order the procurement period can be vastly reduced and subsequently the actual delay that occurs is restricted to two weeks only.

In these circumstances an award six weeks longer than the delay that occurred has been made thus effectively introducing six weeks float into the programme. Should another later relevant event occur then any delaying effect may be reduced by this float as, arguably, it could be taken into account in any further award.

On a project where a series of sequential delays occur it could be argued that any discrepancies between the likely and actual effect of the delaying events will be 'balanced out' and the final overall award will generally reflect the actual entitlement due. However problems may well occur where the contractor's own culpable delay utilises any such introduced float prior to the occurrence of further relevant events. Arguments are likely to arise in respect of the ownership of this introduced element of programme float.

Although the contract may require awards of extension of time to be based on prospective _likely_ effect, most contract forms also allow the employer's agent a period, following completion of the works to review the extensions of time awarded. Therefore, there will be some retrospective consideration of the _actual_ delay attributable to the delaying events. However, in general, extension of time awards already granted can only be reduced to account for later omissions from the works.

The likely impact of a delay on completion must be estimated by reference to the contractor's forward-looking plan through to completion. There are two delay techniques that can be used to predict a future completion date – the 'as-planned impacted' and the 'time impact' analysis. Both of these methods involve impacting the delay event onto the planned programme with the 'as-planned impacted' method impacting delays onto the original planned programme and the 'time impact' analysis impacting delays on to the updated planned programme. Although the 'as planned impacted' technique can be used in this prospective manner it is mainly employed retrospectively.

The plan for the works

As discussed in chapter 5, the as-planned programme may lack certainty for a number of reasons. Also the lack of detail in planned activities means a straight comparison between the as-built and as-planned activities may not be of great benefit.

If there is insufficient information to undertake a detailed review, a comparison between the plan and what actually happened may provide no more than a useful first step to see where delays might have occurred.

The as-planned programme and the discipline of planning are about the investigation of possibilities and the management of uncertainty. In *Principles and Polices in Delay Analysis*, Keith Pickavance pointed out that for a number of reasons the planned programme is unlikely to be followed. He concludes that it represents an educated guess of what may occur in certain circumstances.

Critical path analysis

When preparing or evaluating a prospective claim for an extension of time, the only delays that are of importance are those that affect the end date. If an activity is not critical to the end date it will not matter that it is in delay. For example, a programme for a housing development may have shown that fences were to be erected in five weeks, between weeks 25 and 30 of the programme, and the houses were to be completed by week 40. In this simplistic scenario, fencing could be delayed by ten weeks and, in all probability, it would not matter, providing it was completed by week 40.

Therefore, when making a prospective claim it is the critical activities that are of interest. It is a short step from here to say that delays are identified by the critical path – and, in theory, they usually are – however, it does not follow that a critical path analysis is bound to provide a logical and realistic illustration of what will cause or what has caused delays to the completion. Furthermore, it does not follow that a contractor will only be entitled to delays that are on the critical path, as the contract completion date may be revised even if an event has no affect on the actual completion date (see the case of *Balfour Beatty Building Ltd v Chestermount Properties Ltd* in chapter 8).

Critical path analysis is a highly valuable tool but there are circumstances where it is clearly inappropriate to use. Some of the problems and limitations with critical path analysis were discussed in chapter 5.

Such warnings about the use of critical path analysis contrast sharply with the recommendations set out in the Society of Construction Law Protocol, which states that:

> '... in all but the simplest of projects, [the planned programme] should be prepared as a critical path network using commercially available critical path method project planning software.'[10]

Such a highly prescriptive statement regarding the preparation and acceptance of the planned programme is unusual and most guidance concerning the preparation of planned programmes is less dogmatic.

It is suggested that the foremost consideration when deciding what type of planning technique to use is how best the project can be successfully executed, not how best any subsequent delays might be explained. It is easy to understand the concern expressed by experienced delay analyst Phillip Allington, when he said:

> '... adopting the Protocol could shift project planning fundamentally from a broadly structured common sense activity of looking at possibilities, to one of manipulating for claims.'[11]

As well as these worries, there is some concern over the costs, which some consider unnecessary, associated with the highly prescriptive approach to planning and delay analysis adopted by the Protocol. The viable application of the guidance and recommendation of the Protocol by small subcontractors has also been questioned.[12]

6.2 Retrospective claims

Any of the five delay analysis techniques set out in chapter 5 can be employed to produce a retrospective analysis of delay. As-planned programmes have already been discussed above in the section on prospective claims so this section will focus on as-built and critical path analyses.

Detailed as-built programmes

As-built programmes or records are not only used for simple comparisons of planned and actual progress, they are also required for 'collapsed as-built' analysis, 'windows analysis' and 'time impact analysis'. The only methods that do not use as-built data are the 'planned impacted' approach and prospective use of 'time impact analysis' although even this latter technique requires actual progress data.

An as-built programme is illustrated in figure 38 (overleaf), which shows a straight comparison between the as-planned and actual timing of the perimeter brickwork (activities 1 and 2) and the internal blockwork partitions (activities 20 and 21). However, in this example someone has kept a detailed record of what happened on site, which has enabled the as-built periods to be explained in greater detail in activities 3–19 and 22–29.

In figure 38 it has been possible to plot the timing of architect's instructions and the issue of requests for information (RFIs) as activities 30–38. In other situations it may be relevant to add details such as references to meeting minutes, key correspondence, daywork sheets and other records.

The programme is further enhanced by a histogram of labour resources, noted to have been compiled from the brickwork subcontractor's allocation records. The histogram is plotted to correspond to the time period of the bar chart so that a direct correlation can be made between work activities and labour resources.

From the example at figure 38 it can be seen that the perimeter brickwork was planned to commence at week 27 and be completed during week 37. In the event the programme indicates that commencement was delayed by a period of two weeks and that completion was delayed until week 42.

Activities 3–19, representing an abstract of contemporaneous diary records, indicate likely delay due to the late delivery of special bricks required for cills, as well as time lost due to rain, plant breakdown and non-attendance of labour.

The labour histogram suggests possible insufficient resource levels for the first 2–3 weeks of brickwork, as well as showing a complete lack of bricklaying resources for a two-day period in week 36. However, some caution is recommended when using data compiled in this manner because the apparent lack of resource could be down to a missing allocation sheet for the two days in question.

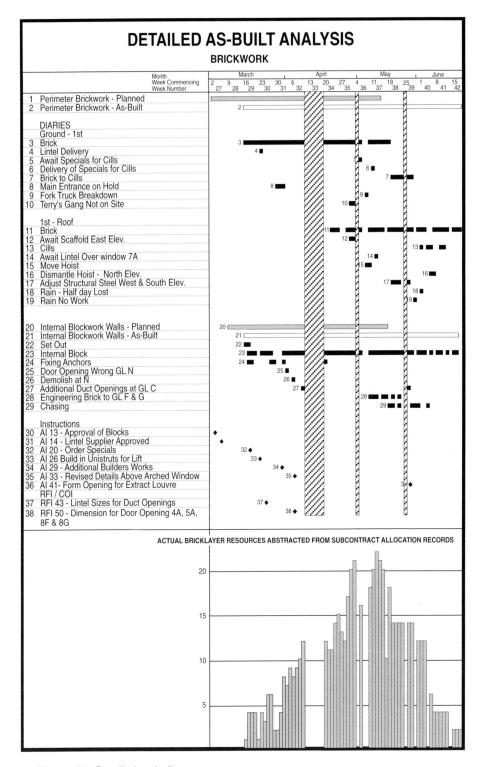

Figure 38: Detailed as-built programme

This example shows how it may be possible to build up an 'as-built' programme for specific elements of work in some detail, indicating what actually occurred on a project. Such analyses can become complex, in which case they may only be understood by the experienced eye of a specialist delay analyst. The level of detail in figure 38 is often adequate to illustrate delays and, particularly when combined with an appropriate narrative, such programmes are likely to provide very useful documents to explain and demonstrate what actually occurred on site.

Reliance on available information

The ability to apply any of the five delay analysis techniques will be dependent on the contemporaneous information available. The table below, which is partly based on one in the Society of Construction Law *Delay and Disruption Protocol*, indicates the factual evidence required to undertake each type of analysis.

Type of Analysis	Programme Information Required			
	As-planned programme without network	Networked as-planned programme	Updated as-planned networked programme	As-built records
1 As-planned v as-built	X	or X	and X	or X
2 Impacted as-planned		X		
3 Collapsed as-built				X
4 Time impact analysis		X	or X	and X
5 Windows analysis		X	or X	and X

As can be seen a networked as-planned programme is required to undertake the 'as-planned impacted', 'time impact' and 'windows' analyses. If the contemporaneous planned programme or programmes are not available in this networked format, logic can be applied retrospectively.

This introduction of logic is not ideal and it can be the subject of disagreement between opposing parties. It is often argued that such additions pre-suppose and make assumptions in respect of the contractor's original planned intent. It can also be alleged that such application is nothing more than manipulation of the planned programme in order to maximise the impact of the delays being analysed.

For the 'windows' and 'time impact' analyses the networked 'as-planned' programme should ideally be available in an updated format – that is in a format that has regularly been updated with progress throughout the course of the project. If it is not available in this format it is essential that the as-built records include such data to enable progress updates to be recreated.

The level of as-built data required for a simple 'as-planned v as-built' comparison is usually less than that required for 'windows' and 'time impact' analyses and as discussed in chapter 5, the quality and type of contemporaneous records may vary throughout the life of project. Therefore the extent and detail of the available information may dictate which delay technique is adopted.

With any analysis the accuracy of the data will obviously be of paramount importance. This is particularly important in respect of critical path analysis, which is highly deterministic and reliant on precise data – critical path analysis is incompatible for use with subjective and uncertain data.

Also the contemporaneous progress updates required by the 'windows' and 'time impact' analyses may have been adequate for project management purposes but may be deemed inadequate to provide satisfactory evidence of actual delay.[13]

6.3 Preparation costs

The 'as-planned v as-built' and the 'as-planned impacted' methodologies are relatively simple to prepare and by implication also relatively cheap. 'Windows' and 'time impact' analyses are somewhat more involved and therefore tend to be more costly to produce. This being the case the cost of undertaking any analysis should be balanced against the strength and validity of the issues being contested and the costs flowing from any extension of time awarded.

The initial costs of preparing a delay analysis, whether it is carried out by an employee or an outside consultant, are generally not recovered from the other side, even if the claim is shown to be entirely justified. The only time that costs are recoverable is if the claim has become a dispute and the dispute had been referred to either arbitration or litigation (not adjudication). Even then the work carried out must have been carried out for the purpose of the arbitration or litigation (not for the earlier negotiations) and the amount recovered is unlikely to be the full cost.

6.4 Supporting information

Most forms of construction contract entitle the employer (or more usually the employer's representatives) to request information to enable an assessment of delays to be made. These contracts are rarely prescriptive about what can and cannot be requested and so, providing they are reasonable, requests can be made for any information. So, for example, a contractor could be asked to provide records such as daily or weekly labour allocation sheets, progress reports, procurement and design status reports, plant records and weather records. Together with these there may be a request for the provision of various programmes.

Unfortunately, many requests for further information are vague in the extreme. Sometimes contractors are simply told they have to prove 'cause and effect' or provide 'further and better particulars'. This is the language of the law courts not construction sites. It is suggested that few, if any, contracts envisage a contractor having to produce a claim suitable for a high court when requesting an extension of time from an employer.

The primary information used to support most delay claims is the delay analysis plus a narrative statement. These primary documents can be enhanced by the provision of relevant supporting information. In this section consideration is given to some of the different types of supporting information that can be provided to assist in illustrating and reinforcing the results of the delay analysis.

Scattergun charts

Significant delays are often caused on construction projects by the cumulative effect of the volume and timing of identifiable repetitive events, such as architects instructions, drawing revisions and/or the late issue of information (evidenced by 'requests for information' sheets or technical queries). Such events are often identified within a claim for delay in the form of schedules, indicating the various dates of issue. Where the problem relates to drawing revisions, schedules generally exist in the form of contract drawing registers and these can be appended to the claim to provide evidence of the recurrence of the problem. These repetitive problems can be plotted on to a programme to produce a 'scattergun chart' (as shown overleaf).

A 'scattergun chart' uses 'milestones' to represent each repetitive instruction, drawing issue or information request. Each event is best shown immediately adjacent to the programme activity it is said was affected. So, for example, lots of instructions relating to brickwork would be plotted under the brickwork activity. The visual result of this process is of random and scattered events, hence the term 'scattergun charts' (or 'measles charts' to some analysts).

Figure 39 (overleaf) shows a typical example of this presentation. Milestones are plotted for each instruction, drawing or information request along side bars showing both the as-planned and as-built activities.

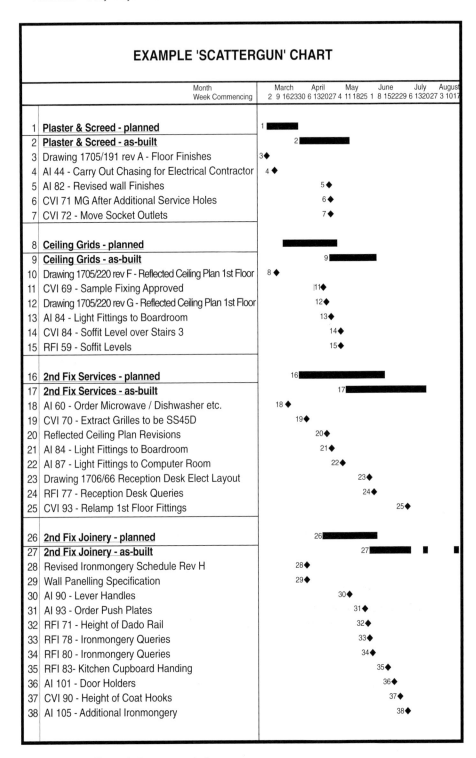

Figure 39: Example 'scattergun' chart

For the sake of clarity figure 39 shows only a limited number of programme activities and a limited number of issues but 'scattergun charts' often contain a lot more information. The purpose of these types of chart is to show the general late and piecemeal issue of information and to indicate that, due to these issues, the contractor was prevented from undertaking the various activities as planned.

This type of presentation is, however, only a graphical comparison and does not link the alleged cause (that is the late and piecemeal supply of information) with the alleged effect (the timing of the activities).

Contractors will often include all issues on a 'scattergun chart', irrespective of whether they were significant and, in many cases, duplicate some of the issues. For example, an architect's Instruction which has apparently been issued late, may be plotted on the chart. However, it may have been that the architect simply issued the instruction retrospectively in order to confirm a number of verbal instructions. Other architect's Instructions may cover the re-issue of drawings that already have been identified separately on the charts.

Therefore, 'scattergun charts' only provide relatively superficial information and will carry little weight if put forward in isolation to demonstrate that works were delayed by the repetitive events identified. Having said that, if there has been a large volume of instructions and a piecemeal release of information, it is likely that the works will have been disrupted to some extent and this may have caused some delay. Furthermore, generally, it will be possible to provide further particularisation of the effects of at least some of the delays identified on a 'scattergun chart'.

'Scattergun charts' can provide a useful and visually impressive secondary level of information but they are unlikely to produce information of primary assistance to justify the delays in most cases.

Scott Schedules

A Scott Schedule is simply a table that lists the issues and records the parties' positions against each issue. The format takes its name from the judge who first used one and although Scott Schedules are generally associated with formal construction disputes, there is no reason why parties should not use them during discussions or negotiations before a dispute has arisen.

A Scott Schedule has no prescribed layout; it will be prepared to suit the circumstances. However, most Scott Schedules will state (or summarise) the parties' views against a list of issues, so they are particularly useful if there is a long list of separate issues – as can be the case with disputes concerning matters of delay.

In a dispute relating to a delay to a construction operation a Scott Schedule may contain:

- a unique delay reference;
- description of the delaying event;
- reference to the relevant contract terms;
- reference to key documents such as instructions or key correspondence;
- quantification of the delay; and
- the effect on the completion date.

Typically a Scott Schedule would be compiled by the party making the claim and issued to the other side for their views to be incorporated. By tabulating the parties' positions on each issue it makes it easier to identify, and hopefully resolve, the differences.

Phasing plans

In certain cases the effect of the delaying events is likely to have had a fundamental impact on the overall sequencing of the works. A comparison between the original planned phasing or sequencing of the works and the way the works were actually undertaken may be difficult to communicate simply by relying on the programme activities.

Graphical illustration and 'planned v as-built' phasing diagrams, using the site layout drawings, can provide a useful and simple means to illustrate deviations to the planned sequencing of the works as a result of the delaying events.

Histograms and 'S' curves

As discussed in chapter 4, histograms and 'S' curves can be used to show and/or compare planned and as-built progress – making them a useful back-up to support the main delay analysis technique.

What is shown or compared will depend on the matters in question but elements such as valuations of the works, placing of concrete, labour resources and general overall progress are often shown on histograms or 'S' curves. These exercises and comparisons are also likely to prove useful in respect of a rebuttal to delays being claimed by the contractor and to indicate culpable delay.

As an example, histograms and 'S' curves can be compiled using the tendered material quantities and based on what the contractor would need to achieve to meet his as-planned programme. These can be compared with the contemporaneous records to indicate in general terms any deficiencies in the contractor's actual achievement.

Visualisation

'Visualisation' is a relatively new development based on computer modelling and at present the utilisation of this technique within the construction industry has been mainly restricted to bid proposals for major projects. 'Visualisation' is the production of a highly detailed computer model of the scheme, which enables the potential end user to take a virtual tour of their proposed new development.

The technique has been used in formal disputes to visually recreate the construction progress and simulate and demonstrate the impact of the delaying events. To create this form of illustration is likely to be prohibitively expensive for most projects and most disputes. Notwithstanding this, at a more simple level the use of graphical presentation packages, such as Microsoft PowerPoint, can be beneficial. Site plans and general architectural layouts and elevations can be created electronically and subsequently overlaid to illustrate how the delaying events influenced the sequencing of the works.

Similarly, histograms, 'S' curves and simple bar charts can be produced electronically and again overlaid to give a visual indication on a weekly or monthly basis of such things as general progress, concrete poured, bricks laid, valuations and the like.

Visual presentations are unlikely, in themselves, to provide sufficient demonstration to support a claim for delay. However they may be very effective in quickly communicating the basis for the claim. Providing the presentation is kept simple, and complex charts, graphs and overlays are avoided, the method may be able to justify its cost in some cases.

6.5 Which method should be used?

There is no straight answer to this question. No one method is appropriate in all cases and each method contains weaknesses.

The **as-planned v as-built** method provides a good graphical comparison of what was planned and what actually happened and such comparisons are always likely to be useful when considering delays. This method combined with a narrative explanation may be suitable for relatively straightforward claims. However, it is unlikely to be enough to persuade a sceptical employer about the merits of a more complex claim without further supporting evidence and analysis.

As-planned impacted methodologies suffer from the drawback that they ignore what actually occurred and the results obtained are entirely theoretical. Use of the technique can be easily dismissed as being inappropriate and unrealistic, particularly if comparison with as-built data shows that the theoretical results and timings are significantly different to what was actually occurring on site. Having said that, all methods are at least partially subjective and so this failing must be kept in perspective.

Some delay claims need no analysis and in this case a review of the planned intent may be sufficient. For example, if a contractor is carrying out the fit-out of two floors of offices and is given a variation to carry out two more floors, on completion of the first two, it would appear logical to simply double the overall contract duration without reference to the as-built progress. This is an unusual and very simple illustration, but it shows that there can be a basic fairness in adjusting the amount of time using the original plan as the benchmark. If it is appropriate in this scenario it may also be appropriate to use the 'as planned impacted' method in other situations too.

The very fact that the 'as-planned impacted' technique is theoretical and does not consider what actually occurred may, of course, be the very reason to use it. The absence of scrutiny over what actually happened on site would benefit a contractor wishing to secure a maximum award of extension of time whilst avoiding the need to highlight his own culpable delay and general inefficiencies.

The **collapsed as-built** technique relies on the application of as-built logic, which will require, to some extent, an element of subjective assessment by the programmer. As-built activity sequencing and resource allocations may or may not be due to the effects of delay – actions may have been taken to mitigate delay. Therefore, apparently logical conclusions about the as-built sequence may be off-the-mark, in which case the results of the delay analysis will be unreliable.

Both the **windows** and **time impact** analyses look at the delaying events on a simulated real-time basis, looking at the progress and project status at the time of the delaying event. These delaying events can be reviewed in detail and encourage a methodical approach. Of all of the techniques they are most likely to provide reasonable results but they come at a relatively high financial cost and are dependant on a level of record keeping not found on the majority of construction projects.

The conclusion might be that, as all the methods contain weaknesses, none of them should be used to prepare a claim. Certainly, all of the methodologies will, to some extent, involve a degree of subjectivity and the way different delay analysts use the methods will vary.

One of the main disadvantages in relying entirely on one all encompassing critical path-based methodology, particularly the 'as-planned impacted' or the 'collapsed as-built' methods, is their vulnerability to attack. For example, if it can be demonstrated that the planned programme was unrealistic or that any retrospectively added logic is flawed, then all of the results of an 'as-planned impacted' technique will be inaccurate and effectively the whole analysis can be discounted. Similarly, if it can be demonstrated that some of the as-built data employed is inaccurate (even if these inaccuracies are fairly minor) it can be alleged that all of the results of a 'collapsed as-built' analysis are flawed and again must be discounted.

With both the 'as-planned impacted' and the 'collapsed as-built' methodologies the demonstration of the delays is dependent upon the relationship between each activity and one commentator suggests that if causation of the first event fails 'the CPA becomes as stable as a house of cards. This is because proof of the later delays depends upon establishing the delays that occurred beforehand.'[14]

There is also a risk that delay analysis results may not be transparent, particularly if a critical path analysis is used, meaning there is a risk that analysis will have been manipulated to provide the answers required. But it would be wrong to make a wholesale dismissal of all the techniques as the main methodologies are well recognised, accepted, to some extent, and they represent the 'only shows in town'.

If you do not use any of these methods, how will you sort through the complex set of facts to see what may have been causing the delay to a project? Each approach has its merits and most of the weaknesses arise not due to flaws in the methodology, but due to the unique difficulties caused by the construction process.

The choice of methodology may be dependent on the contract requirements. It may be a requirement to look at the delaying events and estimate the likely effect and in these cases a methodology suitable for prospective delay analysis will be most suitable – such as the 'as-planned impacted' or a simple form of 'time impact analyses'. Conversely, the contract terms may require entitlement to be based on actual delay and therefore 'as-planned v as-built' and the more detailed and forensic application of 'time impact analysis' may be appropriate.

The final choice of methodology will be determined by many factors, including the information available, contract conditions and the size of claim.

6.6 Assessing the claim and awarding an extension of time

Claims prior to formal proceedings

It would seem reasonable to suggest that the employer's representative has a duty to be aware of the progress of the works and of any ongoing delay, irrespective of any information provided by the contractor. As such it would appear fair to assume that the effect of delaying events referred to in a contractor's claim should be reasonably apparent to the employer's representative.

This being the case, the detail and extent of any analysis required to substantiate the delay being claimed should not have to be extensive and highly detailed. However, all too often, upon receipt of a claim for an extension of time, many employers' representatives behave like strangers to the project and appear incapable or unwilling to use their experience to draw logical conclusions from known facts.

The problems faced by main contractors can also confront subcontractors. In practice a reasonable main contractor will frequently understand why a subcontractor is claiming an extension of time and will not need to see delay analyses and read narratives to know whether the claim is broadly justified, but it does not necessarily follow that subcontractors are given extensions of time without being asked to provide a comprehensive analysis supported by full records and particulars. Given that most subcontractors are small businesses this can, in practice, place an insurmountable obstacle in the way.

Having looked at the situation from the point of view of the contractors, it has to be acknowledged that 'a contractor is probably in a better position than an architect to know the real effect of causes of delay'[15].

Furthermore, it is probably fair to say that some claims submitted by contractors are speculative and seek to disguise their own difficulties and poor performance. In such circumstances it is hardly surprising that more details are requested or that agreement cannot ultimately be reached. It also has to be recognised that most construction delays are based on a complex interaction of events, which cannot be easily assessed. To add to this problem there is often a great deal at stake in terms of monetary damages and professional pride.

If a claim has to be prepared for a formal dispute environment, such as arbitration or litigation, the detail will have to be improved, as the contractor making a claim will have to prove the case to a third-party on the balance of probabilities.

Some contractors might hope that it would be enough to simply bring a complaint to the attention of an arbitrator or judge, who would then serve justice. However, an arbitrator or judge can only decide a dispute by weighing the evidence presented. If the evidence is weak or incomplete the contractor will not be able to prove, on a balance of probabilities, that an entitlement exists.

A delay claim must be supported by robust analysis and, above all, produce a conclusion that does not fly in the face of logic and common sense.

What approach should be adopted?

Most of the standard forms are silent about how the employer's representative should go about determining an extension of time. The JCT forms simply provide that the determination shall be a matter for the architect's opinion.

However, there is usually either an express or implied contractual duty to make a decision that is fair and reasonable. In *Sutcliffe v Thackrah*[16] Lord Reid said:

> 'The building owner and the contractor make their contract on the understanding that in all such matters the architect will act in a fair and unbiased manner and it must therefore be implicit in the owner's contract with the architect that he shall not only exercise due care and skill but also reach such decisions fairly holding the balance between his client and the contractor.'

Further guidance on the approach to be adopted when assessing a delay claim was given in the case of *John Barker Construction Ltd v London Portman Hotel Ltd*[17], where it was said:

> 'In order to make an assessment of whether a particular occurrence has affected the ultimate completion of the work, rather than just a particular operation, it is desirable to consider what operations, at the time the event with which one is concerned happens, are critical to the forward progress of the work as a whole.
>
> On the evidence of [the parties' programming experts] the establishment of the critical path of a particular project can itself be a difficult task if one does not know how the contractor planned the job. Not only that, but the critical path may well change during the course of the works, and almost certainly will do if the progress of the works is affected by some unforeseen event.

[The claimant's expert] frankly accepted that the various different methods of making an assessment of the impact of unforeseen occurrences upon the progress of construction works are likely to produce different results, perhaps dramatically different results. He also accepted that the accuracy of any of the methods in common use critically depends upon the quality of the information upon which the assessment exercise was based.

All of this does, of course, emphasise the vital point that the duty of a professional man, generally stated, is not to be right, but to be careful ... His conduct has to be judged having regard to the information available to him, or which ought to have been available to him, at the time he gave his advice or made his decision or did whatever else it is that he did.'

When it comes to determining an extension of time for late or inaccurate information an architect will be faced with something of a dilemma. In respect of this it has been said that the architect is in an unusual position of being, to some extent, judge in his or her cause[18]. In awarding an extension of time for such events the architect may well be admitting and accepting responsibility for delay to the works.

For this reason contractors probably think claims for extension of time will be viewed more favourably by the architect if the causes of delay relate to such issues as employer generated variations or neutral events such as adverse weather conditions and even the default of other consultants – almost any reason other than those that point the finger at the architect, such as late information release. Such thoughts could encourage a contractor to make a claim that is based more on perceived commercial commonsense than accurate analysis of the events.

The main contractor may find himself in a similar position in relation to claims by subcontractors. A main contractor may be reluctant to award an extension of time to a subcontractor unless an award has been received in relation to the same matter under the main contract or where the main contractor is relatively confident that the subcontractor's claim can be subsequently passed on under the main contract.

Unless the subcontract makes specific allowance for the situation, there is usually no 'back-to-back' arrangement with the main contract in respect of extension of time. The main contractor should therefore view any delay claim from a subcontractor on its own merit, irrespective of any awards made under the main contract.

Concurrent delays

The issue of concurrent delay is a much discussed topic but it remains one of the most difficult areas of construction delay analysis. It is not even certain what 'concurrent delay' means – 'the expression concurrent delay is understood differently in different quarters and definitions are scarce.'[19]

It is suggested that most parties think of concurrent delays as events occurring at the same time, either of which, had they occurred in isolation would have caused a particular delay to the project. The difficulty arises when liability under the contract for the concurrent delays is shared. For example, a contractor is likely to be responsible for delays due to shortages of materials but the employer is usually responsible for delays due to late variations. But, how do you resolve the extension of time claim if these competing delays occur at the same time?

Arguably the case of *Henry Boot Construction (UK) Ltd. v Malmaison Hotel (Manchester) Ltd (1999)*[20] (discussed in chapter 8) provides the answer. In the judgment the judge referred to an agreement made between the parties, who accepted that:

> '… if there are two concurrent causes of delay, one of which is a relevant event, and the other is not, then the contractor is entitled to an extension of time for the period of delay caused by the relevant event notwithstanding the concurrent effect of the other event. Thus, to take a simple example, if no work is possible on a site for a week not only because of exceptionally inclement weather (a relevant event), but also because the contractor has a shortage of labour (not a relevant event), and if the failure to work during the week is likely to delay the works beyond the completion date by one week, then if he considers it fair and reasonable to do so, the architect is required to grant an extension of time of one week. He cannot refuse to do so on the grounds that the delay would have occurred in any event by reason of the shortage of labour.'

Further support for this approach can be found in the Society of Construction Law *Delay and Disruption Protocol*. One of the 'core principles' in the Protocol is that concurrent delay should not reduce any extension of time due. However, the Protocol goes on to qualify the contractor's entitlement. In 'core principle' number 10 it is said:

> 'If the Contractor incurs additional cost that are caused both by Employer Delay and concurrent Contractor Delay, then the Contractor should only recover compensation to the extent it

is able to separately identify the additional cost caused by the Employer … If it would have incurred the additional costs in any event as a result of Contractor Delays, the Contractor will not be entitled to recover those additional costs.'

This approach has become widely adopted and relied on by contractors when making claims for extension of time. Although it represents what can be considered as a fair and reasonable approach, there is a view held by some that it is relied on far too heavily and provides contractors with a 'get-out' clause.

As an example, during the project the design team may have progressively released construction information and introduced minor variations. At the time the contractor did not claim that these issues caused delay, although certain information may have been late in respect of the requirements of the original planned programme.

Retrospectively the contractor may claim that the release of construction information and variations caused delay, so by adopting the *Malmaison* concurrency approach an entitlement to extension of time is valid, as culpable delay should be discounted. Conversely the design team will equally argue that the release of information caused no actual delay and was issued in accordance with the progress of the works at the time.

Whether the *Malmaison* approach would be valid in the above type of scenario is a potential source of argument and as every situation is likely to be different it is difficult to advise of the likely outcome. It must, however be emphasised that *Malmaison* is not the only approach to the difficult subject of concurrent or alleged concurrent delays.

The 'dominant cause' approach considers which of the competing delaying events is the most dominant or predominant. In the above scenario it may could be argued that the dominant cause of delay was caused by the contractor due to a considerable amount of rectification work resulting from poor workmanship and quality control. In this situation the late release of information may be considered to be insignificant and, as claimed by the design team, it may have been released in accordance with the actual progress of the works. As such, it is hard to see how the contractor would have an entitlement to an extension of time.

Perhaps the most equitable approach would be to apportion liability between the parties when concurrent delays occur. However, what ever approach is taken, concurrency in construction delay claims is likely to remain an intractable problem and will often be a cause for disagreement between the parties.

Summary

Any of the delay analysis techniques discussed in chapter 5 can be used when preparing a delay claim, but some methods of delay analysis are best used prospectively and others retrospectively.

Prospective techniques are used to help with the requirement for contractors to notify employers of any delays and to estimate the effect to the completion date. The 'as-planned impacted' and 'time impact' analyses can be used for this although, as discussed, the 'as-planned impacted' technique is mainly used retrospectively.

When preparing or evaluating a prospective claim for an extension of time, in general, the only delays that are of importance are those that affect the end date (activities that are not critical to the end date do not cause delays to completion).

The five analysis methodologies mentioned are all able to show retrospective analysis of delay, but they rely on available contemporaneous information to be effective.

The primary information used to support most claims is in the form of a delay analysis plus a narrative statement, but it may be that in assessing a delay an employer will request further information from the contractor. It can sometimes be helpful to include supporting documents, such as:

- scattergun charts;
- Scott Schedules; or
- visualisation with computer modelling.

No single method of analysis is appropriate in all cases and each method contains weaknesses meaning that the final choice of methodology will be determined by many factors.

Most construction delays are based on a complex interaction of events so evaluating them can be tricky. Any delay claim must be supported by robust analysis and, above all, produce a conclusion that does not fly in the face of logic.

7

Standard forms of contract

Most construction projects in the UK are carried out under a standard form of contract (or subcontract) and all of the standard forms provide clauses for dealing with delays to the project. The techniques for preparing or assessing delay claims described in chapters 5 and 6 are not contract specific and have general application, but each form of contract has its own particular procedures and allocations of risk when it comes to time issues.

There has been an exponential growth in the number of standard forms of contract available for use in the construction industry in the past twenty years. The Joint Contracts Tribunal (JCT) alone now produces over fifty standard forms of building contract, including various main contracts, an intermediate form, a major project form, a minor works form and various subcontract forms. This book cannot come close to considering all the delay clauses in all the different forms of contract and so this chapter focuses on the terms of the most popular standard forms.

The Quantity Surveying and Construction Faculty of RICS produces a biennial survey of 'Contracts in Use'. These surveys indicate that JCT standard forms have been and remain, by a significant margin, the most widely used standard forms of contract for building works in the UK. The standard forms produced by the NEC (which originally stood for New Engineering Contract) are far less popular but, after a slow start, these forms are becoming increasingly used, particularly by the public sector, on building as well as engineering contracts. The standard government form of construction contract is GC/Works 1, produced by the Property Advisors to the Civil Estate and many civil engineering contracts are still carried out under the ICE standard form. In this chapter the delay provisions in the main contract versions of these standard forms are reviewed.

The list of possible delay events in standard forms covers the vast majority of conceivable delays and a few more besides (other than those that are the direct responsibility of the contractor, such as low labour productivity, poor organisation, late ordering or delivery of materials and the like). It is important to have a comprehensive list because, if an event were to occur which was not covered by the contract and which was not a contractor's risk event, then time would become 'at large'.

Time At Large

If the contract does not provide for adjustment of the completion date, or if an event occurs that is not listed in the extension of time provisions of the contract, delays caused by the employer render time 'at large'. In such circumstances a contractor would still be under an implied common law duty to complete within a reasonable period of time, but all previous certainty about the completion date and the amount of damages would be lost.

If time is 'at large' and the employer considers the works were not completed within a reasonable period of time he would have to prove as much. It is not easy to prove delays and the employer's difficulties would not end there because even if it could be established that the contractor was late completing the works, the employer would then have to prove the damages incurred, unless it was held that the liquidated damages clause remained operative even though time was 'at large'. Preparing a claim for and proving the amount of damages suffered due to late completion also presents problems.

7.1 JCT 98

The widely used JCT Standard Form of Building Contract 1998 Edition (which alone is printed in six different forms – Private With Quantities, Private Without Quantities, Private With Approximate Quantities, Local Authority With Quantities, Local Authority Without Quantities and Local Authority With Approximate Quantities) deals with extensions of time at clause 25.

In the 'Local Authorities' forms the term 'Architect/Contract Administrator' is used in lieu of the term 'Architect' but otherwise clause 25 in all six forms is very similar. The quotations in this section are taken from an unamended 'Private With Quantities' form and are reproduced with permission of the Joint Contracts Tribunal and Sweet & Maxwell. © The Joint Contracts Tribunal Limited 1998. Publisher: Sweet & Maxwell.

Relevant Events

The reasons why an extension of time may be given under the JCT 98 form of contract are known as 'Relevant Events'. They are listed under clause 25.4:

25.4 The following are the Relevant Events referred to in clause 25:

25.4 .1 force majeure;

25.4 .2 exceptionally adverse weather conditions;

25.4 .3 loss or damage occasioned by any one or more of the Specified Perils;

25.4 .4 civil commotion, local combination of workmen, strike or lock-out affecting any of the trades employed upon the Works or any of the trades engaged in the preparation, manufacture or transportation of any of the goods or materials required for the Works;

25.4 .5 compliance with the Architect's instructions

25.4 .5 .1 under clauses 2.3, 2.4.1,14.2,14.3 (except compliance with an Architect's instruction for the expenditure of a provisional sum for defined work or of a provisional sum for Performance Specified Work), 23.2, 34, 35 or 36; or

25.4 .5 .2 in regard to the opening up for inspection of any work covered up or the testing of any of the work, materials or goods in accordance with clause 8.3 (including making good in consequence of such opening up or testing) unless the inspection or test showed that the work, materials or goods were not in accordance with this Contract;

25.4 .6 .1 where an Information Release Schedule has been provided, failure of the Architect to comply with clause 5.4.1;

25.4 .6 .2 failure of the Architect to comply with clause 5.4.2;

25.4 .7 delay on the part of Nominated Sub-Contractors or Nominated Suppliers which the Contractor has taken all practicable steps to avoid or reduce;

25.4 .8 .1 the execution of work not forming part of this Contract by the Employer himself or by persons employed or otherwise engaged by the Employ as referred to in clause 29 or the failure to execute such work;

25.4 .8 .2 the supply by the Employer of materials and goods which the Employer has agreed to provide for the Works or the failure so to supply;

25.4 .9 the exercise after the Base Date by the United Kingdom Government of any statutory power which directly affects the execution of the Works by restricting the availability or use of labour which is essential to the proper carrying out of the Works or preventing the Contractor from, or delaying the Contractor in, securing such goods or materials or such fuel or energy as are essential to the proper carrying out of the Works;

25.4 .10 .1 the Contractor's inability for reasons beyond his control and which he could not reasonably have foreseen at the Base Date to secure such labour as is essential to the proper carrying out of the Works; or

25.4 .10 .2 the Contractor's inability for reasons beyond his control and which he could not reasonably have foreseen at the Base Date to secure such goods or materials as are essential to the proper carrying out of the Works;

25.4 .11 the carrying out by a local authority or statutory undertaker of work in pursuance of its statutory obligations in relation to the Works or the failure to carry out such work;

25.4 .12 failure of the Employer to give in due time ingress to or egress from the site of the Works or any part thereof through or over any land, buildings, way or passage adjoining or connected with the site and in the possession and control of the Employer, in accordance with the Contract Bills and/or the Contract Drawings, after receipt by the Architect of such notice, if any, as the Contractor is required to give, or failure of the Employer to give such ingress or egress as otherwise agreed between the Architect and the Contractor;

25.4 .13 where clause 23.1.2 is stated in the Appendix to apply, the deferment by the Employer of giving possession of the site under clause 23.1.2;

25.4 .14 by reason of the execution of work for which an Approximate Quantity is included in the Contract Bills which is not a reasonably accurate forecast of the quantity of work required;

25.4 .15 delay which the Contractor has taken all practicable steps to avoid or reduce consequent upon a change in the Statutory Requirements after the Base Date which necessitates some alteration or modification to any Performance Specified Work;

25.4 .16 the use or threat of terrorism and/or the activity of the relevant authorities in dealing with such use or threat;

25.4 .17 compliance or non-compliance by the Employer with clause 6A.1;

25.4 .18 delay arising from a suspension by the Contractor of the performance of his obligations under this Contract to the Employer pursuant to clause 30.1.4.

The 'Specified Perils' referred to in clause 25.4.3 are defined in clause 1.3 of the contract as:

> '… fire, lightening, explosion, storm, tempest, flood, bursting or overflowing water tanks, apparatus or pipes, earthquake, aircraft and other aerial devices or articles dropped therefrom, riot and civil commotion but excluding Excepted Risks.'

The 'Excepted Risks' in this definition are not matters that trouble most construction projects (and are even less likely to do so now that Concorde has been decommissioned) but, for what it is worth, they are also defined in clause 1.3 as:

> 'ionising radiations or contamination by radioactivity from any nuclear fuel or from any nuclear waste from the combustion of nuclear fuel, radioactive toxic explosion or other hazardous properties of any explosive nuclear assembly or nuclear component thereof, pressure waves caused by aircraft or other aerial devices travelling at sonic or supersonic speeds'.

Duties

When dealing with time issues under clause 25 of JCT 98, both the contractor and the architect have to comply with certain duties. These duties are set out in clauses 25.2 and 25.3.

Clause 25.2 sets out the contractor's duty to give a notice of delay to progress. It commences with the following sub-clause:

25.2 .1 .1 If and whenever it becomes reasonable apparent that the delay progress of the Works is being or is likely to be delayed the Contractor shall forthwith give written notice to the Architect of the material circumstances including the cause or causes of the delay and identify in such notice any event which in his opinion is a Relevant Event.

The wording of this clause suggests that all delays must be reported by the contractor, including those caused entirely by the contractor. However, contractors rarely, if ever, notify the employer or his agents of delays caused by their own failings. Generally, notices provided by contractors relate to delays caused by matters that, in their opinion, are 'Relevant Events', which would entitle them to an extension of time.

The next clause in this part of the contract, clause 25.2.1.2, refers to delays involving nominated subcontractors. Given the scarcity of nominations in modern construction agreements no comments are given here about this clause.

Clauses 25.2.2 and 25.2.3 of the contract require that notices given under clause 25.2.1.1 provide certain information:

25.2 .2   In respect of each and every Relevant Event identified in the notice given in accordance with clause 25.2.1.1 the Contractor shall, if practicable in such notice, or otherwise in writing as soon as possible after such notice:

25.2 .2   .1 give particulars of the expected effects thereof; and

25.2 .2   .2 estimate the extent, if any, of the expected delay in the completion of the Works beyond the Completion Date resulting therefrom whether or not concurrently with delay resulting from any other Relevant Event

and shall give such particulars and estimate to any Nominated Sub-Contractor to whom a copy of any written notice has been given under clause 25.2.1.2.

25.2 .3   The Contractor shall give such further written notices to the Architect ..., as may be reasonably necessary or as the Architect may reasonably require for keeping up-to-date the particulars and estimate referred to in clauses 25.2.2.1 ... including any material change in such particulars or estimate.

In practice contractors do not always comply strictly with these clauses probably because they prioritise their efforts to getting the building construction work completed rather than reading the contract and complying with procedural duties. Therefore, they sometimes fail to send the required written notices and particulars.

Sometimes contractors may feel that a formal written notice will appear to be too confrontational and may upset delicate business relationships. In these cases a contractor might simply speak to the architect about the situation.

A contractor may also think that a formal notice pursuant to this clause is not required in practice if the extent and reasons for delays are well known and probably adequately recorded in site meeting minutes. In such circumstances a contractor might see little point in composing a letter simply to notify the architect of what he or she has already been made aware of and probably discussed.

It may be easy to see why, in practice, notices required by the contract are not always given by contractors but it should be borne in mind that if parties fall out they, or their lawyers, will take a close look at the contract terms and it is not uncommon in formal dispute resolution proceedings for complaints to be made that the contractor failed to comply with the delay notification requirements. It may be that genuine extension of time claims are rarely rejected due to a failure to provide a written notice but it is probably also true that, when involved in a dispute, contractors wish they had given all the notices required by the contract.

When disputes over delay occur, parties often have different views about the extent of the information that should be provided by the contractor. Many architects appear to consider that the contractor's various duties under clause 25.2 (especially the requirement to give particulars of the effect of the delay) entitle them to receive a fully documented claim, with a detailed cause and effect narrative, analysis and evidence – such as would be sufficient to persuade a High Court judge of the merits of the claim. The contract does not state that this level of detail is required. As can be seen, the clause 25.2 simply requires the contractor to:

- give notice of delay to progress straightaway ('forthwith');
- state the cause of the delay and whether the cause is a 'Relevant Event';
- give particulars of the expected effects of the delay, either in the original notice or as soon as possible;
- give an estimate of the extent of any expected impact on the 'Completion Date'; and
- send further updates of the particulars and the estimated impact, as and when reasonably necessary or required.

Under clause 25.2.3 an architect has a right to make a request to the contractor for details that are reasonably necessary or reasonably required to make a decision about the reasons for and extent of delays. Such requests are the norm rather than the exception but an architect should use his or her contract specific knowledge and general construction expertise when considering claims for delay.

As explained in this book, delay analysis is fraught with difficulties and when an issue is unclear or uncertain the natural reflex is to ask for more information. However, many architects make clause 25.2.3 requests that are vague and non-specific. Despite this, contractors often respond by producing large and detailed documents, only to find the architect still has difficulties with the claim. In reality, too much detail can be as difficult for an architect to deal with as too little.

It is suggested that both parties should clarify specifically what information is to be provided when a request is made under clause 25.2.3. Constructive discussions at an early stage between contractors and architects about the key facts and appropriate delay methodology ought to help avoid a protracted dispute. Architects ought to have a clear idea how they propose to assess the delay claim and should be able to articulate specifically what they require from the contractor. The provision of clear requests for information should save a great deal of time, cost and effort in the production and review of claim documents.

Once the notices and information required under clause 25.2 have been provided the architect must decide what, if any, alteration should be made to the 'Completion Date'. The specific duties placed on the architect relating to delay claims are set out in clause 25.3:

25.3 .1 If, in the opinion of the Architect, upon receipt of any notice, particulars and estimate under clauses 25.2.1.1, 25.2.2 and 25.2.3,

   .1 .1 any of the events which are stated by the Contractor to be the cause of the delay is a Relevant Event and

   .1 .2 the completion of the Works is likely to be delayed thereby beyond the Completion Date

the Architect shall in writing to the Contractor give an extension of time by fixing such later date as the Completion Date as he then estimates to be fair and reasonable. The Architect shall, in fixing such new Completion Date, state:

   .1 .3 which of the Relevant Events he has taken into account and

   .1 .4 the extent, if any, to which he has had regard to any instructions issued under clause 13.2 which require as a Variation the omission of any work or obligation and/or under clause 13.3 in regard to the expenditure of a provisional sum for defined work or for Performance Specified Work which results in the omission of any such work,

and shall, if reasonably practicable having regard to the sufficiency of the aforesaid notice, particulars and estimate, fix such new Completion Date not later than 12 weeks from receipt of the notice and of reasonably sufficient particulars and estimate, or, where the period between receipt thereof and the Completion Date is less than 12 weeks, not later than the Completion Date.

If, in the opinion of the Architect, upon receipt of any such notice, particulars and estimate, it is not fair and reasonable to fix a later date as a new Completion Date, the Architect shall if reasonably practicable having regard to the sufficiency of the aforesaid notice, particulars and estimate, so notify the Contractor in writing not later than 12 weeks from receipt of the notice, particulars and estimate, or, where the period between receipt thereof and the Completion Date is less than 12 weeks, not later than the Completion Date.

25.3 .2 After the first exercise by the Architect of his duty under clause 25.3.1 or after any revision to the Completion Date stated by the Architect in a confirmed acceptance of a 13A Quotation in respect of a Variation the Architect may in writing fix a Completion Date earlier than that previously fixed under clause 25 or than that stated by the Architect in a confirmed acceptance of a 13A Quotation if in his opinion the fixing of such earlier Completion Date is fair and reasonable having regard to any instructions issued after the last occasion on which the Architect fixed a new Completion Date

- under clause 13.2 which require or sanction as a Variation the omission of any work or obligation; and/or

- under clause 13.3 in regard to the expenditure of a provisional sum for defined work or for Performance Specified Work which result in the omission of any such work.

Provided that no decision under clause 25.3.2 shall alter the length of nay adjustment to the time required by the Contractor for the completion of the Works in respect of a Variation for which a 13A Quotation has been given and which has been stated in a confirmed acceptance of a 13A Quotation or in respect of a Variation or work for which an adjustment to the time for completion of the Works has been accepted pursuant to clause 13.4.1.2 paragraph A7.

25.3 .3 After the Completion Date, if this occurs before the date of Practical Completion, the Architect may, and not later than the expiry of 12 weeks after the date of Practical Completion shall, in writing to the Contractor either

.3 .1 fix a Completion Date later than that previously fixed if in his opinion the fixing of such later Completion Date is fair and reasonable having regard to any of the Relevant Events, whether upon reviewing a previous decision or otherwise and whether or not the Relevant Event has been specifically notified by the Contractor under clause 25.2.1.1; or

.3 .2 fix a Completion Date earlier than that previously fixed under clause 25 or stated in a confirmed acceptance of a 13A Quotation if in his opinion the fixing of such earlier Completion Date is fair and reasonable having regard to any instructions issued after the last occasion on which the Architect fixed a new Completion Date

- under clause 13.2 which require or sanction as a Variation the omission of any work or obligation; and/or

- under clause 13.3 in regard to the expenditure of a provisional sum for defined work or for Performance Specified Work which result in the omission of any such work; or

.3   .3 confirm to the Contractor the Completion Date previously fixed or stated in a confirmed acceptance of a 13A Quotation.

...

25.3 .6   No decision of the Architect under clause 25.3 shall fix a Completion Date earlier than the Date for Completion stated in the Appendix.

Therefore, by virtue of clauses 25.3.1.1 and .2 the architect has to give the contractor an extension of time, in writing, if any of the events in the contractor's notice of delay are 'Relevant Events' and if the delay is likely to impact on the 'Completion Date'.

Under these clauses the extension of time awarded has to be 'fair and reasonable' – the contract does expressly state that it has to be the result of detailed analysis and there is no requirement for the architect to justify or explain the decision in a reasoned statement. The only requirement for the award is that it should state which relevant events and contract omissions have been taken into account (clauses 25.3.1.3 and .4).

However, an architect was criticised in the case of *John Barker Construction Ltd v London Portman Hotel Ltd*[21] for not carrying out a logical and methodical analysis of a delay claim and for making an 'impressionistic', rather than a calculated, assessment of the extension of time due. This case related to a contract carried out under the JCT 80 standard form but would appear to be of general application to JCT standard forms.

Clause 25.3.1 sets a time limit on the architect to either issue the extension of time or to declare that no alteration will be made to the existing completion date. The time limit is 12 weeks, commencing from either the contractor's notice or from the existing completion date, whichever comes first. The architect can review the time awarded to a contractor retrospectively in the 12 weeks following 'Practical Completion' and, in any event, the architect has a duty to either confirm or adjust the 'Completion Date' within this period (clause 25.3.3). However, an earlier 'Completion Date' than one previously given pursuant to clause 25.3.1 can only be fixed if there are omissions from the contract (clause 25.3.2), otherwise an architect cannot reduce an extension of time once given and cannot set an earlier date than the one originally stated in the contract (clause 25.3.6).

Once an architect makes a decision about whether to award an extension of time during the contract there would appear to be nothing to stop him or her having second thoughts and increasing the period allowed. Indeed, with the restrictions on reducing the time awarded, architects may deliberately or subconsciously err on the side of caution when initially awarding time.

However, despite the difficulties faced by an architect when assessing the future delay to completion of a project, an architect should remember that he or she is under a duty to award a fair and reasonable extension. Failure to do so could lead to successful and expensive claims against the employer who may well look to the architect for recompense.

Mitigation
The contractor's right to an extension of time is subject to complying with certain duties set out in subclauses 25.3.4.1 and .2:

25.3 .4 .1 the Contractor shall use constantly his best endeavours to prevent delay in the progress of the Works, howsoever caused, and to prevent the completion of the Works being delayed or further delayed beyond the Completion Date;

.4 .2 the Contractor shall do all that may reasonably be required to the satisfaction of the Architect to proceed with the Works.

Terms such as 'use constantly his best endeavours' and 'do all that may reasonably be required' are open to interpretation. Some architects take a wide view of what these terms mean but perhaps the better view is that a contractor is only obliged to make such alterations as he can to mitigate delays without incurring additional cost. If a change to the sequence of a programme to resolve a problem can be made, and such change causes no particular difficulty or expense, then perhaps it ought to be undertaken by the contractor.

However, it would appear that there is no duty imposed on the contractor to accelerate the speed of the works to get around delays attributable to a relevant event, for example by increasing resources or working overtime. Therefore, any agreement to accelerate the works would have to be made as a separate contractual arrangement.

7.2 JCT 2005

In 2005 the JCT brought out a new suite of contracts. The Standard Building Contract replaced JCT 98 and like its predecessor, the 2005 form was published in three main versions, namely 'Standard

Building Contract With Quantities', 'Standard Building Contract With Approximate Quantities' and 'Standard Building Contract Without Quantities'. However, unlike JCT 98, the 2005 forms were not split into private and local authority editions.

The clauses in each 2005 version relating to delays are similar (but not identical) to the 1998 versions. The quotations below are from the 'Standard Building Contract Without Quantities (SBC/XQ)' and are reproduced with permission of the Joint Contracts Tribunal and Sweet & Maxwell. © The Joint Contracts Tribunal Limited 2005. Publisher: Sweet & Maxwell.

Relevant events

Under the 2005 form the adjustment of the completion date is dealt with under clauses 2.26 to 2.29. The reasons for the completion date being adjusted are given as relevant events, under clause 2.29, as set out below:

Relevant Events

2.29 The following are the Relevant Events referred to in clauses 2.27 and 2.28:

   .1   Variations and any other matters or instructions which under these Conditions are to be treated as, or as requiring, a Variation;

   .2   instructions of the Architect/Contract Administrator:

      .1 under any of clauses 2.15, 3.15, 3.16, 3.23 or 5.3.2; or

      .2 for the opening up for inspection or testing of any work, materials or goods under clause 3.17 or 3.18.4 (including making good), unless the inspection or test shows that the work, materials or goods are not in accordance with this Contract;

   .3   deferment of the giving of possession of the site or any Section under clause 2.5;

   .4   suspension by the Contractor under clause 4.14 of the performance of his obligations under this Contract;

   .5   any impediment, prevention or default, whether by act or omission, by the Employer, the Architect/Contract Administrator, the Quantity Surveyor or any of the Employer's Persons, except to the extent caused or contributed to by any default, whether by act or omission, of the Contractor or of any of the Contractor's Persons;

   .6   the carrying out by a Statutory Undertaker of work in pursuance of its statutory obligations in relation to the Works, or the failure to carry out such work;

   .7   exceptionally adverse weather conditions;

   .8   loss or damage occasioned by any of the Specified Perils;

.9 civil commotion or the use or threat of terrorism and/or the activities of the relevant authorities in dealing with such event or threat;

.10 strike, lock-out or local combination of workmen affecting any of the trades employed upon the Works or any of the trades engaged in the preparation, manufacture or transportation of any of the goods or materials required for the Works or any persons engaged in the preparation of the design for the Contractor's Designed Portion;

.11 the exercise after the Base Date by the United Kingdom Government of any statutory power which directly affects the execution of the Works;

.12 force majeure.

The list in clause 2.29 is in a different order to the list in clause 25.4 of JCT 98 and there are fewer numbered subclauses, but this is largely because some of the events listed individually in JCT 98 are grouped together in the 2005 form. The list of relevant events remains comprehensive and is likely to cover all employer-risk events that are likely to occur.

Duties

As with JCT 98, the 2005 form imposes certain duties on the contractor and architect. The contractor has to give notice of delay to progress under clause 2.27, which states:

Notice by Contractor of delay to progress

2.27 .1 If and whenever it becomes reasonably apparent that the progress of the Works or any Section is being or is likely to be delayed the Contractor shall forthwith give written notice to the Architect/Contract Administrator of the material circumstances, including the cause or causes of the delay, and shall identify in the notice any event which in his opinion is a Relevant Event.

.2 In respect of each event identified in the notice the Contractor shall, if practicable in such notice or otherwise in writing as soon as possible thereafter, give particulars of its expected effects, including an estimate of any expected delay in the completion of the Works or any Section beyond the relevant Completion Date.

.3 The Contractor shall forthwith notify the Architect/ Contract Administrator in writing of any material change in the estimated delay or in any other particulars and supply such further information as the Architect/Contractor Administrator may at any time reasonably require.

The architect has to amend the completion date under clause 2.28, which states:

Fixing Completion Date

2.28 .1 If, in the opinion of the Architect/Contract Administrator, on receiving a notice and particulars under clause 2.27:

.1 any of the events which are stated to be a cause of delay is a Relevant Event; and

.2 completion of the Works or of any Section is likely to be delayed thereby beyond the relevant Completion Date,

then, save where these Conditions expressly provide otherwise, the Architect/Contract Administrator shall give an extension of time by fixing such later date as the Completion Date for the Works or Section as he then estimates to be fair and reasonable.

.2 Whether or not an extension is given, the Architect/Contractor Administrator shall notify the Contractor in writing of his decision in respect of any notice under clause 2.27 as soon as is reasonably practicable and in any event within 12 weeks of receipt of the required particulars. Where the period from receipt to the Completion Date is less than 12 weeks, he shall endeavour to do so prior to the Completion Date.

.3 The Architect/Contract Administrator shall in his decision state:

.1 the extension of time that he has attributed to each Relevant Event; and

.2 (in the case of a decision under clause 2.28.4 or 2.28.5) the reduction in time that the has attributed to each Relevant Omission.

.4 After the first fixing of a later Completion Date in respect of the Works or a Section, either under clause 2.28.1 or by a Pre-agreed Adjustment, but subject to clauses 2.28.6.3 and 2.28.6.4, the Architect/Contract Administrator may by notice in writing to the Contractor, giving the details referred to in clause 2.28.3, fix a Completion Date for the Works or that Section earlier than that previously so fixed if in his opinion the fixing of such earlier Completion Date is fair and reasonable, having regard to any Relevant Omissions for which instructions have been issued after the last occasion on which a new Completion Date was fixed for the Works or for that Section.

.5 After the Completion Date for the Works or for a Section, if this occurs before the date of practical completion, the Architect/Contract Administrator may, and not later than the expiry of 12 weeks after the date of practical completion shall, by notice in writing to the Contractor, giving the details referred to in clause 2.28.3:

.1 fix a Completion Date for the Works or for the Section later than that previously fixed if in his opinion that is fair and reasonable having regard to any Relevant Events, whether on reviewing a previous decision or otherwise and whether or not the Relevant Event has been specifically notified by the Contractor under clause 2.27.1; or

.2 subject to clauses 2.28.6.3 and 2.28.6.4, fix a Completion Date earlier than that previously fixed if in his opinion that is fair and reasonable having regard to any instructions for Relevant Omissions issued after the last occasion on which a new Completion Date was fixed for the Works or Section; or

.3 confirm the Completion Date previously fixed.

.6 Provided always that:

.1 the Contractor shall constantly use his best endeavours to prevent delay in the progress of the Works or any Section, however caused, and to prevent the completion of the Works or Section being delayed or further delayed beyond the relevant Completion Date;

.2 in the event of any delay the Contractor shall do all that may reasonably be required to the satisfaction of the Architect/Contract Administrator to proceed with the Works or Section;

.3 no decision of the Architect/Contract Administrator under clause 2.28.4 or 2.28.5.2 shall fix a Completion Date for the Works or any Section earlier than the relevant Date for Completion; and

.4 no decision under clause 2.28.4 or 2.28.5.2 shall alter the length of any Pre-agreed Adjustment unless the relevant Variation or other work referred to in clause 5.2.1 is itself the subject of a Relevant Omission.

Clauses 2.27.1 to .3 are very similar to JCT 98 clauses 25.2.1 to 3 and clauses 2.28.1 to.6 are similar to JCT 98 clauses 25.2.1 to 6. The main differences between the two forms are that JCT 2005 omits any reference to nominated subcontractors and introduces two new terms – 'Pre-agreed Adjustment' and 'Relevant Omission'. These new terms are defined in clause 2.26.2 and .3, as follows:

Related definitions and interpretation

2.26 In clauses 2.27 to 2.29 and, so far as relevant, in the other clauses of these Conditions:

...

.2 'Pre-agreed Adjustment' means the fixing of a revised Completion Date for the Works or a Section in respect of a Variation or other work referred to in clause 5.2.1 by the Confirmed Acceptance of a Schedule 2 Quotation;

.3 'Relevant Omission' means the omission of any work or obligation through an instruction for a Variation under clause 3.14.

Given the similarity between the JCT 2005 and JCT 98 clauses relating to time issues the general comments made in connection with JCT 98 apply equally to the 2005 form.

7.3 NEC 3

The NEC 3 engineering and construction contract dated June 2005 deals with programming and delay issues in 'Core Clause 3', which deals with 'time', and in 'Core Clause 6', which deals with 'compensation events'.

The quotations are reproduced with permission of NEC Contracts and publisher Thomas Telford.

The Programme

Unlike the JCT standard forms, the NEC forms incorporate provisions relating to a programme for the works. These provisions are in some detail – for example Clause 31 in 'Core Clause 3' (set out in full below) not only requires a programme to be provided and identified (in the 'Contract Data' section) but also specifies what the programme must show.

Words in italics in this form of contract relate to terms defined in the 'Contract Data' section of the standard form and words with capital letters refer to terms defined in 'Core Clause 1' of the contract.

31

31.1 If a programme is not identified in the Contract Data, the *Contractor* submits a first programme to the *Project Manager* for acceptance within the period stated in the Contract Data.

31.2 The *Contractor* shows on each programme which he submits for acceptance

- the *starting date*, *access dates*, Key Dates and Completion Date,
- planned Completion,
- the order and timing of the operations which the *Contractor* plans to do in order to Provide the Works,
- the order and timing of the work of the *Employer* and Others as last agreed with them by the *Contractor* or, if not so agreed, as stated in the Works Information,
- the dates when the *Contractor* plans to meet each Condition stated for the Key Dates and to complete other work needed to allow the *Employer* and Others to do their work,
- provisions for float,
- time risk allowances,

- health and safety requirements and
- the procedures set out in this contract,
- the dates when, in order to Provide the Works in accordance with his programme, the *Contractor* will need
- access to a part of the Site if later than its access date,
- acceptances,
- Plant and Materials and other things to be provided by the *Employer* and
- information from Others,
- for each operation, a statement of how the *Contractor* plans to do the work identifying the principal Equipment and other resources which he plans to use and
- other information which the Works Information requires the *Contractor* to show on a programme submitted for acceptance.

31.3 Within two weeks of the *Contractor* submitting a programme to him for acceptance, the *Project Manager* either accepts the programme or notifies the *Contractor* of his reasons for not accepting it. A reason for not accepting a programme is that

- the *Contractor's* plans which it shows are not practicable,
- it does not show the information which this contract requires,
- it does not represent the *Contractor's* plans realistically or
- it does not comply with the Works Information.

As can be seen, clause 31.2 not only requires the programme to show dates, durations and sequences of works, but also to show items such as 'float', 'time risk allowances' and dates when information will be required to complete the works. Programmes must also be accompanied by method statements and 'other information'.

Clause 31.3 requires the programme to be accepted or rejected by the project manager within two weeks and any rejection must be notified and explained to the Contractor.

The NEC 3 Guidance Notes define 'float' as 'any spare time within the programme after the time risk allowances have been included'. 'Float' attached to programme activities can be used to mitigate the effects of 'compensation events' but 'float' between the contractor's planned completion date and the contract 'Completion Date' is not used to mitigate 'compensation events'.

The Guidance states that 'time risk allowances' are durations allowed within programme activities to cover contractors' 'realistic' risks. Therefore, these allowances are not used to off-set the effects of 'compensation events'. If the 'time risk allowances' are not 'realistic' the project manager has the power, under clause 31.3, to refuse to accept the contractor's programme but cannot later adjust the periods when reviewing delays.

The project manager can also reject a programme under clause 31.3 if he or she thinks it is impractical and/or unrealistic. Given the number of variables upon which a construction programme is prepared, it is probably rare for a project manager to confidently assert that a contractor has been impractical or unrealistic, unless there has been a fundamental error in the programme.

The NEC 3 Guidance Notes point out that acceptance of a programme is not a condition precedent to the contractor proceeding and failure to accept a revised programme does not require the contractor to stop work. However, the importance to the contractors of getting programmes approved is that, in the event of delays, the 'accepted programme' will be used as the baseline for assessing delay events and their impact on the completion date.

Updating the programme

The contractual requirements relating to the programme do not stop with the issue of the original plan. The programme has to be updated and revised, by virtue of clause 32, and, again, the NEC 3 contract specifies the requirements for and timing of the revisions:

32

32.1 The *Contractor* shows on each revised programme

- the actual progress achieved on each operation and its effect upon the timing of the remaining work,
- the effects of implemented compensation events and of notified early warning matters,
- how the *Contractor* plans to deal with any delays and to correct notified Defects and
- any other changes which the *Contractor* proposes to make to the Accepted Programme.

32.2 The *Contractor* submits a revised programme to the *Project Manager* for acceptance

within the *period for reply* after the *Project Manager* has instructed him to,

- when the *Contractor* chooses to and, in any case,
- at no longer interval than the interval stated in the Contract Data from the *starting date* until Completion of the whole of the works.

As can be seen, clause 32.2 provides for revised programmes to be issued:

- on the instruction of the project manager;
- when the contractor decides; or
- at regular internals defined in the 'Contract Data' section (regardless of the state of progress of the works).

The provisions of this clause put a heavy burden on both the contractor and project manager in terms of planning resources during the works. However, the theory is no doubt that, by updating and approving programmes, the parties are reducing the risk of delays to completion and also providing a useful pool of data if delays do occur.

Compensation events

The NEC 3 contract deals with delays to completion as 'compensation events' in Core Clause 6. The NEC 3 Guidance Notes define 'compensation events' as those that 'entitle the Contractor to be compensated for any effect the event has on the Prices and the Completion Date or a Key Date'.

There are four different places in the NEC 3 standard form of contract where compensation events are listed. The primary list of events is provided in Core Clause 6 at clause 60.1:

60

60.1 The following are compensation events.

(1) The *Project Manager* gives an instruction changing the Works Information except

- a change made in order to accept a Defect or
- a change to the Works Information provided by the *Contractor* for his design which is made either at his request or to comply with other Works Information provided by the *Employer*.

(2) The *Employer* does not allow access to and use of a part of the Site by the later of its *access date* and the date shown on the Accepted Programme.

(3) The *Employer* does not provide something which he is to provide by the date for providing it shown on the Accepted Programme.

(4) The *Project Manager* gives an instruction to stop or not to start any work or to change a Key Date.

(5) The *Employer* or Others

- do not work within the times shown on the Accepted Programme,
- do not work within the conditions stated in the Works Information or
- carry out work on the Site that is not stated in the Works Information.

(6) The *Project Manager* or the *Supervisor* does not reply to a communication from the *Contractor* within the period required by this contract.

(7) The *Project Manager* gives an instruction for dealing with an object of value or of historical or other interest found within the Site.

(8) The *Project Manager* or the *Supervisor* changes a decision which he has previously communicated to the *Contractor*.

(9) The *Project Manager* withholds an acceptance (other than acceptance of a quotation for acceleration or for not correcting a Defect) for a reason not stated in this contract.

(10) The *Supervisor* instructs the *Contractor* to search for a Defect and no Defect is found unless the search is needed only because the *Contractor* gave insufficient notice of doing work obstructing a required test or inspection.

(11) A test or inspection done by the *Supervisor* causes unnecessary delay.

(12) The *Contractor* encounters physical conditions which

- are within the Site,
- are not weather conditions and
- an experienced contractor would have judged at the Contract Date to have such a small chance of occurring that it would have been unreasonable for him to have allowed for them.
- Only the difference between the physical conditions encountered and those for which it would have been reasonable to have allowed is taken into account in assessing a compensation event.

(13) A *weather measurement* is recorded

- within a calendar month,
- before the Completion Date for the whole of the *works* and
- at the place stated in the Contract Data

  the value of which, by comparison with the *weather data*, is shown to occur on average less frequently than once in ten years.

Only the difference between the *weather measurement* and the weather which the *weather data* show to occur on average less frequently than once in ten years is taken into account in assessing a compensation event.

(14) An event which is an *Employer's* risk stated in this contract.

(15) The *Project Manager* certifies take over of a part of the *works* before both Completion and the Completion Date.

(16) The *Employer* does not provide materials, facilities and samples for tests and inspections as stated in the Works Information.

(17) The *Project Manager* notifies a correction to an assumption which he has stated about a compensation event.

(18) A breach of contract by the *Employer* which is not one of the other compensation events in this contract.

(19) An event which

- stops the *Contractor* completing the *works* or
- stops the *Contractor* completing the *works* by the date shown on the Accepted Programme,

and which

- neither Party could prevent,
- an experienced contractor would have judged at the Contract Date to have such a small chance of occurring that it would have been unreasonable for him to have allowed for it and
- is not one of the other compensation events stated in this contract.

Further compensation events are included in some of the Main Option Clauses. If Option B or D is chosen there are the following additional clauses:

60

60.4 A difference between the final total quantity of work done and the quantity stated for an item in the Bill of Quantities is a compensation event if

- the difference does not result from a change to the Works Information,
- the difference causes the Defined Cost per unit of quantity to change and
- the rate in the Bill of Quantities for the item multiplied by the final total quantity of work done is more than 0.5% of the total of the Prices at the Contract Date.

If the Defined Cost per unit of quantity is reduced, the affected rate is reduced.

60.5 A difference between the final total quantity of work done and the quantity for an item stated in the Bill of Quantities which delays Completion or the meeting of the Condition stated for a Key Date is a compensation event.

60.6 The *Project Manager* corrects mistakes in the Bill of Quantities which are departures from the rules for item descriptions and for division of the work into items in the *method of measurement* or are due to ambiguities or inconsistencies. Each such correction is a compensation event which may lead to reduced Prices.

The application of these events is clarified or restricted by the following clauses.

60.2   In judging the physical conditions for the purpose of assessing a compensation event, the *Contractor* is assumed to have taken into account

- the Site Information,
- publicly available information referred to in the Site Information,
- information obtainable from a visual inspection of the Site and
- other information which an experienced contractor could reasonably be expected to have or to obtain.

60.3   If there is an ambiguity or inconsistency within the Site Information (including the information referred to in it), the *Contractor* is assumed to have taken into account the physical conditions more favourable to doing the work.

...

60.7   In assessing a compensation event which results from a correction of an inconsistency between the Bill of Quantities and another document, the *Contractor* is assumed to have taken the Bill of Quantities as correct.

There are also further compensation events stated in the 'Secondary Option Clauses' X2.1, X14.2, X15.2 and Y(UK)2.4 and yet further events can be listed by the employer in the Contract Data section.

Early warning

If there is a delay to the project that could have an impact on the completion date, an early warning notice must be given, under clause 16 (in 'Core Clause 1'). And, by virtue of clause 63.5, if the contractor fails to give early warning, 'which an experienced contractor could have given', the delay is assessed as if an early warning had been given. Notwithstanding this sanction in clause 63.5, the responsibility to give an early warning does not rest solely with the contractor; clause 16.1 says:

'The *Contractor* or the *Project Manager* give an early warning by notifying the other as soon as either becomes aware of any matter which could ... delay completion'.

Here, as elsewhere, the NEC 3 form does not stop after stating a duty or obligation; it goes on, in clauses 16.2 and 16.3, to say not only that a 'risk reduction' meeting can be called to discuss the early warning event but it also specifies what the parties must do at that meeting.

16

...

16.2 Either the *Project Manager* or the *Contractor* may instruct the other to attend a risk reduction meeting. Each may instruct other people to attend if the other agrees.

16.3 At a risk reduction meeting, those who attend co-operate in

- making and considering proposals for how the effect of the registered risks can be avoided or reduced,
- seeking solutions that will bring advantage to all those who will be affected,
- deciding on the actions which will be taken and who, in accordance with this contract, will take them and
- deciding which risks have now been avoided or have passed and can be removed from the Risk Register.

Examples of the sort of problems that may lead to an 'early warning' are given in the NEC 3 Guidance Notes including:

- discovery of unexpected ground conditions;
- potential delay in the supply of crucial materials or plant;
- potential delay caused by the work of public utilities or other contractors;
- effects of bad weather;
- failure by a subcontractor to perform; and
- design problems.

Notification of delay

In addition to the early warning clause, the NEC 3 deals with the notification of delays in clause 61 (in 'Core Clause 6'). Under clause 61.1, the project manager is obliged to notify the contractor of any delay (the 'compensation event') arising from an instruction, at the time the instruction is given. If the project manager gives no notice of an event, the contractor is required by clause 61.3 to notify the project manager of an event 'which has happened, or which he or she expects to happen as a compensation event'.

The contractor has eight weeks from becoming aware of the event to give this notice. If the contractor fails to give notice within eight weeks, the entitlement to a change to the 'Completion Date' is waived (unless the project manager should have notified under clause 61.1 but did not do so).

After receipt of a compensation event notice, the project manager has just one week under clause 61.4 to notify the contractor of the decision as to whether the event is a compensation event or not, although this short time period can be extended by agreement of the contractor. Failure by the project manager to comply with this provision, entitles the contractor to confirm the failure, at which point the project manager then has a further two weeks to reply. If no reply is made the event is deemed to be a compensation event.

Clause 62 deals with the contractor's quotations for 'compensation events'. If a 'compensation event' will have an impact on the programme, the quotation has to include a revised programme (clause 62.2). The procedure and timetable for submitting and agreeing quotations is set out in clauses 62.3 to 62.6.

In the NEC 3 Guidance Notes it is acknowledged that producing a new programme for every minor change may be 'counter-productive' and so, if several minor events occur within a short period of time, some project managers allow the effects of such changes to be shown on one revised programme.

Assessing delays

There is a straightforward explanation of how to assess of delays in general at clause 63.3, which states:

63.3 A delay to the Completion Date is assessed as the length of time that, due to the compensation event, planned Completion is later than planned Completion as shown on the Accepted Programme. A delay to a Key Date is assessed as the length of time that, due to the compensation event, the planned date when the Condition stated for a Key Date will be met is later than the date shown on the Accepted Programme.

Therefore, the baseline for assessing delays under this standard form is the 'Accepted Programme' and the NEC 3 Guidance Notes state that the 'Completion Date' is adjusted by the overall period of delay to the programme caused by a 'compensation event'.

Clause 64 deals more specifically with the project manager's assessments of 'compensation events':

- 64.1 explains the circumstances under which a project manager would make an assessment;
- 64.2 describes what happens if there is no agreed programme;
- 64.3 deals with the notification of the assessment; and
- 64.4 (which echoes clause 61.4 referred to above) states what happens if the project manager fails to meet the time period allowed for assessment.

The full clause is set out below:

64

64.1 The *Project Manager* assesses a compensation event
- if the *Contractor* has not submitted a quotation and details of his assessment within the time allowed,
- if the *Project Manager* decides that the *Contractor* has not assessed the compensation event correctly in a quotation and he does not instruct the *Contractor* to submit a revised quotation,
- if, when the *Contractor* submits quotations for a compensation event, he has not submitted a programme or alterations to a programme which this contract requires him to submit or
- if, when the *Contractor* submits quotations for a compensation event, the *Project Manager* has not accepted the *Contractor's* latest programme for one of the reasons stated in this contract.

64.2 The *Project Manager* assesses a compensation event using his own assessment of the programme for the remaining work if
- there is no Accepted Programme or
- the *Contractor* has not submitted a programme or alterations to a programme for acceptance as required by this contract.

64.3 The *Project Manager* notifies the *Contractor* of his assessment of a compensation event and gives him details of it within the period allowed for the *Contractor's* submission of his quotation for the same event. This period starts when the need for the *Project Manager's* assessment becomes apparent.

64.4 If the *Project Manager* does not assess a compensation event within the time allowed, the *Contractor* may notify the *Project Manager* to this effect. If the *Contractor* submitted more than one quotation for the compensation event, he states in his notification which quotation he proposes is to be accepted. If the *Project Manager* does not reply within two weeks of this notification the notification is treated as acceptance of the *Contractor's* quotation by the *Project Manager*.

By virtue of clause 65.2, the assessment of a delay ('compensation event') is not revised if a forecast upon which it is based is shown by later recorded information to have been wrong.

Clear and simple?

The NEC 3 standard form of contract aims to be clear and simple to understand, but some of the provisions set out above might be considered to be convoluted and some of the unique terminology (such as 'compensation events', 'early warning notices', 'key dates' and 'weather measurement') may, at least initially, cause confusion rather than produce clarity.

Some clauses may appear to be convoluted because NEC 3 does not merely set out to be a set of contract conditions, it also attempts to be a 'stimulus to good management' (see page 3 of the NEC 3 Guidance Notes). As a result, some of the clauses referred to above are highly prescriptive about what each party should do and when it should be done by.

Acceleration

If the works are in delay, one of the options is to accelerate progress. Under clause 36.1 the project manager may instruct the contractor to submit a quotation for accelerating the works and the quotation provided must include detailed cost information and a revised programme. If the quotation is not accepted (or provided) the contractor cannot be instructed to complete early.

According to the NEC 3 Guidance Notes, the idea of acceleration under this clause is to complete earlier than the 'Completion Date' – it is not intended as a means of speeding up so as to complete by the 'Completion Date'. The project manager can instruct the contractor to revise the programme to recover lost time under clause 32.1.

7.4 GC/Works/1

The Property Advisors to the Civil Estate (PACE), produce a standard form of contract known as GC/Works/1. There are two editions of GC/Works/1: 'Without Quantities (1998)' (referred to below) and a 'With Quantities' edition.

Crown copyright material is reproduced with the permission of the Controller of HMSO and the Queen's Printer for Scotland.

In this form of contract time issues, falling under the heading of 'commencement, programme, delays and completion', are referred to in one section spanning clauses 33 to 39:

- Clause 33 deals with the programme.
- Clause 34 deals with the notification of commencement and the calculation of the 'Date for Completion'.
- Clause 35 requires the contractor to attend regular (generally monthly) progress meetings and to submit progress reports five days before meetings (clause 35.3). The project manager has to provide a progress statement seven days after each meeting (clause 35.4).

- Clause 36 is the extensions of time clause.
- Clause 37 deals with all the implications of the employer taking early possession of part of the works.
- Clause 38 deals with acceleration and cost savings.
- Clause 39 sets out the procedure for certifying completion.

The programme

In terms of duties for the programme, clause 33 (1) states,

> 'The Contractor warrants that the Programme shows the sequence in which the Contractor proposes to execute the Works, details of any temporary work, method of work, labour and plant proposed to be employed, and events, which, in his opinion, are critical to the satisfactory completion of the Works; that the Programme is achievable, conforms with the requirements of the Contract, permits effective monitoring of progress, and allows reasonable periods of time for the provision of information required from the Employer; and that the Programme is based on a period for the execution of the Works to the Date or Dates for Completion.'

The contractor may amend this programme at any time under the provisions of clause 33(2). However, an amended programme showing a completion date beyond the contract date for completion shall not constitute a notice requesting an extension of time and amendments are subject to the agreement of the 'PM' (which is the abbreviation in this contract for project manager). The agreement of the PM to any such amendment 'shall not constitute, or be evidence of, or in support of, any extension of time'.

Extensions of time

The reasons why an extension may be given are set out in clause 36(2):

36. Extensions of time

(2) The PM shall award an extension of time under paragraph (1) only if he is satisfied that the delay, or likely delay, is or will be due to –

    (a) the execution of any modified or additional work;

    (b) any act, neglect or default of the Employer, the PM or any other person for whom the Employer is responsible (not arising because of any default or neglect by the Contractor or by any employee, agent or subcontractor of his);

    (c) any strike or industrial action which prevents or delays the execution of the Works, and which is outside the control of the Contractor or any of his subcontractors;

    (d) an Accepted Risk or Unforeseeable Ground Conditions;

(e) any other circumstances (not arising because of any default or neglect by the Contractor or by any employee, agent or subcontractor of his, and other than weather conditions), which are outside the control of the Contractor or any of his subcontractors, and which could not have been reasonably contemplated under the Contract;

(f) failure of the Planning Supervisor to carry out his duties under the CDM Regulations properly; or

(g) the exercise by the Contractor of his rights under Condition 52 (Suspension for non-payment).

'Accepted Risk' or 'Unforeseeable Ground Conditions' referred to in clause 36(2)(d) are defined in clause 1 of the form. The number of events in this clause is fewer than other standard forms but, particularly by virtue of the catchall wording of subclause 2(e), this contract, like other standard forms, provides a very wide ranging list.

The duties of the PM and the contractor are referred to in subclauses 36(1), (3) and (4), which state:

36. Extensions of time

(1) Where the PM receives notice requesting an extension of time from the Contractor (which shall include the grounds for his request), or where the PM considers that there has been or is likely to be a delay which will prevent or has prevented completion of the Works or any Section by the relevant Date for Completion (in this Condition called 'delay'), he shall, as soon as possible and in any event within 42 Days from the date any such notice is received, notify the Contractor of his decision regarding an extension of time for completion of the Works or relevant Section.

...

(3) The PM shall indicate whether his decision is interim or final. The PM shall keep all interim decisions under review until he is satisfied from the information available to him that he can give a final decision.

(4) No requests for extensions of time may be submitted after completion of the Works. The PM shall in any event come to a final decision on all outstanding and interim extensions of time within 42 Days after completion of the Works. The PM shall not be entitled in a final decision to withdraw or reduce any interim extension of time already awarded, except to take account of any authorised omission from the Works or any relevant Section that he has not already allowed for in an interim decision.

As can be seen, under this form of contract the contractor may give notice requesting an extension, giving the grounds for the request, but it is also open to the PM under clause 36(1) to award time without a notice. The PM has a duty to decide whether an extension of time is due within 42 days of the contractor's notice (clause 36(1)).

Clause 36(3) in isolation might appear to allow a provisional extension of time to be given but an 'interim decision' cannot be withdrawn or reduced, by virtue of clause 36(4), unless it is to take account of an omission that has not been accounted for.

Following on from the above clauses, clause 36(5) provides a timetable for dealing with dissatisfaction with a project manager's extension of time decision and clause 36(6), like other standard forms, confirms the contractor's duty to mitigate the effects of the delay and, for the avoidance of doubt, also confirms that extensions of time are not awarded where the delay is attributable to the negligence, default, improper conduct or lack of endeavour of the Contractor.

Acceleration and cost savings

By virtue of clause 38(1) the employer can direct the contractor to submit a priced proposal for achieving an accelerated completion date and by virtue of clause 38(3) the contractor may submit, at any time, proposals for completing early.

A contractor's priced proposal for acceleration must include an amended programme (clause 38(1)(a)) along with an explanation as to how the acceleration can be achieved (clause 38(1)(b)). Interestingly, if the employer accepts the proposal under either of these clauses it is for the employer (not the contractor) to specify 'the amendments to the programme, including any relevant critical paths' (clause 38(2)(b)). Whether a project manager will be able to identify the critical path on a contractor's programme and whether this would serve any effective purpose are moot points but it is noteworthy that the contract programme (required by clause 33) refers to critical details but not specifically to 'critical path'.

7.5 ICE 7th Edition

The ICE standard form of contract has a long history, with the first edition dating back to 1945. New editions came out regularly to start with, but the fourth edition, published in 1955, and the fifth edition, in 1973, each lasted for eighteen years. The seventh edition was first published in 1999, although it was reprinted with amendments in 2003. It is the 2003 amended edition of the ICE form that is referred to in this section.

The quotations are reproduced with permission of the Institution of Civil Engineers and publisher Thomas Telford.

The majority of the provisions relating to time issues in the ICE standard form of contract are found in clauses 41 to 48 but there are a number of other important subclauses dealing with the programme, delay and extra cost scattered throughout the document.

The programme

Clause 14 provides that the contractor shall submit programming information to the engineer, within 21 days after the award of the contract. The programme has to show the proposed order in which it is planned to carry out the work (clause 14(1)(a)) and a general description of the proposed arrangements and methods of construction (clause 14(1)(b)). The engineer has a further 21 days to either accept of reject the programme (clause 14(2)). The engineer must give reasons if he or she rejects the programme (clause 14(2)(b)) and a request must be made to the contractor to provide further information or clarification (clause 14(2)(c)). If the engineer fails to meet the deadline for responding the programme is deemed to have been accepted.

The engineer has power to require the contractor to produce a revised programme during the works if, 'at any time', progress does not conform with the accepted programme (clause 14(4)).

Extensions of time

The clause dealing with delays and extensions of time (clause 44) is set out in full below. Clause 44(1) deals with the provision by the contractor of full and detailed particulars of the claim and clauses 44(2) and (3) deal with the assessment and granting of an extension by the engineer. Clauses 44 (4) and (5) impose further duties on the engineer at, and shortly after, completion of the works.

Extension of time for completion

44   (1) Should the Contractor consider that

  (a) any variation ordered under Clause 51 (1) or
  (b) increased quantities referred to in Clause 51(4) or
  (c) any cause of delay referred to in these Conditions or
  (d) exceptional adverse weather conditions or
  (e) any delay impediment prevention or default by the Employer or
  (f) other special circumstances of any kind whatsoever which may occur

be such as to entitle him to an extension of time for the substantial completion of the Works or any Section thereof he shall within 28 days after the cause of any delay has arisen or as soon thereafter as is reasonable deliver to the Engineer full and detailed particulars in justification of the period of extension claimed in order that the claim may be investigated at the time.

Assessment of delay

(2) (a) The Engineer shall upon receipt of such particulars consider all the circumstances known to him at that time and make an assessment of the delay (if any) that has been suffered by the Contractor as a result of the alleged cause and shall so notify the Contractor in writing.

(b) The Engineer may in the absence of any claim make an assessment of the delay that he considers has been suffered by the Contractor as a result of any of the circumstances listed in sub-clause (1) of this Clause and shall so notify the Contractor in writing.

Interim grant of extension of time

(3) Should the Engineer consider that the delay suffered fairly entitles the Contractor to

an extension of the time for the substantial completion of the Works or any Section thereof such interim extension shall be granted forthwith and be notified to the Contractor in writing with a copy to the Employer. In the event that the Contractor has made a claim for an extension of time but the Engineer does not consider the Contractor entitled to an extension of time he shall so inform the Contractor without delay.

Assessment at due date for completion

(4) The Engineer shall not later than 14 days after the due date or extended date for completion of the Works or any Section thereof (and whether or not the Contractor shall have made any claim for an extension of time) consider all the circumstances known to him at that time and take action similar to that provided for in sub-clause (3) of this Clause. Should the Engineer consider that the Contractor is not entitled to an extension of time he shall so notify the Employer and the Contractor.

Final determination of extension

(5) The Engineer shall within 28 days of the issue of the Certificate of Substantial Completion for the Works or for any Section thereof review all the circumstances of the kind referred to in sub-clause (1) of this Clause and shall finally determine and certify to the Contractor with a copy to the Employer the overall extension of time (if any) to which he considers the Contractor entitled in respect of the Works or the relevant Section. No such final review of the circumstances shall result in a decrease in any extension of time already granted by the Engineer pursuant to sub-clauses (3) or (4) of this Clause.

Clause 51, which is referred to in clause 44(1), relates to alterations, additions and omissions to the works. This list of reasons for an extension under clause 44(1) is enlarged by:

- clause 7(4) – failure by the engineer to issue the necessary drawings, specifications;
- clause 12(6) – unforeseen 'physical conditions' or 'artificial obstructions';
- clause 13(3) – compliance with instructions;
- clause 14(8) – late approval of construction methods or unforeseen limitations imposed by design criteria; and
- clause 31(2) – provision of site facilities for others.

Acceleration

This standard form includes, at clause 46(1), a power for the engineer to effectively require the contractor to accelerate in the event that the works are likely to overrun due to contractor delays.

Rate of progress

46 (1) If for any reason which does not entitle the Contractor to an extension of time the rate of progress of the Works or any Section is at any time in the opinion of the Engineer too slow to ensure substantial completion by the time or extended time for completion prescribed by Clause 43 and 44 as appropriate or the revised time for completion agreed under sub-clause (3) of this Clause the Engineer shall notify the Contractor in writing and the Contractor shall thereupon take such steps as are necessary and to which the Engineer may consent to expedite the progress so as substantially to complete the Works or such Section by that prescribed time or extended time. The Contractor shall not be entitled to any additional payment for taking such steps.

Certification of 'substantial completion' is covered by clause 48 and a further certificate of completion is issued at the end of the 'Defects Correction Period' under clause 61.

Contract	Key time provisions
JCT 98 (Section 7.1)	Provides a list of 'Relevant events' under which an extension of time may be given. Includes details of 'duties' for both the contractor and architect to follow – including how a contractor should notify of a relevant event and how the architect should go about altering the completion date.
JCT 2005 (Section 7.2)	As JCT 98
NEC 3 (Section 7.3)	Deals with programming and delay issues in terms of 'time' and 'compensation events'. Incorporates provisions relating to programming not only detailing what the programme must show, but also how it must be updated and revised. Includes a process for early warning of delays with detailed requirements for a risk reduction meeting. Contains procedure for accelerating the works.
GC/Works/1 (Section 7.4)	Provides for the contractor to issue a detailed and 'achievable' contract programme. Requires the contractor to attend progress meetings and the project manager to issue progress reports prior to meetings. Includes a procedure for acceleration of the works
ICE 7th edition (Section 7.5)	Requires the contractor to provide (and update when requested) a simple programme and other information about the planning of the works. Includes provisions relating to extensions of time under a number of separate clauses. Provides for non-reimbursable acceleration of the works so as to recover time lost due to contractor's slow progress.

8

Case law and delay

This section provides a summary of leading cases relating to construction delays that have come before the English courts. The cases are set out in chronological order.

The first three cases are relatively old, but they have been included for two reasons: firstly, they are still referred to in cases heard today, because they set precedents that have not been overturned; and secondly, they provide a useful starting point in the history of cases about construction delays.

In accordance with the normal legal convention, the titles of the cases referred to below contain three parts:

1. The full names of the parties; the first name being that of the claiming party and the second being that of the defending party.
2. The year the case was heard in court; this is given in square brackets.
3. A citation referring to the location of a report on the case; citations contain the volume number of the report, the abbreviated name of the report and the page number where the case can be found. The majority of the cases in this section were reported in either the *Building Law Reports* (BLR) or the *Construction Law Reports* (ConLR) or sometimes both. Other citations are explained below as they arise.

In some cases the claiming parties are referred to as 'the plaintiff' and the defending party as 'the respondent'. Generally, parties are identified by a shortened version of their full name; for example, 'Amalgamated Building Contractors Limited' becomes 'Amalgamated'.

The authors are not lawyers and so any commentary on cases referred to in this chapter should not be relied upon as legal opinion. If the reader wishes to study the general workings of the British legal system, the common law, the hierarchy of the courts or the specific legal principles arising out of the cases referred to below, they should refer to appropriate legal text books or consult a specialist construction lawyer.

8.1 *Holme and Another v Guppy and Another* [1838] 3 Mees. & W. 387

This case pre-dates both the *Building Law Reports* and the *Construction Law Reports* and is referred to in Volume 3 of *Meeson & Welsby's Exchequer Reports*. The report about this case commences as follows,

> 'Assumpsit for work and labour, money paid, and on account stated. The defendants pleaded, first, as to all except £208 18s 4d, non-assumpserunt; secondly, as to £200, other than the £208 18s 4d, actionem non, because the work and labour was done under an agreement, by which the plaintiffs agreed … to build … a brewery.'

Fortunately, and perhaps with readers in the twenty-first century in mind, Meeson & Welsby did go on to explain the case using fewer Latin words and phrases.

The case relates to a contract for construction works at a brewery on the east side of Kent Street in Liverpool. Holme was a carpentry and joinery firm and Guppy was the brewery owner.

Holme agreed to carry out the carpentry and joinery work at the brewery for £1,700, in a period of four and a half months, commencing 19 April 1836. The contract provided for liquidated damages to be levied at the rate of £40 per week if works were not complete by 31 August 1836.

The works were delayed from the very start as Guppy was unable to give Holme possession of the site for a week. During the works Guppy's masons caused Holme another four weeks of delay and Holme also had problems with its own labour that led to a further delay of a week.

In the event, works were completed five weeks late and Guppy deducted £200 liquidated damages. However, Holme argued that Guppy caused the delay to completion and that damages should not be deducted. The matter came before Judge Coltman in the Liverpool Summer assizes of 1837 and the report in Meeson & Welsby's states that 'a verdict was thereupon taken for the plaintiffs for £200.'

Leave was given to appeal and in 1838 the case moved to the Court of Exchequer. Judge Park decided that no deduction for liquidated damages should be allowed because Guppy was found to have prevented Holme from completing on time and, he said:

'There are clear authorities that if a party be prevented, by refusal of the other contracting party, from completing the contract until the time limited, he is not liable in law for that default.'

Therefore, Holme 'were excused from performing the agreement contained in the original contract'. It was also noted that:

'There is nothing to shew that [Holme] entered into a new contract by which to perform the work in four months and a half, ending at a later period'.

Or to put it another way, there was no extension of time clause and the only way the judge could see that Guppy might retain a legal obligation to complete by a specific date was if there had been a new contract.

The judge concluded that the absence of either an extension of time clause or a new contract meant that:

'The plaintiffs were therefore left at large; and consequently they are not to forfeit anything for the delay'.

The phrase 'time at large' has been used many times since this judgment by parties claiming that there is no set contractual date for completion.

8.2 *Wells v Army & Navy Co-op* [1902] 86 LT 764

Sixty-four years after *Holme v Guppy*, Wells, a firm of builders, entered into an agreement to carry out certain construction works for the Army & Navy Co-op. The ensuing dispute was reported in Volume 86 of the *Law Times Reports*.

Clause 16 of the parties' contract, in one simple sentence, sets out the key requirements relating to completion. It said:

'The contractor's are to complete the whole of the works within one year from the day of the date hereof unless the works be delayed by reason of any alteration or addition in or to the works authorised as aforesaid, or in case of combination of workmen or strikes or by the default of the subcontractors the contractor's are not obliged to employ, or other causes beyond the contractor's control, satisfactory proof of all which must at the time of occurrence be at once afforded to the board of directors of the employers, who shall adjudicate thereon and make due allowance therefor if necessary, and their decision shall be final, and then the contractor's are to complete the works within such time as the said board of directors shall consider to be reasonable, and in case of default the contractors are to pay or allow to the employer as and by way of liquidated and agreed damages the sum of £10 per day for every day during which they shall be so in default until the whole of the works shall be so completed.'

The date of the contract was 29 October 1897 and so, by virtue of clause 16, works should have been completed on 28 October 1898. However, Wells was delayed, mainly by the default of other contractors, by late possession of the site and by late issue of drawings by the architect. The works were eventually finished over a year late.

In accordance with clause 16, Wells applied to the board of directors of Army & Navy to adjudicate on its claim for a reasonable adjustment to the date for completion. The board granted Wells only three months extension and set-off damages for the remainder of the overrun at the contractual rate of £10 per day.

Clause 16 provided the board of directors with the express power to adjudicate and make a final decision about certain delays to completion and perhaps that explains why the case was summarily dismissed in the first instance. However, the Court of Appeal overturned the first instance decision. They found that delays to the works had been caused by the employer (late possession) and the architect (late drawings) and held that these were not matters covered by clause 16. Therefore, the board did not have jurisdiction to adjudicate on these causes of delay and the contractual machinery for adjusting the completion date failed. As a result, Army & Navy could not rely on the liquidated damages clause.

In the judgment Lord Justice Vaughan Williams also stressed that the full time period for the works must be made available to the builder. He said:

'... in the contract one finds the time limited within which the builder is to do the work. That means not only that he is to do it within that time, but it means also that he is to have that time within which to do it ... that limitation of time is clearly intended, not only as an obligation, but as a benefit to the builder ... where you have a time clause and a penalty clause (as I see it) it is always implied in such cases that the penalties are only to apply if the builder has, as far as the building owner is concerned and his conduct is concerned, that time accorded to him for the execution of the works which the contract contemplates he should have.'

8.3 *Amalgamated Building Contractors Ltd v Waltham Holy Cross UDC* [1952] 2 All ER 452

Fifty years after *Wells v Army & Navy Co-op*, the case of *Amalgamated Building Contractors Ltd v Waltham Holy Cross UDC* was reported in the 'All England Reports' of 1952. This case arose out an agreement to construct 202 new houses at Princesfield, Upshire. The agreement was based on the then widely used standard form of building contract issued by the Royal Institute of British Architects and the National Federation of Building Trades Employers.

Clause 17 of the contract stated:

If the Contractor fails to complete the Works by the date stated in the Appendix Conditions or within any extended time fixed under Clause 18 of these Conditions and the Architect certifies in writing that in his opinion the same ought reasonably so to have been completed, the Contractor shall pay or allow to the Employer a sum calculated at the rate stated in the same Appendix as liquidated and ascertained damages.

Clause 18 provided that:

If in the opinion of the Architect the works be delayed … (ix) by reason of labour and material not being available as required … then in any such case the architect shall make a fair and reasonable extension of time for completion of the works.

The rate of liquidated damages stated in the Appendix was £50 a week. This may not sound very much now but, at that time, the 202 houses were being built for little more than £1,000 each.

Amalgamated commenced works on 7 November 1946 and was due to complete by 7 February 1949. However, the last of the houses was not handed over until 28 August 1950. Amalgamated had written to the architect requesting an extension of time due to difficulties relating to labour and materials not being available, but the architect did not respond until 20 December 1950, when he revised the completion date to 23 May 1949. Waltham deducted liquidated damages for the balance of the overrun, which was for a period of 66 weeks.

Amalgamated argued that the extension of time was invalid, saying that the purpose of the extension of time clause was to give contractors a future date at which they could aim when organising their works. In this case the architect for Waltham Holy Cross had issued an extension four months after completion. The Court at first instance decided that the extension was valid, but Amalgamated appealed.

One of the three appeal judges, Lord Justice Denning, noted that it was strange to find a contractor arguing that an extension (which had been awarded in their favour) was invalid but, as he pointed out, they did so 'because, if the extension of time was invalid, they will be able to avoid paying the liquidated damages altogether.'

However, Lord Denning did not agree that the architect could not give an extension of time to a date that had passed. He referred to a hypothetical situation where a contractor is late completing due to his own risk items and is then faced with a strike, for which he could claim an extension of time under the contract. In that case, Lord Denning said the delay caused by the strike would be added to the completion date to produce a new completion date but one that has already passed. He also suggested that an architect could only give an extension of time retrospectively in circumstances when a continuous delay had operated until the works were complete.

This hypothetical case has similarities to the case of Balfour Beatty *Building Ltd v Chestermount Properties Ltd* (see section 8.11), which was heard years later. The judges in Balfour also considered a hypothetical situation where an employer's risk event occurred during a period of contractor's culpable delay. They gave the example of problems caused by statutory undertakers carrying out works on the site, which under that contract was an event entitling the contractor to an extension of time.

The learned authors of the Building Law Reports point out that the implication of these hypotheses is that the employer continues to carry risk in periods of culpable delay. Whether the judges in these two cases intended to imply this consequence is unknown. It is likely that, if faced with a claim for strikes or problems with statutory undertakers during a period of contractor's delay, the employer would remind the contractor that if it had not been late then the further delays would not have arisen.

In *Amalgamated* Lord Denning concluded that his practical illustration showed that the parties must have intended that the architect should be able to give a certificate that is retrospective, even after the works are completed. Therefore, in his judgment, the extension of time given by Waltham was valid and the judge at first instance was correct. The other two judges of appeal agreed with Lord Denning.

8.4 *Peak Construction (Liverpool) Ltd v McKinney Foundation Ltd* [1970] 1 BLR 111

In 1964 Peak entered into contract with Liverpool Corporation to build a fourteen storey block of flats and garages, on East Lancashire Road, Liverpool. However, a dispute about the delays and damages resulting from defective work arose between Peak and McKinney, a nominated subcontractor, before the first of these fourteen storeys was even commenced.

Although it is not relevant to the delay issues arising out of this case, it is interesting to note the colourful language used by the Court of Appeal to describe the form of contract used at that time by the Liverpool Corporation. It was said:

'... if a prize were to be offered for the form of building contract which contained the most one-sided, obscurely and ineptly drafted clauses in the United Kingdom, the claim of this contract could hardly be ignored, even if the RIBA form of contract was among the competitors.'

Under this contract McKinney was nominated as the subcontractor to carry out the design and installation of foundation piling. Work started in May 1964 and was completed within six weeks. However, on 2 October 1964 it was discovered that some of the piling work was gravely defective and four days later all work on site ceased in order for an inspection to be carried out of the other piles.

Through no fault of McKinney, or Peak, the inspection and report were not completed until 24 May 1965. McKinney then asked for permission to carry out the work recommended in the engineer's report but this was not authorised until 30 July 1965. The remedial work was completed and work recommenced on site on 12 November 1965, meaning that 58 weeks had been lost.

Liverpool Corporation deducted a total of £40,000 for liquidated damages due to the 58 weeks delay and Peak sought to pass this on to McKinney. When the case came before the Official Referee the deduction was upheld. The case moved on to the Court of Appeal. This court decided that a delay of 58 weeks did not flow naturally and in the ordinary course of things from McKinney's breach and that the deduction of £40,000 for liquidated damages was 'beyond all reason'.

On the facts of the case the Court of Appeal decided that part of the 58 weeks delay was the fault of Liverpool Corporation, who had been dilatory in agreeing to the investigation and remedial work. Therefore, the Court of Appeal referred this issue back to the Official Referee. However, the court held that an employer who was responsible for the failure to achieve a completion date could not recover liquidated damages. In such cases the employer would have to prove such general damages as may have been suffered. It was also pointed out by the court that no liquidated damages are recoverable if an architect has failed to extend time when he should have done so.

8.5 *Percy Bilton Ltd v Greater London Council* [1982] 20 BLR 1

This case was heard three times – in the High Court, the Court of Appeal and the House of Lords. The dispute, which concerned the effects of the renomination of the mechanical services subcontractor, was decided one way by the High Court and the opposite way by the Court of Appeal. Therefore, the House of Lords effectively had to decide which court had made the right judgment.

The case arose out of a contract dated 25 October 1976 under which Percy Bilton agreed to build 182 dwellings and ancillary works at an estate on Swains Road, Merton, for the Greater London Council (GLC). The GLC conditions of contract were substantially the same as the JCT Standard Form current at that time and the original completion date was 24 January 1979, which provided a contract period of 27 months.

The mechanical services were nominated to a subcontractor known as WJ Lowdell Ltd. Lowdell fell behind the programme for the works and still had 40 weeks of work to carry out when they withdrew labour from the site and went into liquidation, in July 1978. On 14 September 1978 GLC issued an instruction to Bilton to use Crown House Engineering Ltd but on 16 October 1978 Crown House withdrew their tender. Then, finally, on 31 October 1978 GLC nominated Home Counties and work began on 22 January 1979. Home Counties completed 53 weeks later, on 25 January 1980.

Bilton claimed an extension of time, but GLC only revised the completion date to 1 February 1980 and thereafter deducted liquidated damages. The parties fell out and in the first place the dispute came before Judge Stabb. He decided that GLC were at least partly at fault for the delay and, being as there was no provision in clause 23 of the contract for an extension of time due to delays caused by the repudiation of a nominated subcontract and the time required to re-nominate, time was held to be 'at large'. Therefore, GLC were not entitled to deduct liquidated damages. GLC appealed.

The Court of Appeal upheld the appeal. They decided that the mere repudiation of the subcontract by a nominated subcontractor was not to be regarded as a fault or breach of contract by GLC. An employer had a duty to renominate within in a reasonable time but the events in this case did not give rise to an extension of time. Bilton appealed.

The House of Lords agreed with the Court of Appeal. They noted the rulings in *Holme v Guppy* and *Wells v Army & Navy Co-op* but confirmed that the withdrawal of a nominated subcontractor was not a fault of the employer and was not covered by the extension of time provisions of clause 23, meaning that Bilton carried the risk.

8.6 *Walter Lawrence & Sons Ltd v Commercial Union Properties Ltd* [1984] 4 ConLR 37

Many extension of time claims are made and awarded as a result of the affects of the weather on the planned progress of works on site. The case of *Walter Lawrence v Commercial Union* provided some guidance about the correct approach to the issue.

Walter Lawrence entered into an agreement with Commercial Union to carry out certain construction works in 1982. The agreement was based on the JCT Standard Form of Building Contract, 1963 Edition, and the contract completion date was 14 September 1983, but delays occurred, at least in part, due to the severe weather conditions encountered.

Clause 23(b) of the contract provided for an extension of time to be granted to the contractor in the event that the weather was 'exceptionally inclement'. Therefore, Walter Lawrence applied for an extension of time and the architect obtained records from the Meteorological Office in order to assess the claim. The architect then compared the weather records with the contractor's programme and concluded that the entitlement to an extension of time was only two weeks. In a letter to the contractor he explained that it was his view that he could only take into account weather conditions prevailing when the works were due to be put in hand, not when they were actually carried out.

Walter Lawrence pointed out in reply that the wording of the contract related to actual events not programme dates but the architect thought it was inequitable that a contractor could defer work for his own reasons and yet still recover delays from the employer arising out of inclement weather then encountered.

The dispute was referred to Judge Lewis Hawser QC in the Official Referees' Court. He decided in favour of Walter Lawrence. He held that the correct test was whether the weather was 'exceptionally inclement' so as to give rise to a delay to the works actually being carried out at the time. He noted that the contract imposed an obligation on the contractor to proceed 'regularly and diligently' but that did not create an obligation to programme the work in a strict sense or to work strictly to a programme if one was drawn up.

Judge Lewis Hawser QC also held that the architect was mistaken to view delays pursuant to clause 23(b) in the light of the amount of time lost. The test was not whether the amount of time lost was exceptional; it was whether the weather was exceptional.

8.7 *Yorkshire Water Authority v Sir Alfred McAlpine & Son* [1986] 32 BLR 114

On 1 December 1975 McAlpine submitted a tender, in the sum of £7m, for an outlet tunnel underneath a dam at Grimwith Reservoir. In accordance with the tender document, McAlpine provided a programme 'in bar chart or critical path analysis form', which was later supported by a method statement for the works. The programme and statement were subsequently approved by Yorkshire Water and incorporated into the formal agreement, which was based on the ICE Conditions of Contract (5th Edition).

The tender documents had stipulated that the tunnel should be constructed upstream but, in the event, that proved to be impossible and as a result there was a long delay to the works. When the work recommenced it was from the upstream end working downwards. McAlpine claimed that this was a variation but Yorkshire Water disagreed and the dispute was referred to arbitration. On 30 January 1985 the arbitrator decided in favour of McAlpine and shortly after Yorkshire Water appealed the decision.

The case came before the Commercial Court, where Yorkshire Water argued that the method statement merely formed part of McAlpine's duty under clause 14(1) of the ICE contract to provide 'a programme showing the order of procedure in which [the contractor] proposes to carry out the Works.' Clause 14 also obliged McAlpine to provide 'further details and information as the Engineer may reasonably require.'

Yorkshire Water also pointed out that, by virtue of clause 14(7), 'Approval by the Engineer of the Contractor's programme ... shall not relieve the Contractor of any of his duties or responsibilities under the Contract' and under clause 8(2) the contractor has to 'take full responsibility for the adequacy stability and safety of all site operations and methods of construction.'

McAlpine referred to clause 51(1), which stated:

> 'The Engineer shall order any variation to any part of the Works that may in his opinion be necessary for completion of the Works and shall have power to order any variation that for any other reason shall in his opinion be desirable for the satisfactory completion and functioning of the Works. Such variations may include ... changes to the specified sequence method or timing of construction (if any).'

In his judgment Judge Skinner said 'it would be wholly artificial and unrealistic to regard the method statement as a document expressly provided under clause 14'. He decided that in a 'valuable and important contract like this', Yorkshire Water had 'wanted to tie the contractor to a particular programme and method of working'. He held that clause 8(2) did not apply to the method statement, because the statement reflected the specific requirements of the tender, which were expressly incorporated into the contract.

Therefore, the arbitrator's decision was upheld and the change to the method of working was declared a variation under clause 51 because it was impossible to carry out the works as specified. Judge Skinner noted that the situation would have been different had the method statement been produced as part of McAlpine's duties under clause 14.

8.8 *Glenlion Construction Ltd v The Guinness Trust* [1987] 39 BLR 89

The contractual significance, if any, of programmes issued for a project is frequently debated when contractors rely upon those programmes to support a claim for an extension of time. A contract between Glenlion and the Guinness Trust required that a programme be provided within one week of the start of works. In the ensuing arbitration and court case the significance of this programme was considered.

The contract between the parties, which related to a residential development in Bromley, Kent, was based on the then widely used 1963 JCT Standard Form with Quantities (July 1977 revised edition). The date for possession of the site was 29 June 1981 and the period for completion was 114 weeks. Within one week of the date of possession, Glenlion were obliged to provide 'a programme or chart of the whole of the works ... showing a completion date no later than the date for completion.' The programme had to be kept up-to-date by modifications or redrafting.

The programme showed a completion date of 5 June 1983, which was only 101 weeks following the date of possession. Glenlion claimed that, 'on a true construction' of the contract, the firm was entitled to carry out the works in accordance with the programme but claimed to have been delayed because the professional team working for the Guinness Trust did not provide information to allow the early completion.

The dispute was referred to an arbitrator, who issued an interim award in favour of the Guinness Trust. Glenlion appealed and the matter was heard by Judge Fox-Andrews in the Official Referees' Court. He accepted that Glenlion was entitled to complete earlier than the contract completion date but he decided that this did not impose an implied duty on Guinness to produce information early.

Of course, an employer may well try to assist a contractor who is trying to finish early and must not hinder or obstruct the contractor, but that does not mean an employer has a positive duty to help. Judge Fox-Andrews said, 'The unilateral imposition of a different completion date [by a contractor] would result in the whole balance of the contract being lost.'

This case did not consider the issue of 'float' in a contractor's programme but the judgment would suggest that any time difference between the planned and contractual completion dates is contractor's 'float'. It also seems logical to conclude that if a contractor is not entitled to compensation for delays caused to an optimistic planned programme, an employer is not entitled to deny an extension of time on the grounds that a contractor has 'float' in the same programme.

8.9 *H. Fairweather & Co. Ltd v London Borough of Wandsworth* [1987] 39 BLR 106

For many years, both before and since this case, there has been an understanding that loss and expense payments for prolongation costs under JCT contracts only arise if the contractor has been awarded an extension of time. This case served as a reminder that this understanding has no proper basis in the terms of the contract but is reflected in the practical reality.

Fairweather entered into an agreement with Wandsworth to build 478 dwellings in the Borough on 23 December 1975. The agreement was based on the JCT Standard Form, Local Authorities Edition with Quantities, 1963 edition. The date for possession stated in the appendix was 15 December 1975 and the date for completion was 5 August 1979.

There were significant delays to the works, not least as a result of the general strikes in 1978–79. The architect duly awarded an extension of time of 81 weeks, pursuant to clause 23(d) of the contract. Fairweather argued that 18 of these 81 weeks should have been allocated to clause 23(e) or 23(f). The parties could not agree and the dispute was referred to arbitration. The arbitrator agreed with the architect and allowed the extension of time on the grounds that the dominant cause of delay was the strike. Fairweather appealed against the award on a question of law. Judge Fox-Andrews QC heard the appeal in the Official Referees' Court.

At first, it may appear surprising that a contractor took issue with which clause the extension of time was given under, but Fairweather was not just claiming an extension of time, it was also looking for reimbursement of loss and expense. Fairweather thought that if an extension of time was given under clause 23(e) or 23(f) it would open the door to recovery of loss and expense under clause 24.

Judge Fox-Andrews made it clear that there was no connection between an extension of time under clause 23 and loss and expense under clause 24. He said:

'An extension of time under clause 23(e) is neither expressly nor I find impliedly made a condition precedent to a right to payment'.

However, he recognised the inevitable link made in practice between time and money claims. Therefore, he went on to decide whether or not the arbitrator was correct to allocate a variety of delay events to the dominant cause. It was held that he was not correct. Judge Fox-Andrews said:

'On the assumption that condition 23 is not solely concerned with liquidated or ascertained damages but also triggers and conditions a right for a contractor to recover direct loss and expense where applicable under clause 24 then an architect and in his turn an arbitrator has the task of allocating, when the facts require it, the extension of time to the various heads. I do not consider that the dominant test is correct.'

8.10 *McAlpine Humberoak Ltd v McDermott International (No 1)* [1992] 58 BLR 1

As a general rule, if there are many changes on a project it is likely that a contractor will be entitled to an extension of time, the employer will not be successful with a defence that the contractor ought to have expected those changes and, if there is no extension of time clause, employer delays will render time 'at large'. However, in certain circumstances these general rules do not apply, as in the case of *McAlpine Humberoak Ltd v McDermott International (No 1)*.

McAlpine was a subcontractor to McDermott, who was engaged by Conoco to carry out works at the 'Hutton Tension Leg Platform', an off-shore drilling rig in the Shetland Basin, east of Scotland. McDermott engaged McAlpine to construct boxes or pallets to form the top deck of the rig. Originally McAlpine was to provide pallets referenced W3, W4, W5 and W6 but, in the event, W5 and W6 were omitted from the contract. The pallets were to be fabricated and assembled at McAlpine's base in Great Yarmouth and delivered by barge to McDermott, in Ardersier, Moray of Firth – pallet referenced W4 was due to be delivered on 1 February 1982 and W3 a week later, on 8 February 1982.

Work commenced on 18 November 1981. On 1 December 1981 McDermott sent 45 drawings to McAlpine and on 11 December they sent a further 17. Thereafter further drawings were issued regularly through to 5 August 1982, the date when the twenty-second set of new drawings was issued. As information came through, McAlpine raised technical queries (TQs) and in total forty-five TQs were issued. In addition, McDermott issued eighty three variation instructions, albeit thirty two of these were either cancelled or not pursued.

In the event, the W3 pallets were delivered on 17 July 1982 and W4 on 11 September 1982, which was over five months later than the original contract date for W3 and over seven months late for W4. McAlpine put the delays down to the number of drawings issued, the variations and the slow response to TQs. McDermott accepted that there had been some delay but only allowed McAlpine an additional two weeks for delivery of the W3 pallets and 3 weeks for W4.

The dispute ended up in the Court of Appeal and McAlpine's primary case was that time was 'at large'. They pointed out that time was of the essence of the contract and there was no power for McDermott to fix a new completion date. In support of the claim McAlpine referred to *Wells v Army & Navy Co-op*, *Peak v McKinney* and *Holme v Guppy*.

The Court of Appeal decided that the effect of the delays, which were not accommodated by the express terms of the contract, did not make time 'at large'. They said the judgment in *Peak v McKinney*:

'... was simply that an employer is not entitled to rely on such a clause where the reason for late completion was an act of hindrance or prevention by the employer, at least in the absence of a suitable extension of time clause.'

In this case they did not find that late completion was caused by an act of hindrance or prevention by McDermott.

Wells v Army & Navy Co-op and *Holme v Guppy* appear to have been distinguished from this case because there was no claim for liquidated damages here. Therefore, it was held that the contract completion date could be revised and this would keep alive McDermott's entitlement to recover damages for the period between the revised and actual completion dates. As the damages had not been liquidated and inserted into the contract, McDermott had to counterclaim for unliquidated damages.

Like most parties, McAlpine had a second line of attack when the primary time 'at large' argument failed. McAlpine argued that, if the completion could be revised under the contract, it was entitled to have the date revised to the date the pallets were delivered, which would produce the same nett result as the primary claim. McAlpine pointed out that there had been chaos in its drawing office as the multitude of drawings and variations were issued, because the shop drawings had to be revised. Until these revisions had been completed the production of the pallets could not commence.

The judge in the lower court accepted McAlpine's submission, dismissing McDermott's approach as 'a retrospective and dissectional reconstruction by expert evidence of events almost day by day, drawing by drawing, TQ by TQ and weld procedure by weld procedure, designed to show that the spate of additional drawings which descended on McAlpine virtually from the start of the work really had little retarding or disruptive effect on its progress'.

In contrast, the appeal judges thought McDermott's retrospective and dissectional analysis was just what was required and clearly thought it supported the defence that the drawing and TQ issues were of no greater quantity or complexity than should have been expected for a North Sea rig project. The fact that lots of new drawings were issued and then clarified was not a change to the works, as might be the case on many other construction contracts. This was not like a typical traditional building or civil engineering project, where the contractor could reasonably expect to find that the design was largely complete, with drawings available and queries resolved reasonably well in advance of the works being carried out.

Furthermore, McDermott was able to persuade the judges that the chaos in McAlpine's drawing office was due to lack of supervision and poor management rather than the changes and additional information.

Many parties, when defending against a contractor's claim, will make allegations about poor or even incompetent management but in this case McDermott appeared to have had evidence to support the complaint. It was shown that McAlpine had incorporated revisions into shop drawings in good time and that the delays were due to the time spent checking the shop drawings prior to release for production. McDermott also pointed out that delays would also have been caused by McAlpine's late issue of weld procedures (which had to be approved before welding was carried out) and by the high quantity of weld failures (up to 60%).

Therefore, the claim came down to a review of the effect of the variation instructions on the works. Here, again, holes opened up in McAlpine's case. For example, it emerged at the hearing that McAlpine claimed a full day's delay for a variation which took no more than an hour to carry out and made the assumption that the whole workforce planned for an activity was also actually engaged on that activity from start-to-finish. The facts simply did not support these theories, which had been used as a basis for the £3,548,848 claim made by McAlpine. The quantum of the claim was further undermined by McAlpine's admission that the total of £3,548,848 was greatly in excess of the costs actually incurred.

The Court decided that McAlpine was entitled to an extension of time only until 30 April 1982. This decision was made notwithstanding the fact that McDermott had ordered additional work on 11 June 1982. In a judgment that was to be echoed a year later in *Balfour Beatty Building Ltd v Chestermount Properties Ltd*, (see section 8.11) the Court decided it could fix a revised completion date that preceded the date of an instruction to carry out additional work. Lord Justice Lloyd explained,

'If a contractor is already a year late through his own culpable fault, it would be absurd that the employer should lose his claim for unliquidated damages just because, at the last moment, he ordered an extra coat of paint.'

Unlike some of the other cases considered in this chapter, McDermott was not seeking to uphold a liquidated damages clause in the contract, it was pursuing the ordinary remedy in law for a breach of contract, namely recovery of damages, as can be proven, that flow from the breach.

8.11 *Balfour Beatty Building Ltd v Chestermount Properties Ltd* [1993] 62 BLR 1

In some respects this case merely confirmed the existing case law but it became a landmark judgment because of the way it considered and decided whether the revised completion date should be calculated by use of a 'gross' or 'nett' method and because it related to the widely used standard form of contract, the JCT Standard Form of Building Contract, 1980 Private Edition.

The case arose out of a contract in which Balfour agreed to construct the shell and core of a seven storey office block at 126–137 Houndilch, London. Work commenced on 18 September 1987 and the original Contract Completion Date was 17 April 1989. Liquidated damages were set at the rate of £60,000 per week.

During the works Chestermount issued a variation instructing Balfour to carry out the fit-out works. In the event, the original shell and core was not completed until 12 October 1990 and the fit-out was completed on 25 February 1991. Balfour was originally given an extension of time to 12 September 1989 but later (on 14 May 1991) the completion date was further revised to 24 November 1989. This further extension still meant that Balfour was fifteen months late completing and Chestermount deducted liquidated damages amounting to £3.84million. With this sort of money in dispute it is not surprising that the matter came before the Commercial Court.

One of the questions the court had to decide was whether an architect could, under the terms of this contract, issue an extension of time in respect of a 'Relevant Event', in this case a variation instruction, occurring during a period of culpable delay. The extension of time claim awarded by Chestermount related to an instruction issued after the completion date and, as Balfour pointed out, a future event cannot delay a completion date that has already passed. Balfour also pointed out that clause 25.3.1.2 of the contract required the architect to consider whether 'the completion of the Works is likely to be delayed thereby beyond the Completion Date'.

The purpose of an extension of time clause is to keep alive the liquidated damages provisions. Therefore, if the extension of time clause was to fail, the employer could not deduct liquidated damages. On that point the judge had this to say:

> 'The remarkable consequences of the application of the principle [that an act of prevention would disentitle the employer to liquidated damages] could therefore be that if, as in the present case, the contractor fell well behind the clock and overshot the completion date and was unlikely to achieve practical completion until far into the future, if the architect then gave an instruction for the most trivial variation, representing perhaps only a day's extra work, the employer would thereby lose all right to liquidated damages for the entire period of culpable delay up to the practical completion or, at best, on the respondents' submission, the employer's right to liquidated

damages would be confined to the period up to the act of prevention. For the rest of the delay he would have to establish unliquidated damages. What might be a trivial variation instruction would on this argument destroy the whole liquidated damages regime for all subsequent purposes. So extreme a consequence … could hardly reflect the common intention.'

This echoes the views of judges in previous cases referred to above, not least those of Lord Justice Lloyd in *McAlpine Humberoak Ltd v McDermott International (No 1)*. The judge in this case could not accept that the whole liquidated damages regime could so easily be defeated and found that clause 25.3.3 got around the timing problem highlighted by Balfour. This clause allows a review of the contract completion date within 12 weeks following 'Practical Completion'. By implication that must include a review of delays occurring, as here, between the contact completion date and the date of practical completion. Therefore, it was held that an architect could, under the terms of this contract, issue an extension of time in respect of a 'Relevant Event' occurring during a period of culpable delay.

The case is, however, best known for the judgment as to the correct method of calculating a revised completion date. It was common ground between the parties that the instruction for the fit-out works had caused delay and that Balfour were entitled to an extension of time, but Chestermount calculated the revised completion date to be 24 November 1989 by adding the duration of the delay to the existing contract completion date (this was called the 'nett' method or 'dotting-on' the delays).

Balfour pointed out that the variation instruction relating to the fit-out of the building had not even been issued by 24 November 1989 and so they could not possibly have completed by that date. Therefore Balfour adopted a 'gross' method of calculating a revised completion date, which involved adding the duration of delay to the date when the instruction was given, which in this case was two and a half months after the revised date for completion set by Chestermount.

The judge could see that, at first sight, the award of an extension of time for an event before it had occurred appeared 'distinctly peculiar', because it 'gives rise to a new completion date by which the additional works were supposed to be finished which precedes those additional works becoming part of the contract works!' However, he noted that 'the retrospective postponement of the completion date to a date before the event causing delay was an eventuality contemplated 'with equanimity' by Lord Denning MR in *Amalgamated Building Contractors Ltd v Waltham Holy Cross UDC*.

The 'gross' approach had the effect of removing any liability Balfour may have had for delays up to the time of the variation instruction.

The Judge considered this position had to be wrong as the yardstick for assessing extensions of time under the particular contract was 'what is fair and reasonable' and the 'gross' method was not fair. The Judge noted that:

'... if the architect were to assess the length of time required to carry out the variation works and to refix the completion date at the end of such period starting from the date of the variation instruction, he would produce a result which would be unfair to the employer.'

It would be unfair because:

'... the employer would be deprived of any compensation for the contractor's breach in failing to complete by the earlier completion date. The additional period of time then allowed to the contractor for completion of the works would not be co-extensive with any period of delay caused by a relevant event. The submission that this is not unfair to the employer because he has brought it on himself by requesting a variation during a period of culpable delay is misconceived because it assumes that relevant events in general or variation instructions in particular are to be treated according to different principles depending on whether they occur before or during a period of culpable delay.'

The judge concluded that:

'The underlying objective is to arrive at the aggregate period of time within which the contract works as ultimately defined ought to have been completed having regard to the incidence of main contractor's risk events and to calculate the excess time, if any, over that period which the contractor took to complete the works. In essence the architect is concerned to arrive at an aggregate period for completion.'

Therefore:

'The completion date as adjusted was not a date which the contractor ought to have achieved practical completion but the end of the total number of working days starting from the date of possession within which the contractor ought fairly and reasonably to have completed the works.'

Or, to put it another way:

'What is important is not the chronological date but the working days forward from the original date ... The amount of time by which [the architect] postpones the completion date must correspond with the amount of delay.'

This judgment also contained some useful comments about criticality and concurrency. It was said that, in assessing an extension of time, an architect should:

'... take into account amongst other factors the effect that the relevant event had on the progress of the works. Did it bring the progress of the works to a standstill? Or did it merely slow down the progress of the works?'

The objective must be:

'... to assess whether any of the relevant events has caused delay to the progress of the works and, if so, how much'.

However:

'If the variation works can reasonably be conducted simultaneously with the original works without interfering with their progress and are unlikely to prolong practical completion, the architect might properly conclude that no extension of time was justified.'

8.12 *Pigott Foundations Ltd v Shepherd Construction Ltd* [1994] 67 BLR 48

This case concerns an attempt by a subcontractor to limit the level of damages that could be applied in the event of default. The parties had been involved in a project to erect a fourteen storey office block for Equity & Law Life Assurance plc in Chapel Street, Coventry. Shepherd was the main contractor and Pigott was the piling subcontractor.

Pigott's tender offer dated 14 February 1989 included the following term:

'B9. The period of notice of commencement, programme time for the work and the level or amount of liquidated or consequential damages to apply to this Contract are to be agreed prior to contractual commitment. In this particular connection, and in view of our current and projected level of activity, no guarantee is given or implied as to our availability at the time you may require, or to comply with your stipulated programme requirements.'

The offer also included a sequence of work showing a subcontract period of eight weeks.

On 25 April 1989 the parties had a pre-contract meeting and the minutes record that:

'With regard to B9, it was agreed that damages would only apply in the event of Pigott's (sic) not completing within ten weeks and any sum would be limited to £40,000 (max) at the rate of £10,000 per week.'

On 23 June 1989 Pigott and Shepherd entered into a subcontract agreement based on the JCT Standard Form of Domestic Subcontract DOM/1, 1980 edition with amendments, incorporating Pigott's offer and the pre-contract meeting minutes.

Clause 11.1 of the JCT form stated:

'The Sub-Contractor shall carry out and complete the Sub-Contract Works in accordance with the details in the Appendix, part 4 [subcontract commencement date and period] and reasonably in accordance with the progress of the Works ...'

Pigott started on 26 June 1989 and should have completed on 27 August 1989, but the works commenced very slowly and Shepherd immediately raised concerns about the rate of progress. Problems were then encountered with piles failing to meet the load tests and further delays followed instructions to install additional piles. As a result, the bulk of the works were not complete until 20 October 1989, by which time nine piles remained to be installed. On that day Pigott left site and did not return till April 1990 to complete the outstanding work.

Shepherd sought to make deductions from Pigott's account for delay and disruption. The subsequent fall out ended up before Judge Gilliland QC in the Liverpool Official Referees' Court. Pigott argued that Shepherd could not recover losses suffered due to the rate of progress of works within the original contract period and that their liability for damages due to late completion was, in any event, capped at £40,000. The Judge agreed.

Judge Gilliland held that Pigott was entitled to plan and perform the work as it saw fit, providing completion was within the contract period, in this case eight weeks. Pigott had no liability for costs incurred by Shepherd as a result of the rate of progress within that period. The Judge said:

'In my judgment the obligation of the subcontractor under clause 11.1 ... does not upon its true construction require the subcontractor to comply with the main contractor's programme of works nor does it entitle the main contractor to claim that the subcontractor must ... complete a particular part of the subcontract works by a particular date in order to enable the main contractor to proceed with other parts of the works. "The words 'the progress of the Works" are in my judgment directed to requiring the subcontractor to carry out his subcontract works in such a manner as would not unreasonably interfere with the actual carrying out of any other works which can conveniently be carried out at the same time. The words do not however in my judgment require the subcontractor to plan his subcontract work so as to fit in with any scheme of work of the main contractor or to finish any part of the subcontract works by a particular date so as to enable the main contractor to proceed with other parts of the work.'

Furthermore, it was held that the limitation on damages, referred to at the pre-contract meeting and incorporated as a term of the subcontract, applied a cap that Shepherd could not avoid by claiming general damages for breach of other terms of the contract.

8.13 *Galoo Ltd & Others v Bright Grahame Murray* [1994] 1 WLR 1360

This case had nothing to do with construction in general or delay claims in particular but it has been cited in construction delay cases, such as *Great Eastern Hotel Company Ltd v John Laing Construction Ltd* and papers on construction delay because it considers 'causation' and the 'but for' test.

The case, which is reported in the *Weekly Law Reports*, concerned a professional negligence claim by a company, Galoo, against its accountants, Bright Grahame Murray. Galoo claimed that Bright Grahame Murray had failed to carry out an accurate audit of the company accounts and, as result, they incurred trading losses between 1971 and 1974. Galoo said that the firm would have ceased trading had it been made aware of the true state of the accounts and would, thereby, have avoided the losses incurred. The case reached the Court of Appeal where Bright Grahame Murray asserted that the claim relied upon the 'but for' test, which it said was not a proper test in English contract law. As explained in chapter 5, the 'collapsed as-built' method of delay analysis is also referred to as the 'as-built but for' technique.

One of the three appeal court judges, Judge Glass, accepted that the losses incurred by Galoo through continued trading were, in the broadest sense, a result of a breach of contract by Bright Grahame Murray. The analogy he drew was this:

'If a defendant promises to direct me where I should go and, at a cross-roads, directs me to the left road rather than the right road, what happens to me on the left road is, in a sense, the result of what the defendant has done. If I slip on that road, if it collapses under me, or if, because I am there, a car driving down that road and not down the right road strikes me, my loss is, in a sense, the result of the fact that I have been directed to the left road and not the right road.'

In the same way, Galoo incurred losses that, in a sense, were the result of Bright Grahame Murray's negligently prepared accounts. But Judge Glass said that this link was not sufficient, in isolation, to prove the claim in law. He said Galoo had to show a 'causal relationship' between the breach and the loss but failed to do so. He pointed out that other factors could also have caused or contributed to the loss.

It was held that a breach of contract must be the effective or dominant cause of the loss and that it is necessary to distinguish between a breach that caused a loss and a breach that merely provided the opportunity to sustain the loss. The way for a court to draw the distinction was by the application of common sense.

The common link between a case like this and many construction delay claims is that both have to resolve which of a number of events actually caused the problem complained of, in this case loss of money through continued trading or, in construction delay cases, deferment of the contract completion date.

There will always be competing causes of delay in all but the simplest of construction delay claims, some of which may have been caused by the employer, others by the contractor. This case suggests that the way to deal with the intractable problem of competing and/or concurrent causes of delay is by the simple application of common sense.

8.14 *John Barker Construction Ltd v London Portman Hotel Ltd* [1996] 83 BLR 31

This case would have provided something of a wake-up call to architects and others responsible for assessing delay claims made by contractors. Much of the judgment focuses on what lengths an architect should go to when carrying out a determination of an extension of time claim.

Barker commenced refurbishment and alteration works of floors 2–11 of Block B of the London Portman Hotel in April 1994. The agreement for the works was based on the JCT Standard Form of Building Contract with Quantities, 1980 Edition, incorporating the sectional completion supplement. Floors 9–11 were due to be completed on 16 July 1994, floors 5–8 on 30 July 1994, and floors 2–4 on 14 August 1994. In the event, the architect certified that 'Practical Completion' of the whole works occurred on 23 September 1994.

Barker applied for and was awarded extensions of time but not for the full period. The ensuing disagreement became a dispute, which was referred by Barker to the Official Referees' Court, where it was heard by Recorder Toulson QC.

Barker complained that the architect had failed in the proper discharge of his duties. The architect's duties relative to extensions of time are set out in clause 25 of the JCT 80 form. By virtue of clause 25.3.1.2 the architect has a duty to estimate a fair and reasonable extension of time and to communicate this assessment to the contractor in writing. Clause 25.3.1.3 required the architect to state which 'Relevant Events' have been taken into account in the award.

In this case the architect received a notification of a delay of six-weeks from Barker on 1 December 1994. The notification was supported by a narrative, various programmes in bar chart format and either lists of or copies of architect's instructions and confirmation of verbal instruction sheets. The architect requested certain additional information and met with Barker. Then, on 6 January 1995, he produced a report on the extension of time for discussion with other members of the employer's team. This report listed twenty one items considered to be 'Relevant Events' and concluded that an extension of nine days should be awarded for floors 9–11 and seven days for floors 2–8. In a letter dated 2 February 1995 the architect awarded Barker an extension of time for these periods.

The report did not show how the time durations had been arrived at but the architect had annotated a copy of the report with references to relevant instructions and the period of delay for each item. The architect considered that he had analysed Barker's claim methodically and had taken account of the planned programme, the progress of the works at the time and the effect of the relevant events on subsequent work.

The judge accepted that there had been no evidence of 'bad faith' by the architect but he was not persuaded that the architect's assessment was methodical. Court hearings get to a level of detail on issues that most construction professionals would not have envisaged at the time the events took place. In this case, the architect's detailed evidence about what he had done led the judge to conclude that his assessments about the periods of delay were variously unclear, irrational and illogical.

The judge concluded that the extension of time awarded was fundamentally flawed. He said:

'... [the architect] did not carry out a logical analysis in a methodical way of the impact which the relevant matters had or were likely to have on [Barker's] planned programme. He [the architect] made an impressionistic, rather than a calculated, assessment of the time which he thought was reasonable for the various items individually and overall ... Where [the architect] allowed time for relevant events, the allowance which he made in important instances ... bore no logical or reasonable relation to the delay caused.'

Many contractors would have smiled ruefully to learn that extensions of time should be methodically calculated by the architect and should not be impressionistic. No doubt many claims were, and still are, assessed using impression rather than calculation. The key factor in this case appears to have been a rather dramatic disjunction between what the architect honestly thought he had done and what detailed cross examination revealed he had actually done.

Having decided that the architect's assessment was invalid, the judge went on to consider what extension of time should have been awarded. On this point he broadly accepted the approach of the programming expert witness for Barker, who appears to have carried out an 'as-planned impacted' or 'time impact' analysis. The delay analysis was in the form of bar charts which were provided 'to demonstrate how the programme would have been affected if allowance had been made in it for the relevant events'. The charts demonstrated 'the logical links between the various activities shown in the programme' and further charts were produced 'seeking to show the effect on those programmes of the subsequent variations'.

The judge thought Barker's 'planned resources were reasonable for their planned programme' and he accepted,

'... that the subsequent variations were likely to have, and have had, a disruptive effect on that programme, and that the exercise which [the expert] has done is a fair way of calculating a reasonable extension of time.'

Therefore, in this case, a delay analysis based on the planned intent of the contractor appears to have been found to be suitable.

8.15 *Ascon Contracting Ltd v Alfred McAlpine Construction Isle Of Man Ltd* [1999] 66 ConLR 119

Parties have argued about who 'owns the float' in a programme for many years and so when this case touched on the subject it was widely commented on. However, the case also provided very useful guidance on delay analysis and acceleration, and also illustrated the difficulty a main contractor can face trying to pin the blame for project delays onto a subcontractor.

In 1996–97 McAlpine carried out the construction of a five-storey building, known as the Villiers Development, in Douglas, Isle of Man, on a triangular site between Loch Promenade and Victoria Street. Ascon was McAlpine's subcontractor for reinforced concrete floor slabs, basement perimeter walls and columns. The subcontract date for possession was 28 August 1996 and the period was 27 weeks, giving a completion date of 5 March 1997.

Practical completion was in fact achieved on 16 May 1997, just over ten weeks late and Ascon claimed an extension of time of 39 days; 22 days due to water ingress and 17 days due to delays to the lift pit. McAlpine declined to give any extension on the grounds that Ascon were responsible for the delays. Furthermore, McAlpine counterclaimed against Ascon for recovery of its own loss and expense and recovery of £175,000 liquidated damages deducted under the main contract due to a ten-week overrun.

The parties were unable to settle their differences and Ascon brought a claim to the Technology and Construction Court, where it was heard by Judge Hicks QC. The first extension of time claim related to the extent and effect of the incursion of water into the subcontract works. The site was separated from the sea front by little more than the width of Loch Promenade and until the permanent waterproofing was complete, tidal water would percolate into the excavation. The contractual responsibility for keeping the works free from water ingress lay with McAlpine but the works were often flooded. McAlpine countered that the real cause of delay at this time was not the presence of water but Ascon's failure to provide enough steel-fixers.

Judge Hicks accepted that there probably were insufficient steel fixers but he decided that it was not necessary to decide the point because McAlpine's argument 'fallaciously seeks to reverse the burden of proof'. It was held that Ascon was disrupted and put to extra work by water ingress and damage but Ascon had to show that the 22 days of delay were caused by this problem, which was essentially a factual question. Judge Hicks found Ascon's case contained 'gaping holes' and only allowed an extension of six days for this issue.

Judge Hicks allowed a further eight days for Ascon's second claim, relating to the late handover of the lift pit and variations. The reduction to the claim here was partly because it was found that Ascon 'could and should have made more progress' and because certain remedial works were necessary. In other words, Ascon did not do enough to mitigate the effects of the delay and were partly culpable.

It is interesting to note Judge Hicks' comments about the evidence of McAlpine's expert witnesses on the extension of time issues. The expert relied upon a comparison between a logic-linked bar-chart programme and an as-built programme to support his report on the causes of delay. The bar-chart showed all activities as critical, which meant that any delay at an early stage of the works would remain operative throughout. When questioned on this at the hearing, the expert admitted that the situation was not, in reality, so inflexible. However, this late 'attempt to disown the implications of his own bar chart' did not impress Judge Hicks.

Perhaps this provides two lessons: firstly, it is dangerous to try to modify previous evidence when in the witness box; secondly, it is dangerous to place too much reliance on rigid 'logic-linked' programmes when dealing with construction delay claims.

Judge Hicks then considered the claim for acceleration. Ascon claimed that it had been instructed to accelerate and had increased working hours and plant resources because of instructions from McAlpine and sought reimbursement of costs. Judge Hicks said:

> ' "Acceleration" tends to be bandied about as if it were a term of art with a precise technical meaning, but I have found nothing to persuade me that that is the case. The root concept behind the metaphor is no doubt that of increasing speed and therefore, in the context of a construction contract, of finishing earlier. On that basis "accelerative measures" are steps taken, it is assumed at increased expense, with a view to achieving that end. If the other party is to be charged with that expense, however, that description gives no reason, so far, for such a charge. At least two further questions are relevant to any such issue. The first, implicit in the description itself, is "earlier than what?" The second asks by whose decision the relevant steps were taken.
>
> The answer to the first question will characteristically be either "earlier than the contractual date" or "earlier than the (delayed) date which will be achieved without the accelerative measures". In the latter category there may be further questions as to responsibility for the delay and as to whether it confers entitlement to an extension of time. The answer to the second question may clearly be decisive, especially in the common case of contractual provisions for additional payment for variations, but it is closely linked with the first; acceleration not required to meet a contractor's existing obligations is likely to be the result of an instruction from the employer for which the latter must pay, whereas pressure from the employer to make good delay caused by the contractor's own default is unlikely to be so construed.'

Ascon admitted that there were no written instructions to accelerate but claimed that McAlpine put them under pressure to 'to come up with means of … accelerating the works to recover the time that was lost'. It was contended that an instruction could be 'discerned'.

It might be thought unlikely that a court would consider a significant claim for reimbursement of acceleration costs without a clear instruction but Judge Hicks did not have to decide this point because Ascon did not come up with means of accelerating the works to recover the full delay and the acceleration costs were, in any event, included in the delay claim. On the second point he had this to say:

> 'It is difficult to see how there can be any room for the doctrine of mitigation in relation to damage suffered by reason of the employer's culpable delay in the face of express contractual machinery for dealing with the situation by extension of time and reimbursement of loss and expense. However that may be as a matter of principle, what is plain is that there cannot be both an extension to the full extent of the employer's culpable delay, with damages on that basis, and also damages in the form of expense incurred by way of mitigation, unless it is alleged and established that the attempt at mitigation, although reasonable, was wholly ineffective. That is certainly not how Ascon puts its case here.'

Having decided Ascon's claim, the Judge then had to consider McAlpine's counterclaim. In doing so he addressed a point raised by McAlpine as to the effect of 'float' in the main contract programme. The programme provided for completion of works five weeks before the contractual end date and McAlpine argued that it was entitled to the benefit of this float and could use it at its option to 'cancel' or reduce delays for which it or other subcontractors would be responsible in preference to those chargeable to Ascon. Judge Hicks thought this argument was misconceived. He said:

> 'The float is certainly of value to the main contractor in the sense that delays of up to that total amount, however caused, can be accommodated without involving him in liability for liquidated damages to the employer or, if he calculates his own prolongation costs from the contractual completion date (as McAlpine has here) rather than from the earlier date which might have been achieved, in any such costs. He cannot, however, while accepting that benefit as against the employer, claim against subcontractors as if it did not exist. That is self-evident if total delays as against subprogrammes do not exceed the float. The main contractor, not having suffered any loss of the above kinds, cannot recover from subcontractors the hypothetical loss he would have suffered had the float not

existed, and that will be so whether the delay is wholly the fault of one subcontractor, or wholly that of the main contractor himself, or spread in varying degrees between several subcontractors and the main contractor. No doubt those different situations can be described, in a sense, as ones in which the 'benefit' of the float has accrued to the defaulting party or parties, but no-one could suppose that the main contractor has, or should have, any power to alter the result so as to shift that 'benefit'. The issues in any claim against a subcontractor remain simply breach, loss and causation.

I do not see why that analysis should not still hold good if the constituent delays more than use up the float, so that completion is late. Six subcontractors, each responsible for a week's delay, will have caused no loss if there is a six-week float. They are equally at fault, and equally share in the 'benefit'. If the float is only five weeks, so that completion is a week late, the same principle should operate; they are equally at fault, should equally share in the reduced 'benefit' and therefore equally in responsibility for the one week's loss. The allocation should not be in the gift of the main contractor.'

Although this part of the judgment attracted a lot of attention, perhaps the most important part of this section is not the analysis of who owns the float but the reminder that the key issues 'remain simply breach, loss and causation'.

When deciding whether Ascon caused the delay to the completion of the main contract works, Judge Hicks commented as follows:

'The importance of practical completion as between employer and main contractor, and therefore derivatively as between main contractor and finishing trades, is that it marks the date on which possession returns to the employer, with the opportunity of beneficial use of the property. The relevance of that date to causation of loss from delay is therefore direct, and usually decisive. The date of practical completion will also govern liability for liquidated damages. Here no subcontract liquidated damages clause is relied upon and Ascon was not a finishing trade; the question whether delay on its part caused loss of the kind claimed by McAlpine turns not on any nice question of how practical completion is to be understood or its date identified but on the factual issue whether, and if so by how much, delayed working affected the progress of the following trades and thereby the completion of the main contract.'

Ascon argued that delays to the main contract programme were later recovered, in whole or in part, so that that breach was not causative of the delay in completion of the main contract.

Judge Hicks continued:

'That brings me back to the factual issues of causation. The first is whether it is proper, in the absence of other evidence, to infer that the causes of delay at one stage have a continuing effect so as to produce the same delay at a later stage. I believe that that is in principle a proper inference, but that the probability that it will be drawn, or drawn to its full extent, is likely to diminish with the passage of time and the complexity of intervening events. My reasons for regarding it as being proper, with those qualifications, are first that such an inference, at least over short periods, is tacitly assumed in all negotiation, arbitration and litigation of delay claims, and secondly that it represents the 'neutral' position, in the sense that if all other activities proceeded according to programme ... that would be the result.'

The key factual issues considered by Judge Hicks were primarily the following:

- Practical completion of the main contract occurred on 9 February 1998 (ten months after the commencement of cladding).
- The cladding works, which immediately followed Ascon's work, commenced on 1 April 1997, almost eleven week late because of Ascon's delays.
- Ascon were only entitled to an extension of time of 14 days.
- After practical completion of Ascon's work, McAlpine told its employer that the delay would be reduced to four weeks by completion.
- One of McAlpine's factual witness admitted that the delays to the works as at 16 July 1997 were not Ascon's fault.
- By the end of September 1997 the delay to the main contract was down to five weeks, although 'further difficulties' had arisen
- On 17 December 1997 McAlpine sent a letter to Rotary Services Ltd, who had installed emergency light fittings, stating that 'the faults with these fittings is [sic] the sole reason for our being denied a Practical Completion Certificate'.

Judge Hicks concluded from these facts that while it was 'theoretically possible that all the factors causing the delay in April ... were still fully operative' it was 'an unrealistic supposition'. He decided that the reality was that 'by then the passage of time and the supervention of a multiplicity of new causes had broken the chain of causation' and Ascon was not responsible for more than one and a half weeks of the delay in practical completion of the main contract.

8.16 *Henry Boot Construction (UK) Ltd v Malmaison Hotel (Manchester) Ltd* [1999] 70 ConLR 32

In December 1996 Henry Boot Construction was engaged by Malmaison to construct a new hotel in Piccadilly, Manchester. The subsequent court case provided some very helpful comments to the construction industry about how to deal with concurrent delay events and was also useful for its ruling on the scope of matters that an architect can consider when assessing a claim for an extension of time under JCT 80.

The agreement between Boot and Malmaison was based on the JCT Standard Form of Building Contract, 1980 Edition, Private with Quantities. The original contact completion date was set as 21 November 1997 and liquidated damages for late completion were £25,000 per week or part thereof.

The works were delayed and the architect awarded an extension of time, which took the completion date to 6 January 1998. However, practical completion was not certified as until 13 March 1998 and the employer deducted £250,000 in liquidated damages. Boot claimed an extension of time to the date of practical completion due to delays by a nominated subcontractor and delays caused by late, varied and inadequate information, and by variations. The architect disagreed and the dispute was referred to arbitration.

In the arbitration, Malmaison said the claim was misconceived and flawed. One of the complaints was said to be that Boot had based the delay analysis on a revised programme, which ignored the true state of the works at the date the delays were said to have occurred. Another complaint was that the delays did not affect the critical path or account for culpable delay. In the 'Statement of Defence' Malmaison listed many alleged failings in Boot's performance, which it said were the true causes of the delays. Boot said this defence was irrelevant and outside the scope of the arbitrator's jurisdiction, because it did not relate to the relevant events upon which the architect had to determine the extension of time due under the contract.

The arbitrator gave a decision, which Malmaison appealed, and the case came before Judge Dyson in the Technology and Construction Court. In his judgment Judge Dyson noted two areas of 'common ground' between the parties. Firstly, both sides agreed with the analysis of the extension of time provisions in the contract as set out in *Balfour Beatty Building Ltd v Chestermount Properties Ltd*. Secondly, both sides agreed that:

> '...if there are two concurrent causes of delay, one of which is a Relevant Event, and the other is not, then the contractor is entitled to an extension of time for the period of delay caused

by the Relevant Event notwithstanding the concurrent effect of the other event. Thus, to take a simple example, if no work is possible on a site for a week not only because of exceptionally inclement weather (a Relevant Event) but also because the contractor has a shortage of labour (not a Relevant Event), and if the failure to work during that week is likely to delay the Works beyond the Completion Date by one week, then if he considers it fair and reasonable to do so, the Architect is required to grant an extension of time of one week. He cannot refuse to do so on the grounds that the delay would have occurred in any event by reason of shortage of labour.'

This second agreement is often misquoted (both accidentally and deliberately) as being a statement of the judge rather than a statement in the judgment – the judgment merely records the parties' agreement. Notwithstanding this fact, the position set out is widely considered to be an accurate statement of how concurrency under JCT 80 should be viewed.

On the subject of concurrency Judge Dyson helpfully considered a hypothetical situation where a contractor claims two weeks extension of time due to access to the site being deferred for that period. In this case, he said:

'It would be open to the employer to defend the claim by disputing that access was denied, or by contending that the contractor could and should have been getting on with work off-site ... so as to eliminate the effects of the delayed access. But it is difficult to see how in such a case the employer could rely on poor progress by the contractor generally throughout the contract as a defence to the claim for an extension of time of two weeks for delayed access.'

Having noted the common ground about concurrency, Judge Dyson addressed the issue in dispute concerning the scope of events an architect (or arbitrator) can take into account when assessing delay. The judge accepted Malmaison's argument – an architect is not precluded by clause 25 from considering the effect of events, other than relevant events, when deciding whether to allow an extension of time.

Judge Dyson said:

'It seems to me that it is a question of fact in any case whether a Relevant Event has caused or is likely to cause delay to the Works beyond the completion date.'

8.17 *Royal Brompton Hospital NHS Trust v Frederick Alexander Hammond & Others* [2000] 76 ConLR 148

Unlike most other cases concerning construction project delays the contractor for the project, Taylor Woodrow Construction Ltd, was not involved in the litigation. The claim was made by the Royal Brompton Hospital NHS Trust against the project manager and the architect and the case considered a number of points in connection with the assessment of extensions of time.

The dispute arose out of a contract to build a new six storey hospital, known as 'The National Heart and Chest Centre Phase 1', located at Sydney Street in Chelsea, London. The agreement between the Trust and Taylor Woodrow was based on the JCT Standard Form of Building Contract, 1980 edition, Local Authorities with Quantities. The Completion Date specified was 23 July 1989.

The progress of the Works was delayed and Taylor Woodrow claimed extensions of time pursuant to the provisions of clause 25 of the Main Contract. The architect awarded a number of extensions that produced a revised completion date of 14 January 1990. However, practical completion was not certified as being achieved until 22 May 1990.

Following the issue of the Certificate of Practical Completion Taylor Woodrow continued to make representations about the delays. The architect thought Taylor Woodrow's performance on the project had been 'far from satisfactory' but concluded that there were matters that were not Taylor Woodrow's responsibility, which delayed the works by the full 43 weeks and 2 days. Therefore, the architect ultimately revised the date for completion to 22 May 1990.

It is interesting to note that the architect appeared to consider that clause 25 of the contract, relating to extensions of time, worked in favour of contractors, who he thought were able to avoid liquidated damages despite poor on-site performance.

The Trust claimed that the extension of time awarded to Taylor Woodrow was incorrect and accused both their architect and project manager of negligence. In the event, the case against the project manager failed and so reference below is made exclusively to the architect.

The case came before Judge Richard Seymour Q.C. in the Technology and Construction Court. The particulars of the claim brought by the Trust included allegations that when considering applications for extensions of time the architect had failed to determine the critical path of Taylor Woodrow's works, resulting in extensions being given for non-critical path activities. Furthermore the Trust said the architect had failed:

> '... to determine either at all and/or with reasonable accuracy Taylor Woodrow's actual progress against its programme and/or the reasons for delay against that programme when considering Taylor Woodrow's applications for extensions of time.'

In order to decide the case, Judge Seymour started by looking at the circumstances in which it is proper to grant an extension of time under clause 25 of JCT 80. He identified two conditions that need to be satisfied before an extension of time can be granted:

1   that a relevant event has occurred; and
2   that that relevant event is likely to cause the completion of the works as a whole to be delayed beyond the completion date then fixed under the contract, whether as a result of the original agreement between the contracting parties or as a result of the grant of a previous extension of time.

This led to the more difficult question of how to deal with 'concurrency'. Counsel for the architect cited *Balfour Beatty Building Ltd v Chestermount Properties Ltd* and *Henry Boot Construction (UK) Ltd v Malmaison Hotel (Manchester) Ltd*, which were said to support the approach taken by the architect where relevant and non-relevant events operated concurrently. Judge Seymour thought it necessary to be clear what was meant by 'events operating concurrently'. He said:

> 'It does not mean, in my judgment, a situation in which, work already being delayed, let it be supposed, because the contractor has had difficulty in obtaining sufficient labour, an event occurs which is a Relevant Event and which, had the contractor not been delayed, would have caused him to be delayed, but which in fact, by reason of the existing delay, made no difference. In such a situation although there is a Relevant Event 'the completion of the Works is [not] likely to be delayed <u>thereby</u> beyond the Completion Date.' The Relevant Event simply has no effect upon the completion date.

> This situation obviously needs to be distinguished from a situation in which, as it were, the works are proceeding in a regular fashion and on programme, when two things happen, either of which, had it happened on its own, would have caused delay, and one is a Relevant Event, while the other is not. In such circumstances there is a real concurrency of causes of the delay.'

Judge Seymour noted that there were a number of established delay analysis techniques but, in order to make an assessment of whether a particular occurrence affected the ultimate completion of the work, rather than just a particular operation, he thought it desirable to consider what operations were critical to the forward progress of the work as a whole, at the time the delay event occurs.

The expert witness engaged by the Trust admitted that the establishment of the critical path of a particular construction project can itself be a difficult task and the critical path may well change during the course of the works. The expert also accepted that the various different methods of making an assessment of the impact of unforeseen occurrences upon the progress of construction works are likely to produce different results, perhaps even dramatically different results. He also accepted that the accuracy of any of the delay analysis methods in common use depends upon the quality of the information upon which the assessment exercise is based.

There were four particular extensions that fell under the spotlight in this case. One related to the late possession of part of the site known as the Chelsea Hospital for Women. This delay did not actually cause any delay to the completion of the works because Taylor Woodrow was already so far behind programme that work could not have started earlier than the date upon which full possession was given. However, the architect awarded an extension of time of 11 weeks for this event, being the period of deferred possession. The architect considered that Taylor Woodrow ought to have the full period allowed by the contract to undertake the work in the Chelsea Hospital for Women area.

Judge Seymour had considerable doubts as to whether the architect's view was 'a correct analysis of the position' under JCT 80, as an extension should only be given if the progress of the works has been delayed. However, this point was not argued before him (and had it been perhaps he would have come to a different view).

The issue before the court concerned a claim of professional negligence, not the correct legal interpretation of the contract. At the hearing, experienced witnesses stated that there was a body of opinion among those who have to make decisions on extensions of time to contractors that there was an automatic entitlement to time if access to the site is deferred. The judge decided that the fact that the architect also subscribed to that opinion meant he was not negligent in granting the 11 weeks extension.

The second of the four delays related to an instruction to lay 'Hydrotite' damp proof membrane to the floors. The 'Wall and Floor Finishes' activity, to which the 'Hydrotite' related, was on the critical path and so the extension of time awarded by the architect was equal to the time required to carry out the additional work. The architect's award for this delay was made in two parts. The first decision, of five weeks, given on 19 October 1989, was made at a time when Taylor Woodrow was still expressing confidence that the Works could be completed by mid-February 1990. Judge Seymour said:

'If that expression of confidence was taken at face value, no extension of time at all on the Hydrotite Ground was justified as at 19 October 1989 and, in my judgment, it would have been negligent to have granted one. However, it seems to me that an architect must exercise his or her own judgment as to how realistic or otherwise such expressions of confidence are: he or she does not have to accept what the contractor says, even if the contractor is predicting that there will be no delay.'

Therefore, it was held that this first decision was not made negligently.

The second decision relating to the 'Hydrotite', which was made on 24 November 1989, gave Taylor Woodrow a further seven weeks. By this time the laying of the flooring was virtually complete, three weeks earlier than the target programme. Therefore, by this time it had become apparent that the progress of the works would not be delayed. As a result it was held that in giving a further extension the architect was negligent. Judge Seymour acknowledged that:

'the distinction ... between the first and the second extensions of time granted on the Hydrotite Ground may appear rather artificial' and he did not 'pretend that it is intellectually very satisfactory.'

However, this very important distinction appears to be based on what the architect knew at the time the two awards were made.

The third delay event concerned a late variation to the safety cabinets. The Trust said the safety cabinets were not on the critical path and therefore could not have caused delay to the completion of the works as a whole. Judge Seymour said:

'I have to say that I do not think that it is obvious, just as a matter of common sense, whether the safety cabinets were on the critical path or not ... Ultimately it is the last operation which needs to be carried out on a construction site before it is possible to say that the works are practically complete which is on the critical path, no matter how insignificant in itself. Therefore, subject to any point which can properly be made as to insignificance, fixing the last door handle is on the critical path. While there was evidence from the documentation put before me that commissioning, to which I refer below, was going at the same time as the work to the benches upon which the safety cabinets stood, that does not, of itself, mean that the safety cabinets were not on the critical path. In the absence of clear evidence that the safety cabinets were not on the critical path, I do not feel able to conclude that no reasonably competent architect could possibly have thought that they were.'

The fourth and final issue was the commissioning. It was not in dispute that some extension of time was appropriate – the issue was, what the appropriate length of time was. The architect allowed eight weeks. The result of this decision by the architect was that Taylor Woodrow avoided any responsibility for the failure to complete the works any earlier than 22 May 1990, despite their allegedly poor performance but it was held that,

'... if Taylor Woodrow was delayed in completing the works both by matters for which it bore the contractual risk and by Relevant Events, within the meaning of that term in the Standard Form, in the light of the authorities to which I have referred, it would be entitled to extensions of time by reason of the occurrence of the Relevant Events notwithstanding its own defaults.'

The 'authorities referred to' were *Balfour Beatty Building Ltd v Chestermount Properties Ltd* and *Henry Boot Construction (UK) Ltd v Malmaison Hotel (Manchester) Ltd*.

8.18 Balfour Beatty Construction Ltd v The Mayor and Burgesses of the London Borough of Lambeth [2002] BLR 288

This case concerned the enforcement of an Adjudicator's Decision made on 23 January 2002. It was heard by Judge Humphrey Lloyd QC in the Technology & Construction Court. The judgment contains interesting comments about both the presentation of claims in adjudication and about delay analysis in general.

The adjudication arose out of an agreement made in October 1999 between Lambeth and Balfour. The agreement, which was based on the JCT standard form of building contract 1998 Edition, Local Authorities without Quantities, incorporating amendments and TC/94 and contractor's designed portion supplement 1998, provided for the refurbishment and remodelling of Falmouth House, Penwith Manor Estate, Kennington Park Road, London. The value of the contract was £3,847,231.

The works began in November 1999. There were delays and the architect decided that Balfour was entitled to extensions of time, to 23 October 2000. Practical Completion was achieved seven months later, on 24 May 2001. Lambeth became entitled to, and did, deduct damages for delay totalling £355,831.71.

The adjudicator decided Balfour was entitled to an extension of time of thirty five weeks and one day, creating a revised completion date of 10 April 2001, which reduced the applicable period for damages to six weeks and two days. Lambeth challenged the adjudicator's decision and resisted enforcement, alleging that the adjudicator did not act impartially and the decision was reached 'in breach of contract and without jurisdiction'.

On submissions to adjudication Judge Humphrey Lloyd had this to say:

'This is yet another case in which adjudication has been launched after completion of the works and in which the dispute attracts a simple description but comprises a highly complex set of facts and issues relating to the performance of a contract carried over many months. It may well be doubted whether adjudication was intended for such a situation. If it is to be utilised effectively it is essential that the referring party gives the adjudicator all that is needed in a highly manageable form. From the material available to me it is clear that Balfour did little or nothing to present its case in a logical or methodical way. Despite the fact that the dispute concerned a multi-million pound refurbishment contract no attempt was made to provide any critical path.'

The Judge thought that an adjudicator ought to be able to expect that elementary information regarding the delay would be readily available and that it would be produced in the adjudication. In this case 'elementary information' would include a schedule setting out each Relevant Event, the date of the Event, the activity directly affected by the Event, the nature of the effect (i.e. delay to start, extension of duration, delay to finish) the timing or date of that effect, and any necessary comments.

On the analysis of the delay the Judge commented:

'By now one would have thought that it was well understood that, on a contract of this kind, in order to attack, on the facts, a clause 24 certificate for non-completion (or an extension of time determined under clause 25), the foundation must be the original programme (if capable of justification and substantiation to show its validity and reliability as a contractual starting point) and its success will similarly depend on the soundness of its revisions on the occurrence of every event, so as to be able to provide a satisfactory and convincing demonstration of cause and effect. A valid critical path (or paths) has to be established both initially and at every later material point since it (or they) will almost certainly change. Some means has also to be established for demonstrating the effect of concurrent or parallel delays or other matters for which the employer will not be responsible under the contract.'

It might be concluded from Judge Humphrey Lloyd QC's summary that delay analyses should be based on critical path programmes showing the original intent and the effects of every change. However, it is suggested that due emphasis should be given to the other parts of his statement.

Firstly, the methodology suggested is only for 'a contract of this kind'. This appears to be a reference to the size and complexity of the contract and the ensuing delays. Therefore, it would probably not be suitable for smaller and/or less complex projects.

Secondly, the original programme can only form the foundation 'if capable of justification and substantiation to show its validity and reliability as a contractual starting point'. If the original programme is shown to be invalid or unreliable, there is no foundation for the suggested approach.

Similarly, the success of the approach will 'depend on the soundness of its revisions on the occurrence of every event, so as to be able to provide a satisfactory and convincing demonstration of cause and effect'. If the updates are unsatisfactory or unconvincing the analysis will fail.

Finally, the limitations of critical path analysis (as explained in chapter 3) must also be borne in mind.

The outcome of this case was that the adjudicator's decision was not enforced because it was held that there was a doubt about its impartiality. It was said that:

'... by making good the deficiencies in Balfour's case and by overcoming the absence of a sustainable as-built programme with a critical path ... the adjudicator moved into the danger zone of being impartial or liable to "apparent bias", as it is now recognised'.

8.19 Skanska Construction UK Ltd v Egger (Barony) Ltd [2004] EWHC 1748, TCC

This case is unusual in that it includes consideration of certain computer programmes widely used in construction delay analysis, namely 'Power Project' and 'Primavera'. It also confirmed some of the essential ingredients for an analysis of delay to a construction project.

Despite the interesting points coming out of this judgment, it was not reported in the *Building Law Reports* and *Construction Law Reports*. However, the judgment can be viewed on the website of the British and Irish Legal Information Institute (www.bailii.org). The case reference stands for England and Wales High Court, case reference number 1748, in the Technology and Construction Court (EWHC 1748, TCC).

The dispute arose out of a project carried out in 1997–98 whereby Skanska built a new factory for Egger, an Austrian chipboard manufacturer, on the site of the former Barony Colliery in East Ayrshire. The site required the removal of surface coal spoil to make it suitable for development. Egger entered into a separate contract with an earthworks contractor to have preparatory works undertaken, prior to Skanska's involvement. The guaranteed maximum price originally stood at £12million.

During the course of construction the floor slab of the warehouse of the factory cracked and it broke up when subjected to the weight of loaded vehicles driving over it. This resulted in disruption and delay being caused to the works, the costs of which were claimed by Skanska in their final account totalling £24.5million – Egger's valuation was £13.5million and from this sum they sought to deduct £4.1million in respect of allegedly defective work, as well as liquidated and ascertained damages. With such significant sums in dispute, it is not surprising that the matter came before Judge David Wilcox in the Technology and Construction Court.

One of the disputed sections of the account concerned the subcontractors' claims. The contract works were wholly performed by subcontractors, as the contract scheme provided, and Skanska sought to recover the £1,139,277 paid (or payable) to them for loss and expense. Egger had already been found to be responsible for delays to the works (at an earlier trial) but they argued that no sum was due in respect of these claims because they were insufficiently particularised and may have included monies which were attributable to inefficiencies for which Egger were not responsible.

In order to decide this issue the judge had to consider evidence provided by the delay analysts appointed by each side. Egger's expert produced a large and detailed report which appears to have been based on an 'as-planned impacted' methodology. The original programme had been produced using 'Power Project' and was in a simple bar chart format. In order to produce an as-planned programme that could be rescheduled when impacted with changes, Egger's programming expert had to convert this bar chart into a logic-linked critical path network. He did so using 'Primavera' software.

The result was a programme containing what the judge called 'derived notional subcontract periods' based upon programmes that, in the event, did not reflect what actually occurred on site. The judge did not say whether the analysis was unusable due to this discrepancy between the programme and actual events because there were further fundamental flaws.

The critical path network relied upon information provided to the expert by members of Egger's management team. However, these managers were not called to give evidence at the hearing and so the report was reliant on 'the untested judgment of others', who selected and characterised the data for input into the computer programme. Not surprisingly the judge found that the reliance on untested views of others affected the authority of the computer generated programme, even if the logic used in the programme was impeccable. However, the judge's views about the authority of this programme were further undermined when, during evidence, it was positively shown that the programme relied on 'facts' that were incorrect. As noted by Judge Wilcox: '… the reliability of [a] sophisticated impact analysis is only as good as the data put in.'

That left the court with the analysis prepared by Skanska's expert. Egger argued that the analysis of Skanska's expert should not be relied upon because the 'Power Project' software used to prepare it was incapable of producing a reliable analysis. Egger pointed out that 'Power Project' 'is primarily a planning tool creating a graphic representation, it is a dated system and does not have the sophistication of [Egger's expert's] system.' Egger also said that the effective application of 'Power Project', with its inherent limitations, was dependent upon the 'intuition' of its user, in that it allowed 'the power of selection of facts and interpretive judgment of them'.

Skanska accepted that 'Power Project' was not suitable for carrying out the kind of impact analysis carried out by Egger's expert but it was suitable for the purpose it was used, namely 'the forward-looking and creative aspect in the planning of a project'.

The judge was satisfied that 'Power Project' had a significant capacity for logical connections and for identifying critical paths and for rescheduling activities to show how events change. As regards the power of selection of facts and interpretive judgment of them, the judge could not see how this criticism differed from the process followed and applied by Egger's expert.

The expert engaged by Skanska impressed the judge:

> '… as someone who was objective, meticulous as to detail, and not hide bound by theory as when demonstrable fact collided with computer programme logic. His analysis was accessibly depicted in a series of charts accompanying his evidence.'

Therefore, although Skanska's expert used a less sophisticated analysis, the judge preferred his evidence because his analysis was relatively transparent and based on accurate facts. But perhaps most tellingly, he appeared to reject a narrow minded reliance on computer logic for construction delay analysis.

When it came to an analysis of the details of the delays the judge found there was no cogent evidence of disruption and delay caused otherwise than by Egger and so Skanska's claims regarding subcontractors' delays succeeded.

8.20 *Great Eastern Hotel Company Ltd v John Laing Construction Ltd* [2005] 99 ConLR 45

From the title of this case it may appear to be another employer/contractor dispute. In fact it is a dispute brought by an employer against a construction manager. In order to review the claim the judge had to consider the periods and causes of delays to the project.

Great Eastern engaged Laing as construction manager of a major project to refurbish and extend the Great Eastern Hotel at the junction of Liverpool Street and Bishopsgate, in the City of London. Works included the demolition and rebuilding of the upper floors and the construction of a new structure between two blocks of the existing building. Laing's tender included a proposed programme of 109 weeks, commencing from 2 June 1997 and the budget cost for the works was £34.8million.

The works commenced a few weeks later than planned, on 30 June 1997, and soon fell into delay. The procurement of the temporary roof, which covered a large section of the existing building, took three weeks longer than programmed and erection took 35 weeks instead of ten weeks. It was agreed that this operation was critical to the whole project.

Practical completion was achieved on 13 July 2000, 346 days later than the original planned date of 2 August 1999. As a result Great Eastern had to make significant additional payments to its professional team and to the trade contractors, meaning that the final cost of the project was £61million.

Great Eastern held Laing responsible for the additional costs and sought to recover £17million by way of damages for breach of contract. The case was heard by Judge David Wilcox in the Technology and Construction Court.

Both parties engaged programming expert witnesses to assist with the delay issues. The expert for Great Eastern assessed the delays by analysing the updated programme on a monthly basis to measure the impact of events as they proceeded. The expert for Laing mainly used a retrospective analysis of the as-built programme to determine the critical path and assess the periods and causes of delays but also used an 'as-planned impacted' analysis to review concurrent delays.

Both forms of analysis produced a similar principal critical path and similar period of delay (49.5 weeks). However, there were differences as to the route of the critical path and the causes of delay. Laing's expert said that all the delays were due to either the design team and/or the trade contractors.

The research and analyses prepared by the expert for Great Eastern were described by the judge as 'impressive and comprehensive'. They were based on:

> '… contemporary primary documentation which included computer records and timed site photographs depicting the actual progress … This data was objectively evaluated and reflected in [the expert's] expressed opinion.'

This analysis appears to have assisted the judge in deciding that Laing:

- failed to ensure that the demolition and roofing package was let on time;
- neglected to use design information provided for the temporary roof;
- failed to manage the temporary roof design and construction package;
- allowed the temporary roof contractor to start on site without agreeing a binding contract;
- overlooked the need to progress the relocation and protection of the existing Railtrack services so that the work became critical and caused five weeks of delay to the project as a whole;

- allowed the temporary roof to be removed early, without putting alternative measures in place to keep the building watertight, causing damage and delays;
- deliberately misrepresented the true period of delay during the works;
- produced a revised programme that was 'attempting the impossible, namely recovery of … seven months [of delay] during a period of nine months'; and
- altered logic links on the contract programme 'to mask delay and management incompetence'.

It is interesting to note that these decisions, which all go to the assessment of the delay to the works, are decisions on factual issues applied to programme analysis, which echoes the views of other decisions including that of Judge Dyson in *Henry Boot Construction Ltd v Malmaison Hotel* who said: '… it is a question of fact in any case whether a Relevant Event has caused or is likely to cause delay to the Works beyond the completion date.'

To the extent that the 'as-planned impacted' analysis was used by Laing, it did not find favour with Judge Wilcox. He said the impacted as-planned delay analysis:

'… takes no account of the actual events which occurred on the Project and gives rise to an hypothetical answer.'

Therefore, he noted, the method fails to take account of the fact that a party may reprioritise tasks when aware of delays actually occurring on the site. In contrast the 'windows' type of analysis by Great Eastern's expert 'took account of the actual events'.

The judge also noted that Laing's expert carefully constructed three critical paths starting at the beginning of the project in July 1977 when the milestone dates did not exist. He found that, at best, these were 'theoretical constructs' identified retrospectively once the project was completed. They were not paths which were identified by either party during the project itself and it was found that the theory regarding the second critical path 'collided with reality'.

Laing also relied on the principle established in Galoo (see section 8.13). They argued that even if breaches by Laing were established, '… that cannot itself establish the necessary causal link …' The judge relied on another part of the judgment, which stated that questions of causation were to be unravelled by the application of the court's common sense.

Case	Summary
Holme and Another v Guppy and Another (1838) (Section 8.1)	Introduced the concept of 'time at large' as a term for a situation where there is an act of prevention by the employer and no provision under the contract or separate agreement to alter the completion date.
Wells v Army & Navy Co-op (1902) (Section 8.2)	Considered that it is not only the contractor's responsibility to complete a project in the given time period, but also the employer's responsibility to ensure the contractor has the given period of time.
Amalgamated Building Contractors Ltd v Waltham Holy Cross UDC (1952) (Section 8.3)	Concluded that an architect is able to give an extension of time retrospectively.
Peak Construction (Liverpool) Ltd v McKinney Foundation Ltd (1970) (Section 8.4)	Held that liquidated damages could not be recovered by an employer who was responsible for the failure to achieve a completion date.
Percy Bilton Ltd v Greater London Council (1982) (Section 8.5)	Decided that the repudiation of a subcontract by a nominated subcontractor is not to be regarded as a fault or breach of contract by the employer.
Walter Lawrence & Sons Ltd v Commercial Union Properties Ltd (1984) (Section 8.6)	Found that a contractor is entitled to an extension of time due to inclement weather even if the works were delayed and would not have encountered the weather had they been on schedule.
Yorkshire Water Authority v Sir Alfred McAlpine & Son (1986) (Section 8.7)	Reviewed the status of an approved clause 14 programme and method statement issued under ICE Conditions of Contract (5th Edition) in connection with an enforced change to the sequence of work.
Glenlion Construction Ltd v The Guinness Trust (1987) (Section 8.8)	Considered the contractual significance of programmes issued for a project – in particular whether an employer had a duty to produce information to meet a contractor's planned early completion.

Case	Summary
H. Fairweather & Co. Ltd v London Borough of Wandsworth (1987) (Section 8.9)	Confirmed that an extension of time does not create an automatic right to payment for prolongation costs under JCT 80 and decided that an architect should not decide extensions of time by reference to the dominant cause.
McAlpine Humberoak Ltd v McDermott International (No 1) (1992) (Section 8.10)	In certain circumstances time does not become 'at large' even in the absence of a suitable extension of time clause and a contractor may not be entitled to an extension of time even if there have been many employer design changes.
Balfour Beatty Building Ltd v Chestermount Properties Ltd (1993) (Section 8.11)	Decided that extensions of time should be measured 'nett' not 'gross', thereby putting the emphasis on the period rather than date of the delay event – often referred to as 'dotting-on' the delays.
Pigott Foundations Ltd v Shepherd Construction Ltd (1994) (Section 8.12)	Decided that a subcontractor is entitled to plan and perform work as it sees fit providing completion is within the contract period and upheld a limitation clause on recoverable damages against the subcontractor.
Galoo Ltd & Others v Bright Grahame Murray (1994) (Section 8.13)	Discussed causation and 'but for' analyses, stating that it is necessary to distinguish between a breech that caused a loss and a breach that merely provided the opportunity to sustain loss, by use of common sense.
John Barker Construction Ltd v London Portman Hotel Ltd (1996) (Section 8.14)	Discussed the lengths an architect should go to when deciding on the extent of an extension of time – any calculations should be methodical and not impressionistic.
Ascon Contracting Ltd v Alfred McAlpine Construction Isle Of Man Limited (1999) (Section 8.15)	Considered ownership of 'float' in programmes and highlighted the difficulties trying to pin the blame for delays on one subcontractor, particularly if there is a great deal of work carried out on site after that subcontractor has completed

Case	Summary
Henry Boot Construction Ltd v Malmaison Hotel (1999) (Section 8.16)	Decided that an architect may consider all events (not just 'Relevant Events') when assessing delay. The parties in this case agreed that if there are two concurrent causes of delay, one of which is a 'Relevant Event' under JCT 80 and the other is not, then the contractor is entitled to an extension of time relative to the relevant event notwithstanding the concurrent effect of the other event.
Royal Brompton Hospital NHS Trust v Frederick Alexander Hammond & Others (2000) (Section 8.17)	Held that an architect should make an assessment of delay by reference to the circumstances at the time the delay event occurred. Also commented on difficulties of assessing critical path and dealing with concurrent delays.
Balfour Beatty Construction Ltd v The Mayor and Burgesses of the London Borough of Lambeth (2002) (Section 8.18)	Commented on the information and analysis that should be provided (if possible) by parties making delay claims and also considered the role of the adjudicator.
Skanska Construction UK Ltd v Egger (Barony) Ltd (2004) (Section 8.19)	This case underlined the crucial importance of an accurate analysis of the facts when assessing delay issues – detailed and sophisticated computer delay analyses are only as good as the data input.
Great Eastern Hotel Company Ltd v John Laing Construction Ltd (2005) (Section 8.20)	Confirmed that delay cases turn on the facts, as applied to realistic delay assessments. The 'as-planned impacted' analysis was criticised for giving rise to a hypothetical answer.

9

Dispute resolution

Disputes about construction delays, or for that matter any other construction related issue, are usually resolved by negotiation between the parties. On occasions negotiations fail and when this happens there are a variety of choices available as to how to proceed. One of these choices is to litigate and the other choices can be collectively described as alternative dispute resolution methods.

One of the great attractions of alternative dispute resolution methods to businesses is that the dispute will not appear in the press or in law reports. Unlike litigation, all forms of alternative dispute resolution are private and confidential. However, this means that commentary about the relative merits and the relative success of each of the different alternatives can only be given on the basis of anecdotal evidence and personal experience.

For many years arbitration was the construction industry's preferred alternative to litigation but now the majority of disputes in the UK are referred to adjudication. Mediation is also regularly used and expert determination is another alternative.

In this chapter only the most popular methods of dispute resolution are discussed but there are other options, such as early neutral evaluation, mini-trial and dispute review boards.

9.1 Negotiation

Differences and disputes always have and always will occur on construction projects, often relating to how long the works have taken, but also about cost and quality. Most of these differences are resolved by negotiation.

There are many advantages to resolving disputes by negotiation, including speed, cost and usually the retention of commercial relationships. Perhaps the most important and distinctive aspect about negotiation (as opposed to the formal methods of dispute resolution) is that there are very few rules.

Providing parties stay on the right side of the criminal law they can conduct the negotiations in a manner and at a speed to suit themselves and parties can provide as much or as little evidence to support their positions as they wish. Because of the informal nature of negotiation, parties may be able to put the facts, the terms of the contract and the case law all to one side, and to 'horse-trade' (that is to settle the dispute on commercially acceptable terms, regardless of the merits of the case).

Negotiation is also relatively inexpensive, as, in general, parties to a negotiation do not engage consultants or lawyers and do not have to appoint a tribunal. Therefore, the main expense is measured in time rather than money.

However, it is not always possible to find a commercially acceptable compromise and in most cases parties to a construction dispute cannot simply conclude negotiations without at least some correlation between the merits of the case and the amount of the settlement, not least because they are often answerable to either shareholders, public bodies, other business partners and/or the bank.

Although most disputes are settled by negotiation, many negotiations ultimately fail, particularly where the differences are large. This failure can occur for a variety of reasons, including

- intransigence;
- commercial necessity;
- greed;
- ignorance;
- poor advice;
- unrealistic assessment of the case;
- misunderstandings;
- lack of factual records;
- absence of clear contractual terms;
- job preservation; and/or
- professional credibility.

Negotiations may also fail because one party runs out of time, due to impatience or commercial pressures. Therefore, the absence of a formal set procedure for negotiations and the possible absence of specialists to advise on and organise the case can be a problem, as well as a benefit.

9.2 Litigation

From a young age we see dramatic figures in gowns and horse hair wigs in courtroom dramas on TV and in films and so we develop a broad understanding that a dispute can be referred to a court where the judge has the power to right a wrong. However, unless we happen to be personally involved in litigation in one way or another there is no reason why we should have anything more than a vague idea of court procedure.

Most people associate courts with criminal law but, with the exception of the relatively small number of cases involving fraud, most construction cases are matters for the civil court. Civil litigation involves actions brought by one person or body, such as a limited company, against another, with the aim of being compensated if the claim is proved. In criminal cases the action is brought against the person by the state, in the name of the Queen, with the purpose of punishing the person, if found guilty.

In criminal cases the state has to prove the case beyond all reasonable doubt. It would appear that many people think that this is also the standard of proof required in civil matters. For example, it was noted in the judgment in the case of *John Barker Construction Ltd v London Portman Hotel* (1996)[22] that the employer had thought that if the contactor were to challenge the architect's extension of time award in court, then it would 'be required to prove beyond reasonable doubt that the extensions offered are fair'. In fact the standard of proof in civil cases is the balance of probabilities. This is a lower threshold and a contractor does not have to prove a loss and expense, delay or valuation claim 'beyond all reasonable doubt'.

As well as differences, there are a number of similarities between the civil and criminal courts in the UK. For example, unless you represent yourself in court, you will have to engage a lawyer to appear on your behalf. In both types of court an adversarial system is operated, where the lawyers put the case in the most favourable light for their clients, and the judge or jury weigh the factual evidence and apply the law in order to decide the matter. A case will be decided on the balance of the evidence presented and it is not for the judge to carry out investigations to discover the truth of the matter – it is for the parties to present their evidence and provide persuasive proof.

Some claimants in civil actions go to court to get 'justice', but their idea of justice is generally rather subjective and usually irrelevant. A court must decide a case on the basis of the parties' contractual agreement, not on a vague concept of 'fairness'. If a party has entered into a legally binding contract that contains terms that appear to be unfair, the judge cannot rewrite the agreement to make it 'fair'.

There are many different civil courts in the UK. Most litigation of construction disputes is referred to the TCC (the Technology and Construction Court). This is, as the name suggests, a specialist court, with judges who understand construction projects. Like the courts, legal practices also fall into specialisms and construction parties who intend to refer a dispute to litigation are well advised to seek out a lawyer who is a construction specialist.

Construction disputes generally concern issues of time, cost and/or quality of works and so most cases involve both witnesses of fact and expert witnesses – such as programmers, architects, engineers and/or surveyors. Both types of witness (factual and expert) usually give evidence orally at the hearing and/or in a sworn written statement or report. Witnesses of fact give factual evidence about what they saw, said, wrote, heard, smelt or touched; whereas expert witnesses give opinion evidence based on analysis and/or experience concerning the information provided to them.

Litigation is governed by the CPR (Civil Procedure Rules). These rules bring some certainty and fairness to the proceedings but this is at the expense of flexibility.

Disputes decided by courts will be meticulously examined by lawyers, experts and finally the judge, although that is not always the end of the matter. In certain circumstances judgments of the TCC can be appealed to the Court of Appeal and from there judgments can be appealed to the House of Lords.

Litigation provides for a very thorough review of the dispute and ultimately a binding and enforceable decision – but it will take time and cost money. It is not unusual for the costs of litigation of construction disputes to exceed the amount finally awarded but, unlike adjudication, the successful party can at least claim reimbursement of legal costs from the other party. In practice it is unlikely that 100 per cent of the costs expended on legal fees will be recoverable from the other side, but a successful party may recover between 65–80 per cent of its costs.

9.3 Adjudication

Construction industry adjudication is an alternative dispute resolution procedure introduced into the UK construction industry in May 1998 by virtue of section 108 of the *Housing Grants, Construction & Regeneration Act* 1996. This Act requires most types of construction contract to provide parties with an *opportunity* (not obligation) to have disputes or differences under their contract decided by an independent adjudicator. If the parties' contract does not comply with the Act then certain terms are implied into their agreement, by virtue of the government Scheme, more properly known as *The Scheme for Construction Contract (England and Wales) Regulations* 1998, or in Scotland *The Scheme for Construction Contract (Scotland) Regulations* 1998, or in Northern Ireland the *Construction Contracts (NI) Order* 1997.

An adjudicator is usually a construction industry professional – quantity surveyor, engineer or architect – or a lawyer who specialises in construction. The Act requires that an adjudicator is appointed within seven days of a notice of adjudication and he or she generally decides the dispute 28 days later. However, with the consent of the referring party, time for the decision can be extended by 14 days and with the consent of both parties it can be extended beyond 42 days.

Therefore, the adjudication process is intended to be quick and relatively cheap. It is an ideal procedure for dealing with arguments about interim payments and discreet contractual issues. However, parties also regularly choose to have major final account, loss and expense and extension of time disputes referred to adjudication.

Given the time constraints on the parties and adjudicator, it is inevitable that some decisions amount to rough justice. However, the on-going success of adjudication in the UK construction industry suggests that many parties are prepared to put up with, or at least take the risk of, a 'rough' decision. This may be because a dispute referred to adjudication is only temporarily binding. By and large, an adjudicator's decision cannot be appealed and will be enforced on application to the court but a party can have the same dispute tried afresh if it is unhappy with the decision. A decided dispute cannot be referred back to adjudication for a second time but it can be referred to the court (or to arbitration if that is the method agreed by the parties for resolving their contractual disputes).

Since the introduction of adjudication into the UK construction industry in 1998, the role of the adjudicator has been clarified (some may say curtailed) by court decisions. Broadly speaking that role is to make an impartial decision on the basis of evidence provided by the parties, as opposed to making a decision on the basis of analysis and investigation conducted by the adjudicator.

Typically an adjudicator will receive two written submissions in the first week or so of the 28 day adjudication period (a referral from the claiming party and a response from the defending party). Sometimes further written submissions or comments are made by the parties and sometimes there is a meeting at which the adjudicator can 'get up to speed' with the dispute and to clarify any queries. Usually the last week or two of the adjudication period is the time when the adjudicator goes through the submissions in detail and makes a decision. Most decisions are provided with reasons set out briefly in writing.

It would appear that the cost of taking a matter to adjudication is on the increase, particularly as claims become larger and more sophisticated but, in the vast majority of cases, a party cannot recover its costs from the other side, even if it is eventually successful in the action. Depending on your point of view, this may be considered to be an advantage or a disadvantage in using adjudication.

Is adjudication suited to resolving delay claims?

In chapter 8 there is a commentary about the case of *Balfour Beatty Construction Ltd v The Mayor and Burgesses of the London Borough of Lambeth* (2002)[23], which concerned a delay claim referred to adjudication. In that case the judge said:

> 'the dispute attracts a simple description but comprises a highly complex set of facts and issues relating to the performance of a contract carried over many months. It may well be doubted whether adjudication was intended for such a situation.'

Most construction delay claims are complex and given the short timeframe for adjudication it must be that the merits of a delay claim are likely to be more fully and more carefully considered in arbitration or litigation. However, this will come at a significant cost, both in terms of time and money and it may be felt that a quick assessment by an experienced professional, who understands the subject, is better than a slow and expensive analysis that may ultimately come up with a similar answer.

As said by the judge in *Balfour Beatty v Lambeth*, if adjudication is to be utilised effectively 'it is essential that the referring party gives the adjudicator all that is needed in a highly manageable form'.

9.4 Arbitration

Arbitration is a procedure whereby two parties agree to refer their dispute for decision by a third party. This third party is generally a respected senior figure involved in the same trade as the disputing parties. Therefore, most construction arbitrators are, like adjudicators, from the quantity surveying, engineering or architectural professions, or lawyers with construction industry knowledge and expertise.

Arbitration, as a means of resolving trade disputes, has been around for many hundreds of years, with the first arbitration act in England passed in 1698. The current statute governing the law of arbitration in England, Wales and Northern Ireland is the *Arbitration Act* 1998. Until the advent of adjudication, arbitration was the most popular means of formal dispute resolution in the construction industry in the UK. It is still widely used in many countries around the world.

It is open to parties to agree to arbitrate, instead of going to court, at any time. However, agreements to arbitrate disputes are generally included as a term of the written contract for the works. Unlike adjudication, arbitration is not optional if it has been included as a term of the contract and a defendant can apply to the court to 'stay' any legal proceedings commenced by the claiming party. (In general, a court will grant a stay under section 9 of the *Arbitration Act* 1996.) Like an adjudicator, an arbitrator in a construction case decides the facts and the law, in order to resolve the issues – he or she does not instigate and undertake his or her own investigations unless given the power to do so by the parties.

Arbitration has a number of advantages over litigation as it is:

- a private and consensual process;
- decided by someone who understands the technical aspects of the matter;
- less formal and more flexible than court proceedings; and
- it should be quicker and cheaper than litigation.

It also has the advantage that the procedure can be agreed by, rather than imposed on, the parties (which is also an advantage of arbitration over adjudication). Therefore, in a number of key respects, arbitration would appear to be an ideal forum for dealing with delay claims but, as stated above, it has gained a reputation in the UK construction industry for being too expensive.

The *Arbitration Act* 1996, which updated the law of arbitration in the UK, was widely acclaimed for its clarity and for its capacity to make arbitration more efficient and effective. It was also enacted at a time when the training of construction arbitrators was better than ever before. However, by 1996, arbitration had developed a reputation in the UK construction industry for being too expensive and too drawn out – in short it was considered to be too much like litigation. This perception and the introduction of adjudication into the UK has seen a decline in the number of construction disputes referred to arbitration, but it is still regularly used as an alternative to litigation.

If arbitration is the agreed option for resolving disputes in the original agreement, then the procedure for the appointment of an arbitrator will generally be set out in the contract. Many standard forms of construction contract provide for the appointment to be made by the President of one of the industry's professional bodies, such as RICS, the Chartered Institute of Arbitrators, the RIBA or the ICE. However, it is always open to the parties to agree to make their own choice as to who should be appointed.

There is no prescribed procedure or timetable for arbitration. The parties may agree a procedure and timetable (either in the contract or subsequently) or it may be decided by the arbitrator. In construction cases it is not unusual to have written submissions (claim, defence and reply), statements from factual witnesses, reports from expert witnesses, and a hearing at which evidence is tested. At the end the arbitrator makes an award that, in general, will be upheld by the courts and will only be subject to appeal on limited grounds. Therefore, unlike adjudication, the decision is generally final and binding.

Most parties to arbitration will require the assistance of solicitors, expert in the field of construction law, expert witnesses and quite possibly barristers to settle pleadings and to act as advocates at the hearing. The work these people carry out will have to be thorough and so it will not be cheap – it is hard to imagine many construction arbitrations where the final costs are less than several tens of thousands of pounds and it is not unusual for costs to be in the hundreds of thousands. In addition to this the arbitrator's fees will have to be met.

However, unlike adjudication, the successful party can seek recovery of its costs. As with litigation, it is highly unlikely that there will be a 100 per cent recovery of costs. After assessment successful parties typically recover 65–80 per cent of the total spent.

9.5 Mediation

Mediation is an alternative method of resolving construction disputes and, with the encouragement of the courts, it is being used more now than ever before. It boasts high success rates (in terms of cases settled) but, compared to the number of disputes settled by negotiation, adjudication or litigation (and, in the past, arbitration) the number of construction mediations is still relatively low.

Mediation is, in many respects, at the opposite end of the dispute resolution spectrum to adjudication, arbitration and litigation. It might be thought of as being one step away from negotiation. Like negotiation, there are no set rules and settlement is not reached by the decision of a third party, it is reached by the agreement of the disputing parties. Therefore, like negotiation, the merits of the dispute do not have to be the deciding factor – commercial considerations can be (and usually are) a major driving force.

It is often pointed out by advocates of the process that mediation can produce solutions to claims that are not available in formal proceedings. For example, a party may be prepared to reach a settlement in mediation for far less than it thinks the claim is actually worth if, in return, the defending party agree to negotiate a future contract with them. An adjudicator, arbitrator or judge cannot order this sort of compromise when deciding the legal rights and wrongs of a claim.

It is also pointed out that mediation produces fast results at a fraction of the cost of arbitration or litigation. Even on a large or complex dispute, parties may agree to prepare for the mediation in a matter of weeks, with the mediation meeting lasting just one day. In comparison, complex disputes can take months or even years of preparation in litigation or arbitration and the hearing may last for weeks. Having said that, the costs of preparing for mediation are generally not recoverable and, unlike formal dispute resolution procedures, there is no certainty that mediation will produce a positive outcome. Therefore, if the case does not settle as a result of the mediation, the whole process will have been a great waste of time and money.

There is no set procedure for mediation but it is not unusual for the meeting to start with both parties briefly outlining their positions in front of the mediator. After this, the parties are likely to retire to private rooms and the mediator will visit both to seek clarifications and perhaps make suggestions that may help bring about a settlement of the dispute.

The mediator does not ordinarily offer an opinion about the merits of the parties' arguments but will prompt discussion about areas that may provide a breakthrough to the impasse that has existed. He or she remains neutral and, unless given permission to disclose information to the other side, the mediator will not divulge details of closed meetings (or private 'caucuses') with the parties.

It is not unusual for mediations to go on late into the night and some people feel the first few hours of the day are often a time for posturing ahead of the 'real' negotiations later, as time runs out and pressure builds. One of the features of mediation is that the process is 'without prejudice' because it is an attempt to settle the dispute. Therefore, anything said or written down at the mediation is not admissible in any subsequent court or arbitration proceedings.

Mediators may be construction professionals or construction lawyers but, as the mediator's role is to facilitate a settlement rather than decide a dispute, it is perhaps more important to choose a mediator for his or her skills in that facilitative role than because of his or her knowledge or professional background.

The popularity of mediation has increased with the encouragement of the courts. The cases of *Dunnett v Railtrack plc* (2002)[24] and *Hurst v Leeming* (2003)[25] showed that courts were prepared to penalise a party in costs if the opportunity to mediate a settlement had been declined in favour of pressing ahead with litigation. Pre-trail mediation was later considered in the Court of Appeal for the case of *Halsey v Milton Keynes General NHS Trust* (2004)[26]. The following is an extract from the judgment:

> 'As was explained in Lord Woolf's final report Access to Justice (1996), for some time before the Civil Procedure Rules (CPR) came into force, resort by parties involved in litigation to ADR [alternative dispute resolution] had been encouraged by the courts in various ways. The CPR, practice directions and pre-action protocols have built on these early developments.
>
> ...
>
> We heard argument on the question of whether the court has power to order parties to submit their disputes to mediation against their will. It is one thing to encourage the parties to agree to mediation, even to encourage them in the strongest terms. It is another to order them to do so. It seems to us that to oblige truly unwilling parties to refer their disputes to mediation would be to impose an unacceptable obstruction on their right of access to the court ... it seems to us likely that compulsion of ADR would be regarded as an unacceptable constraint on the right of access to the court .... We would adopt what the editors of Civil Procedure 2003 say at vol. 1, para. 1.4.11: 'The hallmark of ADR procedures, and perhaps the key to their effectiveness in individual cases, is that they are processes voluntarily entered into by the parties in dispute with outcomes, if the parties so wish, which are non-binding. Consequently the court cannot direct that such methods be used but may merely encourage and facilitate.
>
> If the court were to compel parties to enter into a mediation to which they objected, that would achieve nothing except to add to the costs to be borne by the parties, possibly postpone the time when the court determines the dispute and damage the perceived effectiveness of the ADR process.
>
> ...
>
> In deciding whether to deprive a successful party of some or all of his costs on the grounds that he has refused to agree to ADR, it must be borne in mind that such an order is an exception to the general rule that costs should follow the event. In our view, the burden is on the unsuccessful party to show why there

should be a departure from the general rule. The fundamental principle is that such departure is not justified unless it is shown (the burden being on the unsuccessful party) that the successful party acted unreasonably in refusing to agree to ADR.'

9.6 Expert determination

Expert determination of construction disputes is comparatively rare but it certainly has the potential to be an effective and attractive option for single issue or relatively straightforward disputes. Expert determination should not be confused with the role of an expert witness in litigation or arbitration proceedings, which is an entirely different role.

Expert determination is fundamentally different to adjudication, arbitration or litigation. Many people unfamiliar with dispute resolution techniques assume that the role of an adjudicator or arbitrator is to find a just and fair answer to the claim, almost regardless of the submissions made. They assume that the adjudicator or arbitrator, once notified of the issues, will make enquiries, seek further information and carry out investigations and analyses to get to the 'truth' of the matter. In fact, in general, the role of adjudicator or arbitrator is similar to that of a judge, who has to weigh the evidence provided by the parties – the role is not to create evidence to assist one or other of the parties.

In expert determination, however, the expert is expected to apply his or her knowledge and experience and carry out his or her own investigations in order to determine the correct answer. An expert may receive little or nothing by way of supporting submissions and evidence from the parties.

Unlike adjudication, arbitration or litigation, there are no specific legislation or rules to be complied with. The appointment of an expert to carry out a determination is like the appointment of any professional to carry out a service – it is based upon a contract of appointment, which is likely to set out the duties, tasks, timetable and remuneration. As a result, an expert's determination cannot be enforced like an adjudicator's decision or an arbitrator's award, but, subject to the terms of the parties' contract, it is possible that failure to comply with the expert's determination may be a breach of contract, in which case the parties will have the usual legal remedies available to them for breach.

An expert might be asked to determine the value of a variation, a final account or an extension of time. The person chosen by the parties to carry out the determination is likely to be known to be a highly competent independent practitioner in the field of the matter in dispute.

Expert determination is likely to be relatively inexpensive and could produce a satisfactory resolution of a dispute. However, more than any other process, this one involves handing over the dispute to a third party and, as a result, parties may feel they lose control of matters. Parties may feel the same way about disputes that go to court but at least in litigation they have a representative pleading their case on the basis of instructions given. If the expert is given free reign, all control is handed over. And depending on the terms upon which the parties agree the appointment, it may be that the expert's determination is binding upon them.

One of the difficulties with expert determination is that there are no standard or default provisions, rules or regulations (such as the adjudication 'Scheme', the Arbitration Act or the CPR). Therefore, the parties have to ensure that all aspects of the appointment and all eventualities are catered for in their agreement. This may be difficult to achieve, particularly by parties already involved in a dispute. If matters are not clarified then one dispute (settled by the expert) could lead to another (about the meaning and effect of the determination).

The prospect of a third party unilaterally providing a binding determination may be unattractive to some but it is certainly an economical alternative and should not be quickly dismissed when considering how best to resolve delay claims and other construction related disputes that are likely to rely on expert analysis as opposed to points of law.

9.7 Expert witnesses

Expert witnesses do not resolve disputes but they are key figures in both criminal and civil litigation and arbitration. Expert witnesses are people with skills, experience and competence within a particular field of operation who give opinion evidence based on their technical knowledge as applied to the matter in dispute.

The role of an expert witness is to assist the judge or arbitrator by explaining and interpreting technical issues. Their duty is to act impartially and honestly. An expert must not seek to advance the case of one of the parties; to do so would not only be a breach of duty but it would also be counter-productive – a judge or arbitrator will give little or no weight to the evidence of an expert who is obviously advocating a parties' case, rather than giving honest and unbiased opinions.

In construction delay disputes programmers are frequently appointed as experts to report on the causes and extent of the delay and to give evidence at the hearing. Sometimes expert programmers are appointed by the court, the arbitrator or jointly by the parties but, more frequently, each side will be given permission to appoint its own expert.

Experts can also be engaged to assist as advisors in negotiations, mediation and adjudication.

Summary			
	Process	**Pros**	**Cons**
Negotiation	Usually carried out by the parties in correspondence, meetings and/or telephone conversations.	No cost Parties retain complete control Not essential to argue the merits of the case in full detail Can usually retain commercial relationships even if negotiations are heated	Can drag on over long period of time No certainty of positive resolution of dispute.
Litigation	Procedure is set by court rules and parties are represented by lawyers. A Judge decides the dispute on the facts and the law based on evidence provided, particularly as tested at the hearing.	Thorough review of the issues and the merits of the case resulting in binding judgment The 'winner' can recover wasted costs	Expensive, time consuming and stressful May be subject to appeal to a higher court Judge may not have practical understanding of technical issues.
Adjudication	Procedure is set by the Contract or the Government 'Scheme' and parties may use lawyers or claims consultants to present the case. A decision is reached within 28 days, generally based solely on written submissions made by the parties.	Quick and relatively inexpensive Adjudicator should be a person who understands the technical aspects of the dispute	Can amount to 'rough' justice No recovery of costs Decision only temporarily binding (the same matter can be referred to litigation or arbitration)

	Process	Pros	Cons
Arbitration	The *Arbitration Act* 1998 allows parties or an arbitrator to decide a suitable procedure. Parties are often represented by lawyers and most cases involve a hearing. The arbitrator's award is based on evidence provided.	Dispute usually decided by person who understands the technical aspects Parties not obliged to use lawyers at hearings Procedure to suit the case Winner can recover wasted costs	Can be expensive, time consuming and stressful Arbitrator may not have adequate expertise to deal with difficult legal points
Mediation	The Mediator tries to facilitate a settlement agreement during a meeting typically lasting one or two days.	Quick and relatively inexpensive Parties stay in control Offers a wider range of solutions	Can be a waste of time and money if no settlement materialises Reliant on willingness of parties to make concessions
Expert determination	An expert carries out investigations and uses knowledge to determine the dispute and the parties decide the procedure.	Relatively inexpensive Not dependent on the quality of submissions of the parties	Parties lose control of the process No procedural rules unless agreed by the parties May be problems with enforcement
Expert Witnesses	An Expert is appointed to provide impartial opinion evidence on specialist technical matters. Even though the expert is usually appointed by the parties he or she has a strict duty to be impartial in all circumstances.	Good experts can help save a great deal of time and cost	Experts can be very expensive to employ If advice is biased or poor it can cause a party to lose a 'good' case.

10
Conclusion

In providing practical advice about the evaluation of claims for delays on construction projects it has been necessary to highlight the many difficulties and shortcomings of the various commonly used delay analysis techniques. But, as stated from the outset, it is not difficult to pick holes in delay claims – the difficulty is finding an approach that can withstand robust examination.

It has been pointed out that all construction projects involve many different activities and, on all but the simplest, some form of methodical analysis of the facts will be required. This is likely to involve the use of computer generated programmes, but too often this task captures the interest of the delay analyst and, as a consequence, there is a failure to properly interrogate and particularise the facts giving rise to the problems.

As a result, construction delay claims are too frequently presented in the form of copious quantities of multi-coloured programmes and critical path networks with little narrative explanation or evidence of the facts to support the analysis. This produces a claim that ultimately requires a leap of faith whereby the ability of the programmer and the programme are trusted implicitly.

A computer generated analysis should be the first, not the only, step towards evaluating the delay and blind reliance on the results produced by computerised delay analysis techniques should be avoided. When an objective scientific analysis of the delay has been carried out, it is suggested that a subjective common-sense review of the facts should be undertaken and compared to the conclusions of the computer analysis.

The idea that it is inappropriate to approach delay analysis as a purely scientific discipline was given judicial approval in *Skanska*

Construction UK Ltd v Egger (Barony) Ltd (2004)[27]. In this case the judge pointed out that the reliability of a computer generated 'sophisticated impact analysis' was only as good as the data put in. The judge was far more impressed by logical opinions based on an accurate and transparent analysis of the facts than by theoretical conclusions based on computer programme logic that was not supported by factual evidence.

In an article entitled 'Garbage In, Garbage Out', about the Skanska case, which was published in *Building magazine*[28], construction lawyer Dominic Helps noted that although a computer provides a useful tool for use in delay analysis, it is only 'a glorified calculator and is certainly no substitute for the direct application of professional experience and objective judgement based on a clear understanding of the facts.'

Similarly, in *Great Eastern Hotel Company Limited v John Laing Construction Ltd* 2005[29] the judgment was based on a comprehensive and objective analysis of the facts – the judge rejected the 'theoretical constructs' of one side's computer generated programming analysis, which at least in part 'collided with reality'.

The problem of computer generated programmes colliding with reality is certainly not unique to this case. Programming experts who have the knowledge and skills to be able to look behind the immaculate colour printouts presented with a claim often find gaping flaws in the logic and factual basis of a claim and, because of the way activities are linked together, even a relatively minor error can cascade across the programme to produce a major discrepancy.

These cases support the view that delay analysis should be based not only on thorough research, but also on a sensible interpretation of the factual evidence. Too often, the commonsense view of the facts is not given sufficient priority.

The vast majority of delay claims do not end up before a judge and rarely will parties have to undertake the type of painstaking expert analysis required to prove a delay claim in a court. However, the combination of analysis and a sensible, common sense interpretation applies in all cases.

That is not to say that anyone who possesses common sense will be able to decide upon a reasonable extension of time if presented with a thorough, logical and well presented analysis. In order to determine an extension of time, common sense must be combined with an understanding of the construction process in general and the project in particular – and in order to make a fair and reasonable determination it is necessary to be objective and impartial, which may not be easy if you are employed by one of the parties.

It is also suggested that the approach to delay analysis must not be overly pedantic. Perhaps one of the reasons that parties find it difficult to settle delay claims is that they find it hard to accept imprecision. Contractors, architects, engineers and surveyors live in a world where information given or received is generally required to be precise and unambiguous. Contractors have to build to tight tolerances, architects and engineers have to produce designs that allow contractors to know precisely what size, colour, quantity and quality is required for every component of a building, and quantity surveyors generally have to measure in accordance with standard rules and, in the final analysis, value work to the nearest penny. Therefore, construction professionals are used to working with precise information and so, when it comes to delay analysis, it is perhaps difficult to accept that the best answer that can be given is often merely approximate.

Of course, a claim will ultimately have to be made and decided by reference to a precise and exact period of time, but delay analyses are based in part on subjective interpretation – they are not based entirely on fixed and incontrovertible facts. Therefore, it has to be accepted that delay periods cannot be determined with absolute precision.

It also has to be accepted that claims arising under a contract do not have to be proved beyond all reasonable doubt – that is the test applied in criminal trials and even if a delay claim goes to court the test is only 'on the balance of probabilities'. And perhaps it is of some comfort to remember that the duty of a professional man, generally stated, is not to be right, but to be careful – the fact that he is in the event proved to be wrong is not, in itself, evidence that he has been negligent.

This leaves open the question of what sort of analysis should be undertaken. There is much published commentary in respect of the delay analysis techniques and their application and many commentators have particular favourites. However, construction projects and construction delays are all unique, to some extent, and, it is suggested, there is no one technique that suits all. The quality and quantity of contemporaneous information may make certain techniques difficult or impossible to use.

In some cases it may be appropriate to consider delay against what was planned, in other situations it may be more appropriate to consider what the situation would have been 'but for' the occurrence of the delaying event. In other circumstances looking at the delay in a discrete window of time or leading up to a specific project milestone, such as the completion of the building envelope and the achievement of a weather tight environment, may be the best approach. So, it is generally a case of 'horses for courses'.

Practical tips

When dealing with claims always make it clear whether you are using calendar days or working days. If the latter, state how many days constitute a working week and which days are excluded from the reckoning due to bank or trade holidays. Once a decision has been made be consistent – sometimes working days are mixed up with calendar days in the same claim.

It is often useful to state the day and the date, not just the date, when referring to start, completion or key dates.

If using lots of different colours to depict different activities on a programme, remember that many people are to some extent colour blind. Therefore, it is best to stick with primary colours or to add different textures as well as colours to provide a clear code for the programme. This will also assist when the programmes are printed or photocopied in black and white.

If a claim contains lots of programmes, include a clear and brief summary programme so that the reader can get a quick overview.

Ensure that all programmes have a unique title and/or reference number (including revision number where applicable) and that the date and author of the programme is stated.

Make sure that programmes supplied with claims are explained in jargon-free language (stating how and why they were produced and, most importantly, what do they show?). Do not assume they will be easily understood or studiously examined by an architect, engineer, adjudicator or judge.

Ensure that programmes display only the pertinent facts and that superfluous detail is excluded. It is often advantageous to include summary level programmes within the main body of the claim with more detailed programmes included within appendices.

If one of the recognised critical path analysis based methodologies is employed a detailed explanation of how actually it has been undertaken should be provided. This is particularly important in respect to such aspects as the retrospective addition of programme logic and logic amendments carried out during the analysis.

If a large programme is reduced in size be careful not to reduce it so much that it is either difficult or impossible to read (this is not a rare occurrence!).

As a general rule if there have been a lot of variations on the project and/or the value of the works have increased, then it is highly likely that some delay to completion will have occurred. In these cases the starting point will usually be 'how much' not 'if'.

Unless as-built records are not available, a delay analysis should include a review of what actually happened on site. Therefore, in most cases, an 'as-planned impacted' analysis will not be sufficient.

Perhaps the best approach is to consider the delays from differing perspectives applying differing techniques to provide a cross-check. This is more likely to produce a conclusion that is realistic, pragmatic and, above all, both fair and reasonable.

Glossary

In this book there has been a deliberate attempt to avoid jargon and abbreviations but, when the subject of delay to construction projects is discussed, certain words and phrases that are not part of everyday language will crop-up. A list of some of these words and phrases is provided below with a brief note of explanation.

Condition Precedent: A legal term referring to a provision in a contract that must be fulfilled prior to another clause becoming effective. For example, it is a condition of many contracts that a notice of delay must be served before an entitlement to an extension of time arises.

Concurrent delays: Two or more delay events occurring at the same time. For example, a project may be delayed simultaneously due to bad weather, a late variation instruction and labour problems.

Culpable delay: A delay that is the fault of, or at the contractual risk of, the named party, for example reference is often made to 'the contractor's culpable delay' when claims are being discussed.

Damages: A legal term referring to a sum of money claimed or adjudged to be due as compensation for loss or injury due to breach of contract or a tort (negligence).

Dominant cause: A reference to the primary and overriding reason for the occurrence of an event. Used in delay claims to distinguish and prioritise a specific delay event, particularly in circumstances where there have been concurrent or culpable delays.

Float: A term used by programmers to define the amount of time available to carry out a non-critical activity before it becomes critical.

Liquidated damages: Often abbreviated to LDs, liquidated damages are damages as described above but which have been estimated and fixed in advance. Most construction contracts provide liquidated damages figures to apply in the event of late completion. The amount of liquidated damages inserted into a contract must be a genuine pre-estimate, not a penalty charge.

Liquidated and ascertained damages: Often abbreviated to LADs, these are the same as liquidated damages, described above, but with the emphasis that the amount has been ascertained or carefully estimated.

Official Referees' Court: A specialist English court that used to hear most of the major building and engineering disputes – replaced in 1998 by the Technology and Construction Court.

Practical completion: A term used in many construction contracts to refer to the state of completion at the time the works are ready to be handed back to the employer. Similar to 'substantial completion' in other forms of contract, this needs to be distinguished from 'final completion', which usually refers to the time when any defects that have appeared post practical completion have been rectified ('Final Completion' typically occurs 6–12 months after practical completion).

Prospective delay analysis: An analysis looking forward to delays that may occur in the future as a result of current or recent delay events.

Queen's Bench Division: One of three divisions of the English High Court (the others being the Family and Chancery Divisions). The High Court is superior to the County Courts in the hierarchy of the civil courts but below the Court of Appeal and the House of Lords.

Relevant event: A term used in JCT standard forms of building contract to refer to an event that may give rise to an extension of time.

Retrospective delay analysis: An analysis looking back at delays that have occurred in the past.

Scott schedule: A table setting out side by side a list of each party's contentions on each issue. Named after the judge who introduced them into court proceedings.

Snagging: Finishing, repairing and/or rectifying works prior to practical completion.

Technology and Construction Court: A High Court of Justice, in the Queen's Bench Division, specialising in construction cases and other technical disputes – replaced the Official Referees' Court in 1998.

Time at large: A situation where there is no fixed contractual completion date, generally because there is no mechanism in the contract to vary the completion date or the reasons for the delay are not events for which the contract provides for the granting of an extension of time.

Time is of the essence: 'Time being of the essence means that one or more stipulations as to time are conditions breach of which discharges the other party from the obligation to continue to perform any of his own promises. Delay in performance is treated as going to the root of the contract without regard to the magnitude of the breach.' From *Keating on Building Contracts*, Seventh Edition, para. 9–04.

Unliquidated damages: As damages above. Referred to as unliquidated to emphasis the distinction with liquidated damages.

Further information

Cooke, B. and Williams, P., *Construction Planning Programming and Control* (2nd edition), Blackwell Publishing, July 2004 (ISBN 1 40512 148 3)

Harris, F. and McCaffer, R., *Worked examples in Construction Management*, Granada Publishing Limited (now Blackwell Scientific Publishing), 1978 (ISBN 0 24611 370 7)

Planned Progress Monitoring, Property Services Agency, Department of the Environment , 1980

Harris, F. and McCaffer, R., *Modern Construction Management*, Blackwell Scientific Publishing, July 1995 (ISBN 0 63203 897 7)

Wake, S., *Earned Value The Power & The Glory*, *Project* (Magazine of the APM), February 2002

Briggs, S. C., *History of Critical Path Analysis*, Trett Digest, www.trett.com/digest

McCaffrey G., *Practical Planning and the SCL Delay and Disruption Protocol 'The Devil is in the Detail'*. A talk given to Adjudication Society, Edinburgh, 27 February 2003

Lumsden, N.P., *Line of balance method*, Pergamon, Oxford, 1968

Pickavance, K., *Delay and Disruption in Construction Contracts* (2nd Edition), LLP Reference Publishing, July 2000 (ISBN 1 85978 508 5)

Society of Construction Law, *Delay and Disruption Protocol*, October 2002, www.scl.org.uk

Wickwire, J.M. and Ockman, S., *Use of Critical Path Method on Contract Claims*, The Construction Lawyer, October 1999

Helps, D., *Garbage In, Garbage Out, Building*, 05 November 2004

Farrow, T., *Delay Analysis – Method and Mythology*. A paper based on a talk given to a meeting of the Society of Construction Law, Manchester, 06 November 2001

Palles-Clark, R., *The Value of Critical Path Analysis in Proving Delay Claims, Construction Law Review, 2002*

Palles-Clark, R., *Problems with Using Critical Path Analysis for Proving Delay Claims, Construction Law Review, 2003*

Driver, S. *Extensions of Time and Acceleration, Construction Law Review, 2003*

Birkby, G. and Brough, P., *Construction Companion to Extensions of Time*, RIBA Publishing Ltd, 2002

McCaffrey, G., *The Devil is in the Detail*, A paper based on a talk given to the Adjudication Society, Edinburgh, 27 February 2003.

Masson, D., *Following the Critical Path, Contract Journal 1995*

Fenwick Elliott, R., *Delay and Disruption Claims*, Fenwick Elliott Articles and Papers, 1996

Winter, J. and Johnson, P., *Resolving Complex Delay Claims*, A paper based on a lecture given to the Society of Construction Law, 06 June 2000.

Blackler, T., *Delayed Gratification, Building*, 18 January 2002.

Pickavance, K., *Principles and Policies in Delay Analysis*, A paper presented to the Society of Construction Law,06 February 2002

Starr, P., *Timed Delay, The Witness*, January/February 2003

Henchie, N., *Just Cool It, Building*, 05 July 2002

Burr, A. and Lane, N., *The SCL Delay and Disruption Protocol: Hunting* Snarks, *Construction Law Journal,* Sweet & Maxwell, 14 February 2003

Marrin, J., *Concurrent Delay*, A paper given at a meeting of the Society of Construction Law, 05 February 2002.

Stokes, M. and McKibbin, R., *Float, Now You See it Now You Don't!*, ICE CLR, 2003

Endnotes

1 Wickwire, J., M., and Ockman, S., *Use of Critical Path Method on Contract Claims*, *The Construction Lawyer*, October 1999

2 Wickwire, J., M., and Ockman, S., *Use of Critical Path Method on Contract Claims*, *The Construction Lawyer*, October 1999

3 Society of Construction Law, *Delay and Disruption Protocol*, October 2002

4 Wickwire, J., M., and Ockman, S., *Use of Critical Path Method on Contract Claims*, *The Construction Lawyer*, October 1999

5 Society of Construction Law, Delay and Disruption Protocol, October 2002. P49

6 Society of Construction Law, Delay and Disruption Protocol, October 2002. P48, paragraph 4.16

7 Society of Construction Law, Delay and Disruption Protocol, October 2002. P46, paragraph 4.3

8 Wickwire, J., M., and Ockman, S., *Use of Critical Path Method on Contract Claims*, *The Construction Lawyer*, October 1999

9 Society of Construction Law Delay and Disruption Protocol. P11, Para 1.2.4 & P12 Para 1.2.13

10 The Society of Construction Law *Delay and Disruption Protocol*, October 2002

11 Starr, P., *Timed Delay*, *The Witness*, January/February 2003

12 Burr, A. and Lane, N., *The SCL Delay and Disruption Protocol: Hunting Snarks, Construction Law Journal 2003*

13 Burr, A. and Lane, N., *The SCL Delay and Disruption Protocol: Hunting* Snarks, *Construction Law Journal 2003*

14 Masson D. Following the Critical Path. Contract Journal 16 February 1995. P34–35

15 8.10 *Balfour Beatty Building Ltd v Chestermount Properties Ltd* (1993) 62 BLR 1

16 *Sutcliffe v Thackrah* [1974] AC 727

17 *John Barker Construction Ltd v London Portman Hotel Ltd* (1996) 83 BLR 31

18 Birkby, G. and Brough, P., *Construction Companion to Extensions of Time,* RIBA Publishing Ltd, 2002

19 Marrin, J., *Concurrent Delay,* A paper given at a meeting of the Society of Construction Law, 05 February 2002

20 *Henry Boot Construction Ltd v Malmaison Hotel* (1999) 70 ConLR 32

21 *John Barker Construction Ltd v London Portman Hotel Ltd* (1996) 83 BLR 31

22 *John Barker Construction Ltd v London Portman Hotel Ltd* (1996) 83 BLR 31

23 *Balfour Beatty Construction Ltd v The Mayor and Burgesses of the London Borough of Lambeth* (2002) 2002 BLR 288

24 *Dunnett v Railtrack plc.* (2002) 2 ALL ER 850
25 *Hurst v Leeming* (2003) EWHC 499 (Ch)
26 *Halsey v Milton Keynes General NHS Trust* [2004] EWCA (Civ) 576
27 Skanska Construction UK Ltd v Egger (Barony) Ltd [2004] EWHC 1748, TCC
28 Helps, D., *Garbage In, Garbage Out, Building*, 05 November 2004
29 8.19 *Great Eastern Hotel Company Ltd v John Laing Construction Ltd* [2005] EWHC 181 (TCC)

Index